ISBN 978-1-333-57322-5
PIBN 10521495

English
Français
Deutsche
Italiano
Español
Português

www.forgottenbooks.com

Mythology Photography **Fiction**
Fishing Christianity **Art** Cooking
Essays Buddhism Freemasonry
Medicine **Biology** Music **Ancient**
Egypt Evolution Carpentry Physics
Dance Geology **Mathematics** Fitness
Shakespeare **Folklore** Yoga Marketing
Confidence Immortality Biographies
Poetry **Psychology** Witchcraft
Electronics Chemistry History **Law**
Accounting **Philosophy** Anthropology
Alchemy Drama Quantum Mechanics
Atheism Sexual Health **Ancient History**
Entrepreneurship Languages Sport
Paleontology Needlework Islam
Metaphysics Investment Archaeology
Parenting Statistics Criminology
Motivational

AN INTERIOR BY MR. LUTYENS.

THE HOUSE AND ITS EQUIPMENT

EDITED BY LAWRENCE WEAVER

LONDON :

PUBLISHED AT THE OFFICES OF COUNTRY LIFE
20, TAVISTOCK STREET, COVENT GARDEN, AND BY
GEORGE NEWNES, LTD., 8-11, SOUTHAMPTON STREET,
STRAND.   NEW YORK : CHARLES SCRIBNER'S SONS

CONTENTS.

INTRODUCTION.

THE welcome given to *Small Country Houses of To-day*, which dealt with the planning and archi-tectural treatment of about fifty typical houses by well-known architects, seems to justify the publication of this, a companion volume.   In the former book the aim was to consider each house as a definite architectural conception.   It was shown how many and how greatly differing are the *motifs* that may justly be employed in giving form to needs which are, in the main, the same for all houses.   Though six of its chapters were given to the description of old buildings which had been repaired and altered to meet new conditions and needs, the design of new houses received the lion's share of consideration.   The scheme of the present volume is altogether different, though the aim is the same, viz., to enlarge the healthy interest, already widespread, in all questions that concern the practical equipment and decorative amenities of the house.   Many volumes have been published in which a single writer has endeavoured to cover the whole field, but such a course seems to demand an amount of knowledge and critical ability which it is unreasonable to expect.   The method here adopted, of securing contributions from twenty-three writers, between whom the forty-three chapters have been divided, is obviously more likely to secure expert advice on subjects so diverse.   It will, however, be found that the general attitude of all the contributors is the same, in so far as they plead with the public 'to approach all questions relating to the house and its equipment in an architectural spirit.   The book roughly divides itself into three sections.   The first fourteen chapters deal with the treatment of various rooms and with different means of beautifying them by plaster-work, panelling, and furniture aptly designed and chosen.   The next seventeen are devoted to practical questions, such as drainage and lighting.   The last twelve take us from the house to its encircling garden, in consonance with the plea (set out by Mr. Ernest Newton in the first chapter) that house and garden should be considered together as constituent parts of an artistic whole.   While no one book, or, indeed, anything short of a library, can include all the subjects involved in so vast a problem as the equipment of the house, it is hoped that this volume will stimulate and help those who are not wholly satisfied with their homes and desire to better them.   LAWRENCE WEAVER.

DOMESTIC ARCHITECTURE OF TO-DAY

The New Renaissance of English House-building—The Smallish House—Arts and Crafts Movement— Garden Design—Relations of Architect and Client.

THE history of the English race is very clearly written in its domestic architecture. We are a home-loving people, and from the earliest settled times we have given serious attention to the art of house-building. Well into the last century our traditions were practically unbroken, and it is possible to date without much difficulty every house that was built up to that time, and to trace from their houses the changes and developments in the manner of life of the people who lived in them. These changes were slow and leisurely, as became a quiet and naturally rather conservative people. Railways, more than anything else, killed this traditional art, but there were, of course, many other contributory causes. The nineteenth century began an era of change in the outlook and the mode of life of the whole country. Communities which from time immemorial had lived remote from the greater centres of activity, content in their seclusion, suddenly found themselves caught in the stream of modern developments, and their pleasant, uneventful existence rudely invaded. Home industries were transplanted to factories, and the craftsman had to give way to the mechanic. It was exciting, but no sort of time for the further development of traditional archi- tecture. In the sixties and seventies we began to settle down again, but by that time traditional architecture was practically dead.

This is very rough-and-ready his- tory, but it is near enough for the purpose of dating

I.—"THE SMALLISH HOUSE."

with more or less accuracy the renaissance of English domestic architecture. The pioneers of this renaissance— Norman Shaw, Nesfield, Philip Webb, Devey and some few others—each picked up the thread of traditional design arbitrarily and gave to his buildings a personal character, so that their designs, although based on old work, were in no sense mere copies ; they aimed at catching the spirit of the old building rather than at the literal reproduction of any defined style. This was the starting-point of the great development that has taken place in domestic architecture during the last forty years. Circumstances were favourable. The great commercial activity of the period produced almost a new class—men who from small beginnings had made large fortunes and were fired with an ambition to " found a family." Their first step towards this object was to buy land and build a house. Since that time to the present day almost every note in the possible scale of house design has been struck. We were asked forty years ago to invent a new style, and we have invented a dozen. We have had houses recalling the buildings of the seventeenth and

2.—"THE FARMHOUSE MOTIF."

eighteenth centuries, and of earlier periods ; we have made full play with building materials, concrete, stone, tiles, pebbles, rough-cast, in all sorts of skilful or playful combinations of colour, form and texture ; we have used all motifs, from adzed beams and rough stone to gilded and painted ceilings and marble floors ; we have even tried our hands at the Art Nouveau : though it has not taken so much hold of England as of the Continent. Doubtless it has its place in the general development of things, and, in fact, the work of some of its ablest exponents has a certain directness, reticence and refinement which gives it a character of its own that is not unattractive. But in the hands of the wilder spirits it seems to me simply a bizarre sort of nightmare, defying every law of construction and natural form, and even decency.

As we review this half-century of house-building there are, perhaps, four points especially noticeable. In the first place, it is the day of the smallish house. The Nash of our time would find the " country seats " and " noblemen's mansions " no longer being built. And this smallness of the house has resulted in a peculiarly intimate touch. Perhaps the most marked feature of our modern domestic architecture is its individual character. Every part of a building from start to finish is minutely designed. The projection, depth and contour of each moulding is carefully drawn ; the colour and texture of walling and roofing materials, and the manner in which they shall be used, are carefully considered and made to contribute to the general effect; mantel-pieces, grates and panelling, door handles and hinges, even nails, are all drawn and made to our liking. The inevitable drawback to this intensely personal practice of architecture is that, while it develops the art of design, it does little or nothing for the craft of building. The architect has, so far as he can, gathered up the lines of traditional building, and conscientiously or capriciously follows one or the other just as his fancy for the moment dictates. The builder of the ready-made house is totally unmoved by this intensive architectural culture ; and while the con-

3.—AN ARCHITECT'S GARDEN.

scientious architect is striving after perfection, the speculating builder gaily devastates whole districts, his only ideal being the greatest apparent accommodation for the least actual cost. It is all a little bewildering, and it is difficult and not very profitable to attempt to forecast the future.

In the second place, this revival of domestic architecture has been accompanied by a parallel revival in the arts subservient to house design—by what is known as the " arts and crafts " movement. Those who can remember the pre-Morris days know to what depths the arts of house furnishing and decoration had fallen—wall-papers of a ghastly green, with gold fleur-de-lys dabbed on at regular intervals ; the " suite " upholstered in crimson or sky blue repp ; the distressing carpets and amber-dyed sheepskin mats. Morris changed all this and gave us fine colour and pattern. It is impossible to over-estimate his influence, both direct and indirect. He created a standard both in design and workmanship, and although, of course, his views and dogmas were not universally accepted, he opened people's eyes to possibilities of which they had not even dreamed. Those who had been vaguely oppressed by their surroundings became conscious of the cause of their discomfort, and demanded something better, even if they were not prepared for a complete reversal of their former views. This demand created a supply. Makers of stuffs and wall-papers really did what they could to meet these new requirements ; naturally, with varying success. Many architects assisted the manufacturers by designing wall-hangings, carpets and other fabrics.

The third point is the revival of the lost art of garden design. The " House Beautiful " still required a setting. The architect who had given so much thought to the building was forced regretfully to resign the laying-out of the garden to alien hands ; the cult of the curly path, of the kidney-shaped bed and clump of pampas grass was well established and not easy to dislodge. Gradually, however, people's interest was aroused by garden books and illustrations of the fine old gardens scattered up and down the country. Now the architect plans the garden almost as a matter of course. The dethronement of the nursery garden designer and the installation of the architect in his place has come about rather suddenly. The architect is sometimes a little embarrassed by the confidence reposed in him as a garden-maker. His knowledge of planning and his powers of designing an effective " lay-out " may in some cases exceed his horticultural learning. Of course, he need not be a specialist in this line, but he must have a fair working knowledge of plants and their habits, of when and where to put them, or his garden will be shorn of more than half its interest. It is the contriving of cunningly-sheltered nooks for one kind of plant and the naked exposure of others that is three-quarters of a well-conceived garden plan. This applies much less, of course, to the arrangement of large and quite formal gardens than to the small garden, which requires a far more delicate and intimate handling.

All this is rather a tremendous result to have achieved in so short a time, especially when it must be remembered that for perhaps the larger half of that time architects had but little support from the public. There were many unrecorded and, fortunately, bloodless battles before the architect and his client saw eye to eye. I should be claiming too much to

4.—LOCAL MATERIALS: WELSH SLATES IN WALES.

assert that victory is ours all along the line even now ; but the growth of public interest and appreciation is very marked, fostered and dictated, no doubt, as much by the attention drawn to domestic architecture by books, magazines and weekly papers as by the direct influence of the architect. The omniscient daily Press alone lags behind, and has still to discover the art of architecture. With a few notable exceptions architectural criticism in the daily papers has not advanced much beyond the penny-a-line stage ; and there is no doubt that the architecture of public buildings, with which the daily Press is chiefly concerned, has not made quite the same kind of advance as domestic work. The reason for this is that in the latter architect and client are in touch ; they discuss requirements and details : there is a sort of partnership. Public architecture, on the other hand, is generally the result of a competition. The architect has no direct employer, but has to work to hard-and-fast printed directions ; there is no elasticity of give and take ; and it is all " in the air." Elaborate drawings have to be made showing many details and features if a competitor is to have a chance of success ; and when successful he cannot leave these features out ; he is the slave of his fine drawings. In the case of a house there is opportunity for much personal explanation, which, indeed, is often required. The client certainly is in many instances not attracted by the elevation of a house, which is quite right when built, but not, as a drawing, sufficiently effective to get a chance if it were subject to the conditions of a competition. The fourth and the most important point is the genuineness of the progress. It is quite clear that if the revival had been merely a revival of externals—a sort of Christmas-card architecture—it would have had no vitality, and would have deservedly died out long .ago. But it has been a real attempt to grapple with the requirements of modern life. Of course, it was hardly to be expected that it should have been wholly free from extravagances and affectatioñs. We have. perhaps, used the farmhouse motif beyond its proper limits. For a house of moderate size, and for people of simple habits, it is, of course, legitimate ; but it is a common-place of house-building that, as far as possible, the wishes and requirements of those who are going to live in the house should be met. I say "as far as possible" because people's wishes are sometimes rather chaotic, and an architect has occasionally to invent their requirements for them. But, speaking generally, we may say that domestic architecture will progress more naturally and soundly if the architect honestly faces the often difficult problems set him, instead of enforcing his own individual views. The ordinary man who wants a plain, simple house, with well-lighted rooms, carpeted floors and all that goes to the making of a comfortable home, is rather hardly used when he finds that he has to sit in a sort of low, farmhouse kitchen, with a gritting floor and a reluctant log fire. And yet, if the architect has duties to his employer, the employer no less has duties to his architect. A certain give-and-take is necessary. The architect, with his experience, should be left full freedom in details. But if the employer has definite views as to the way in which he wants to live, it is no part of the architect's duty to tell him that he is mistaken. Perhaps he will like many rooms, one for every part of the business of life, or he may prefer one big room for general family use. That is his business ; but it is the architect's business to make a whole of these units. Some wholly incongruous feature is often introduced and insisted on after the general scheme is complete and the work begun, and the result is deplorable ; whereas if a point had been made of it at first, the architect would have had a chance of making it the pivot on which the whole of his design turned.

But, on the whole—and this is the most encouraging point about the present position in domestic architecture—the real progress made has been the result of interaction between architect and client. It has been a real attempt to solve new problems. Practical needs, instead of being ignored or overlooked, have brought about new types of plans. Considerations of aspect have settled the position and sequence of rooms. The materials available for building in different parts of the country have imposed limitations, and suggested certain methods of using them. The proper lighting and most convenient arrangement of domestic offices ; the position of fireplaces ; the disposition of beds and other furniture—all these practical problems are of the essence of any scheme for the planning of a house, and each in its turn, when successfully solved, has helped towards the realisation of the vision which is always enticing us to further efforts, the ideal house which everyone wants—a house compact but spacious, noiseless, light, airy and cheerful, cool in summer and warm in winter, well ventilated but free from draughts, a house that costs little to build and less to keep in repair, yet "built for eternity" and comely and pleasant to look upon.

ERNEST NEWTON, A.R.A.

COLOUR IN , THE HOUSE.

The Love of Colour Inextinguishable—Nature a Storehouse, rather than a Guide—The Colouring of Wall and Ceiling—The Influence of Aspect and Lighting—The Sterility of Undue Caution in Choice of Colours

IT is said that " truth will out even in an affidavit," and the love of colour seems as inextinguishable. In spite of its being treated as an indulgence, at which the virtuous hands of academic authority are lifted in grave reproof, and its being guarded in anxious privacy lest its owners' reputation should be sent tottering from its polished base, the joy in colour breaks out every now and then in defiance of the austerity of our education. Love of colour is an emotional matter, like the love of melody and the magical rhythm of some literature and poetry ; it is a gift independent of race or chime. Other passions there are, weightier, more moral, more self-conscious, where the intellect has been tampering with the emotions and deflecting them in various deliberately dug channels to fertilise some theory or philosophy of life—where the artist calls on man to probe with him into the storm and stress, the problems of existence. When such big issues are afoot colour shrinks—for shelter—into the unobtrusive security of low tones and prudent selection of tincture, or else takes on a special poignancy akin to the broken searching melodies of Beethoven's later works. But these agitations of the heart are private—not for our sleeves, still less for our walls. And yet our walls reflect ourselves, our care and our indifference ; their harmonies are of our own making, and so are the discords. True, there are houses built whose walls are for ever incapable of being resolved or modulated into the beauty of fair proportion. If the first function of the house is to be a shelter, its second is to be a bower. Driven beyond the pale of Eden, tossed into the blind forces and destructions of that grim epitome of inhumanity—Nature—man's first work was to shield himself and his from the violence of her methods, and then next to turn some of her activities to account on his behalf. For we must remember always that Nature is man's mortal enemy—untiring, unsleeping ; not actively vindictive, but having established, after æons of tentative effort, a working equilibrium of blind forces, she resents any interference with her delicately adjusted balance. She is man's antagonist, but also his nurse. All that he knows of beauty of form and of colour he has got from her ; his ideals of power, grandeur and spaciousness he has learnt from her ; the joy of life and the tragedy of death are ever before his eyes ; the beating of the infinitely old winds and the infinitely old sea upon this infinitely old world, and the tranquil swinging of the watchful stars around the pole, showed him influences so immeasurably beyond his own that they became for him his religion, his apprehension of good and evil. Armed with these convictions, he defies her ; defies her ideals. With Nature, motion is the prime fact of the universe ; friction is so much interference, and her activities are bent to lessen and eliminate friction. Man sets himself to oppose these aims : he had, at the outset, to fight for his existence ; and that, by a system of compact social vigilance, being to some degree assured, he creates, as his standard of good, the qualities of permanence, rest and completion. In this conflict of ideals, he has to use weapons other than those employed by Nature ; his whole life is one unending interference with her processes, and in the matter of vigilance he is no match for her. She never sleeps ; never rests. Based on his observations of her method, her expansions and her results, he has to achieve his ends by quite other means. He sets himself to secure in some definite form her wayward, fluctuating charm and beauty ; he has to synthesise her lavish profusion, endless resources, variety of detail, gradations of light and colour, complexity of forms, graces of movement and so forth, and, like the drawing of a flickering flame of fire, has to evolve forms and colours that shall be symbols, and yet give the delight that the actualities themselves afford.

Nature, then, is a storehouse, but—except in a very limited sense—no guide. We move in a smaller circle, with fewer resources, speaking another language. Her invocation to Spring, her farewell to Summer, are not to be caught and reproduced in distemper, and yet, somehow, we have got to colour our walls. Have we ? It wants considering. By colouring I include also the use of panelling, unpainted and painted. The first condition to seize upon is the aspect of the house and the nature of the windows and sources of light. The walls of a room that looks to the south may be almost colourless, whereas in the rooms facing the north you should pile on as much colour as you can. It is in such aspects that the rich warm brown of oak panelling tells so effectively, giving the comfort and friendliness of colour. Windows should count as pictures—stained-glass pictures—and all hopes of making the walls compete with them in colour must be dismissed. Even the use of patterns becomes a difficulty—such incident and disturbance of the big, wide wall spaces as may be needed can often best be provided by means of pictures and other works of art, very sparingly used. A useful maxim to employ is, in colouring follow the light ; put light colours where there is plenty of light, and rich colours where the light is not so dominant. By rights, the window space on the north side of the house should not be so ample, and if—as like it may —the north window should count as one full of colour, one must play up to it with some full colour, like purple, brown or deep gold, to preserve the steady dignity of the room. It is not always remembered that the outlook from a north room is generally a more brilliant and highly-coloured affair than the view on the sunny side. With one's back to the sun, one views the landscape undisturbed by its rays, and as the sun wears down to the horizon, the features of the prospect are accentuated by strong colour and shadow, vibrating and concentrating in the splendour of the sunset and the tranquillity of the after-glow. Strong light blanches colour ; you see it at its richest and its strength in twilight. It is enough to recall the pictures of the Old Masters in the National Gallery—especially of the Venetian and Florentine (Umbrian) schools—to exemplify this ; their richest tints they exhibit in a twilight calm. For sheer comfort and satisfaction in colour, it would be impossible, I think, to surpass the decoration of the Sala del Cambio at Perugia or the Chapel of St. Giorgio degli Schiavoni at Venice. They are both what might be called dark rooms, and if the eye chose, there is much for it to rest on and discover ; but treated merely as a piece of colour decoration, and without attempting to dwell on the storied structure of the painting, one carries away in one's recollection the lasting impression that they are the two pleasantest rooms it has been one's fortune to linger in. Simplicity of colour, especially in a light room, is a high quality. So often far too many colours are used, half-a-dozen different tints in the curtain and a score in the carpet, and fresh distractions in the upholstery of the furniture. Moreover, a decision must be made as to whether the pictures or the wall-paper are to furnish the wall. If the former, then there need be no pattern on the latter, if the latter is used at all. On the other hand, if the paper is to take charge of the walls, it need be of some strong, vigorous pattern, capable of clothing the spaces like so much arras. Unless the room is a low one, the ceiling should not be the blank white so generally and complaisantly accepted. A dark ceiling is restful ; it links together the four walls and carries across overhead their colour and their quality without attracting any notice or comment. Few people are conscious how this sense of restfulness has been obtained, although they are quite sensible of its effect. Even where the walls are white, a tinted ceiling, unless the room is a low one, tempers any tendency to glare and distributes an opalescent bloom on the walls themselves. There is, however, a kind of sterile caution in this tame use of white walls and white woodwork, which argues a self-conscious shrinking from playing one's part in the world, and, in consequence, making mistakes. Many are the cases where it is exactly the right thing, if all the accessories are carefully kept subservient ; but there comes an instance where something should be attempted and risked, and it is not a healthy state of affairs to be too neurotically sensitive to fine shades and harmonies. The real artist can allow for mistakes, as the real musician for false notes ; it is the amateur who cannot listen to any music unless it is perfectly played.

We have travelled a long way from that robust acceptance of definite colour that suffused the people of the Middle Ages. In their downright demand for blue, for red, for gold—without stickling for fine shades and subtle varieties—they got good blue, good red, good gold ; blue of the lapis, vermilion from the Orient. Better colours have never been. We cannot judge of their wall painting, for time and man's hand have obliterated most and disfigured the rest ; but their books and their manuscripts remain to speak for their delight in and their use of fine colour. There we can recover the rich hangings, the bright heraldry, the gay apparel of the people who live on the pages of the missals and who were, to all appearance, scarce conscious of the extravagance of their hues. They thought nothing of those discords, those conflicts of colour, that rack our frightened senses ; in their quantity there was variety and gradation enough to blend the juxtaposition into harmony.

Besides being sterile, the issues at stake do not warrant such scrupulous refinement. A man will spend an hour in a tailor's shop and possibly an unquiet night afterwards, choosing the exact sprinkling of the pepper and salt mixtures of his clothes from a multitude of patterns almost identical. What does it matter how his choice is made ? It quite conceivably did in the days when half a man's cloth hose was red and half was blue, and a slashed doublet topped his parti-coloured legs ; and yet it would seem that they were pretty indifferent then to any special niceties. The blazoning on a shield was a more compromising thing than the precise shade of an umbrella ; but the mind of to-day is more exercised over the latter than the knight's care for his shield in the time of Edward III. Such hesitation is not respectable. It indicates the exhaustion of the colour sense. The hope for a virile school of colour decoration must be grounded on a robuster attitude, concerned with broader considerations, and eager to use failure as stepping stones to higher efforts and as the necessary means of education. I hardly dare propose to let these young enthusiasts (the scholars) loose in the country house of a quiet man, whose one wish about his home is for it to escape criticism ; they must find other and larger fields for their operations, say, in the village halls and schools ; but what they achieve and the tradition that they create will inevitably affect, and affect greatly. our conceptions as to the colour-treatment of the interiors of houses.   HALSEY RICARDO.

PLASTER-WORK

A Short Historical Survey—Ethics of Copying Old Examples—The Worship of Styles—Quandary of the Thoughtful Designer.

THE craft of plaster-work is a very ancient one. In the form of gesso, which is a branch of the same art, it was practised by the Egyptians, but merely served as a fine ground for painting on. The Greeks used plaster in the same way to form a smooth surface on their finely-hewn but rough-textured stone, as a basis for polychromatic decoration. In mediæval times, again, a plaster more nearly akin to the material as we know it at the present day was used over the interior walling of buildings, so as to get a suitable ground for decoration. In Roman times plaster or stucco was at first used as a basis for colour decoration. The modelling of the plaster surface into relief ornament appears to have developed later ; but there remain many examples of this type, such as those from the garden of the Villa Farnesina, and there are fragments in the British and South Kensington Museums. In Byzantine churches the art was practised to

5.—MODERN VERSION OF XVII. CENTURY MOTIF.

some extent ; but in mediæval times it appears to have fallen into the background, eclipsed by the transcendent and universal outburst of the stonemason's art. Plaster-work, however, was not quite extinguished. It smouldered and peeped out at intervals. Even the man who put the plain plastering on the inside of the stone walls had his little bit of fun. The coating of plaster used was very thin, not at all the modern " three-coat work." The plasterer of the Middle Ages was not ashamed of the surface left by his trowel, and avoided bringing the plaster face

6.—AT WYCH CROSS PLACE.

to dead uniformity. Not being burdened with the thickness of three coats of plaster, he would stop when he came to the dressed stone-work of a window with a pretty little zigzag wrought with his trowel— a pleasant finish even without the

7.—FRIEZE WITH HUNTING SCENE.

decoration which usually followed. In the fourteenth and fifteenth centuries modelled plaster-work was revived in France for interior decorations. Some of those wonderful chimney hoods, usually built of stone, in the great châteaux, are framed up in timber and entirely covered inside and out with plaster, elaborate figure-work and other modelled ornament appearing on the front. About the same period "post and pan" work, as it used to be called, began to be used in house-building. This work is now commonly called "half-timber construction." The pan or panel was the space between the posts or timber framing, filled with a compost of clay and straw, or sometimes with brick, and then plastered. Over the greater part of England, when oak was plentiful, this form of building became very common, and with it the modelling of the plaster was often practised. In cottage work it sometimes went no further than a simple scratching or marking of the surface ; more frequently it was stamped with wooden moulds. But it also developed into marvellously ornate and beautifully-modelled plaster, as in the famous examples at Wyvenhoe, Maidstone, Canterbury and elsewhere.

In the seventeenth century there was a fresh outburst of decoration in plaster in this country, and very beautiful work was done on friezes and ceilings, examples of which are very numerous. It would appear that the introduction in the sixteenth century of Italian workmen had something to do with this revival. Certainly if we set aside the Romans themselves, there were never greater masters of plaster-work than the Italians, who wrought in what was called "stucco duro." Their material was so hard and well tempered as to withstand the effects of weather for centuries. Old Hardwick Hall was unroofed when the new house was built at the end of the sixteenth century ; but even to this day much of the figure-work on the stucco friezes shows an undamaged surface. The English workman appears to have quickly absorbed what was useful to him in the Italian methods, and soon blossomed out on lines of his own which marked the seventeenth century as the high-water level of plaster-work in this country. In the eighteenth century the vigour of the movement gradually expended itself. During the Adams period it passed through a phase quite marvellous and admirable of its kind, based consciously and deliberately on the Roman plaster-work of the time of Pompeii. Only if viewed in comparison with the freer and more robust Elizabethan work can the plaster-work evolved by the brothers Adam be called decadent. When compared with the nemesis that followed in the nineteenth century it stands out as singularly refined, delicate and satisfying workmanship. A side issue of the plasterer's craft, known as "compo" ornament, developed at this period. It is a tough, leathery material, which was frequently applied to wood in place of carving. This form of ornament, perfectly straightforward in itself,

8.—BASED ON EARLY WORK BUT NOT COPIED.

9.—A TREATMENT OF BEAMS.

shows the craftsman balancing on a knife-edge. One little touch in the wrong direction and he produces sham wood-carving ; but kept within bounds, compo ornament is first cousin once removed to gesso.

Before considering the plaster-work that is being done at the present day it is well thus to glance backwards and review the history and development of the art. We are then in a better position to gauge the quality and adjudge the value of modern work-manship and design. In the revival of a moribund craft the instinct of the enthusiastic workman usually carries him straight to the finest period of its historic development. Perhaps this may not always be so, but it is true of the revival of modern plaster-work as evidenced by the beautiful ceiling designs shown in Figs. 5, 6, 7 and 8. All these show to the full the freedom seen in seventeenth century work. They have the same air of being done without wild striving and effort, and are based on, but not copied from, the early work. Of the four the ceiling at Wych Cross Place brings with it more suggestion of having adopted features from Elizabethan times. At this point we enter controversial grounds—how far is it proper to copy and reproduce ? There is no question about the little frieze of a hunting scene being modern— the modelling and shape of the dogs proclaim it (Fig. 7).

10.—IN THE ADAM STYLE.

But when we come to the ceiling designed in the Adam style, where stands our craftsman ? This is a twentieth century revival of an eighteenth century rendering of Roman plaster-work. It could quite easily be a mere rearrangement of the ornaments made from the actual eighteenth century moulds, some of which still exist, and in any case can easily be reproduced from existing examples of the plaster-work. The rooms so decorated may be extremely pleasant, and probably are so, but the work cannot altogether escape the charge of being stage architecture. The fiction, if skilfully executed, may well be so complete that only the radiators and sanitary adjuncts give away the deception created.

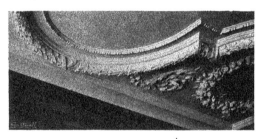

11.—MODERN VARIANT OF GEORGIAN.

This aspect of the modern practice in the plasterers' workshops gives cause for serious thought. It arises from a position so universally taken up by the people who build, and is so often tacitly accepted by the designer or the archi-tect, as to be difficult to combat. It is so "safe" to be able to say, this is "Georgian" or this is "Empire," and many people are so sensitive to the criticism of friends that they wish to be assured that their rooms are "correct." The thoughtful designer is often in a quandary and finds himself accused of the vanity of desiring to produce "original" work. Where is this reproduction of the historical styles to end? It appears to be running through the gamut, and after the earlier revivals of last century to have reached in turn Georgian, Adam and Empire. Early Victorian is already a term to be flirted with. Must we complete the cycle and ultimately reach the *re*-revival of Gothic? Surely such a position for any craft—and it applies to others besides plaster-work—has only got to be succinctly stated to appear as little other than a *reductio ad absurdum*.

Reverting for a moment to the illustrations, Fig. 9 shows a treatment of beams with ornament, which looks as if it had been wrapped round the structural beam almost like wall-paper. The design is a beautiful one in itself, and no canon of art is infringed by modelling the stems and tendrils round the soft angles in plaster; but something is lost in the suggestion of strength and rigidity, which straight lines on the lower edges would at once restore. The wreath round an oval window shown in Fig. 12 is another example of the correct rendering of a historical style, reproducing as it does the kind of work that was carved in wood and stone by Grinling Gibbons and others in Wren's time. It is unsuitable for domestic work owing to the difficulty of keeping it clean and the danger of damaging the work in the attempt to do so. Fig. 11 shows an example of plaster-work in the style usually termed Georgian, although the wreath and scroll in the corner have a flavour of nineteenth century work about them.   F. W. TROUP.

12.—WREATH IN THE WREN MANNER.

WOOD-PANELLING

Fashion in Wall-coverings—Pictures versus Panelling—Inexpensive Modern Panelling--
The Uses of Deal and Inlay.

IT is a truism that nothing is more fickle than Fashion. That it was so in Shakespeare's day we have the incidental testimony of Conrade and Borachio, as they stood talking under the pent-house on that night when Dogberry was unusually alert. The fickleness, it is true, varies according to circumstances; it is more marked, for instance, in the clothing of the body, which is easily changed, than in the clothing of the house, which is somewhat difficult to remove. Nevertheless, the clothing of the house has varied from age to age according to the dictates of Fashion. In Shakespeare's time the commonest form of wall-covering was panelling of wood, although the yet older method of hanging the walls with tapestry was still in vogue, as we learn from many of his allusions. Panelling held the field for more than a century and a-half after his period. It survived, indeed, although reduced in height to a mere dado, until the beginning of the last century; and it was within the recollection of the fathers of middle-aged men that wood dados were removed from their parlours in order to comply with the custom of papering the entire wall. It was the wall-paper that ousted panelling, as being cheaper and brighter (for the restriction of window space in consequence of the window-tax must not be forgotten), and, moreover, as ministering to the ever-present desire for change.

In the Elizabethan period wall-panelling was formed in comparatively small oblongs; but owing to the slight distance which the panel was recessed from the surrounding framework, and the simple repetition of the same

13.—A ROOM THAT COST FIFTY POUNDS TO PANEL.

forms over a large surface of wall space, the effect was restful and quiet; it produced a pleasant, subdued liveliness. In Jacobean work—at least, in its more pretentious manifestations—the result was more fussy; there was a more evident striving after effect. Then came the larger handling of the later half of the seventeenth century; the huge panels and the boldly-projecting mouldings associated with the time of Wren, the kind of work which adorns so many of the City churches. The flat, delicately-arabasqued pilasters of a century earlier became large columns almost disengaged from the wall. The small-membered cornices grew in bulk and carried boldly-designed foliage. The carving, which formerly submitted to the severe restraint of its surrounding framework, cast off such trammels and appealed to the eye not as incidentally enriching the design, but as an independent work of art, to be admired for its own intricacy and marvellous modelling. It was the wonderful skill of

Grinling Gibbons that fostered this development, and the general effect of the treatment can be seen in the accompanying illustration of a modern example in this manner, where emphasis is given to the picture framed in the overmantel by a Gibbons-like composition of fruit and cherubs (Fig 18).

The whirligig of Time brings in its revenges, and the fashion which our grandfathers discarded is now in vogue once more. Nor is the change a mere freak of fickleness; for where there are no fine pictures to be hung, panelling is a highly satisfactory method of covering a wall. To be sure, painters grumble sadly and assert that the prevalence of panelling is depriving them of their occupation; that the man who has his walls panelled wants pictures no more than the man of austere taste would think of adding

14.—AT LONGSTOWE HALL.

jam to his bread and butter. To which the cynic might reply: What kind of a picture is yours if it cannot hold its own against lifeless wood?

However this may be, there is no doubt that, given the desire to obtain a decorative effect, the desire can be gratified more cheaply by panelling than by pictures. Forty or fifty pounds would not go far in pictures, but it would go all round a fair-sized room in the manner shown in Fig. 13. The room is large, nearly thirty feet by twenty feet, and the panelling is over ten feet in height. The area covered was about five hundred square feet, and the cost of the panelling, at one shilling and tenpence a foot, thus worked out at about fifty pounds. Owing to modern methods of doing the work—a suitable combination of machinery and hand labour— it is now possible to produce panelling at less than half the prices prevalent ten years ago. Expensive woods are not necessary for rich effects. Proportion and rhythm may not be easy to obtain, but they are not costly in execution. It is, therefore, worth anybody's while, when building or altering his house, to consider the use of this charming method of decoration in one or more of the rooms.

It is not necessary to employ oak or other hard woods. Delightful

15.—DESIGNED BY MESSRS. SIMPSON AND AYRTON.

16.—DFAL PANELLING DESIGNED BY MR. LUTYENS.

effects can be secured not only with painted deal, but with deal left clean from the tool, as in the smoking-room at Temple Dinsley, with its panelling designed by Mr. Lutyens (Fig. 16). There is another adjunct to panelling which can be employed ; to wit, inlay. A good example of this is the woodwork that surrounds the hall fireplace at Ditton Place, Balcombe (Fig. 17). The architects of that interesting house, Mr. Cecil Brewer and Mr. Dunbar Smith, have been sparing in their use of inlay, but the little parti-coloured chequers at the points of the square flush panels give a touch of added interest.

If money is no great object, richer and more elaborate effects can, of course, be obtained, such as are shown in the illustrations of panelling

17.—INLAID WORK AT DITTON PLACE.

at Longstowe Hall, Cambridgeshire (Figs. 14 and 15). This is conceived quite in the spirit of old work, and is none the worse for mingling the styles of different periods. The doors, with their shallow panels surrounded by soft and delicate mouldings, recall the early seventeenth century ; the twisted column, itself a piece of old work pleasantly fulfilling a new use, strikes a somewhat later note, and the bold pilaster in the corner is reminiscent of Wren. But the whole effect, heightened as it is by the graceful and charmingly-disposed ironwork, is eminently pleasant, and shows that cultivated designers, such as Messrs. Simpson and Ayrton, can produce work vieing in interest with much of that which, hallowed by age, rouses the enthusiasm of latter-day students.

J. A. GOTCH, F.S.A.

18.—IN THE GRINLING GIBBONS MANNER.

ARCHITECTURAL FURNITURE

Nineteenth Century Ideas of Furniture—Architects and Furniture Design—The Screening of Radiators—
Varying Motifs in Design and Craftsmanship

THE title of this chapter is intended to suggest a name for that type of furniture which is built into the fabric of the house, forming part and parcel of it ; yet it is a little misleading, as all good furniture is architectural, whether it is a fixture or not. The influence of architects on furniture design has, on the whole, been sound, often keeping the cabinet-maker away . from flamboyancy in detail and guiding him in the paths of sensible construction. . This can be readily seen in all the early Gothic work, and especially in the pleasing mouldings which help to finish many a Jacobean cabinet. The influence of later men like Chambers and Adam on the crafts of their period is, of course, well known. So much, then, for the title ; it may remain as preferable to " Fitments," which is jumpy, or " Fitted Furniture," which is not much better ; and the subject is an interesting one whatever we dub it.

The particular significance of people's desire to beautify their houses with architectural furniture is that it is evidence of a certain belief in their own judgment ; that it shows in them the coming again of that home-making instinct which has been supposed to be peculiarly British. Certainly up to the middle of the last century this was the case, and the Englishman's home being his castle, he made it as comfortable as he could. His Turkey carpets were the genuine article, and his mahogany table had no need to be screened by a chenille cover because the legs only were of that wood. Horsehair and repp conveyed the impression that permanency was the aim. In the succeeding generations, it was just this quality that was lacking, and the average home of that day suggested that the owner was a bird of passage who, having bought the effects of a previous migrant, was prepared to pass them on at the shortest notice to a following one. The furniture was deplorably made and very cheap ; far too cheap to have been made under fair conditions, and it appeared to be considered an advantage that so soon as it became shabby, which it very speedily did, it was a matter of trifling expense to renew it. Pretty came into use as an adjective, and a

19.—MORNING-ROOM AT HEATHCOTE, ILKLEY.

more unarchitectural word was never invented. Permanency was not sought. To consider seriously the furnishing of house and home on the basis of the knowledge that the furniture so acquired would have to be lived with for the rest of one's life made the experiment as hazardous as matrimony. Ability to do so reflects an equable and well-trained mind and an amount of knowledge that the layman did not then possess. The connoisseur of the eighteenth century was so appreciative of fine work that he generally managed to obtain it,

20.—FIREPLACE WITH CUPBOARDS AT HEATHCOTE.

and one's hope is that in this twentieth century he may blossom into life again. To be content, then, to go one step further and have one's house fitted with architectural furniture, shows, at least, that the owner has the faculty of being able to make up his mind, that he knows exactly what he wants, and also that he is making a home that shall in each succeeding year be more a part of himself, rather than the mere furnishing of a house taken for a short period. The former state used to obtain, and in most cases a man married and lived all his life in one home. In the turmoil of the mechanical age he seems to have lived mostly in the pantechnicon vans of the remover. Because he was very uncomfortable and miserable, he invented a saying that "Fools built houses, but wise men lived in pantechnicons," and in divers other ways he pretended that the home and its surroundings was no longer of any consequence, and had, in fact, lost all its significance. Then, like the baby in the tale, he tired of seeing the wheels go round, and felt once more the necessity of a resting-place where peace might be enjoyed after turmoil, and strength gathered for the living of his arduous life. So the home came into fashion again, and the

21.—DESIGNED BY SIR ROBERT LORIMER FOR LYMPNE CASTLE.

furniture which was so unhomelike began to be replaced by oddments of other ages, often incongruous in their new surroundings, and not at all fitting to them or their new owner. But this is all of yesterday; the leaven works, and every day the movement gains strength. There are many architects working now on sensible lines, with almost a real tradition of building. That they are able to do so is a tribute to the men like Shaw, Devey and Webb, who so manfully battled against the nineteenth century saying, already

22.—DINING-ROOM AT FRINTON-ON-SEA, DESIGNED BY MR. VOYSEY.

quoted, that they reversed its judgment. So the wise men build houses now, and furnish them in a variety of ways, some of which are illustrated here; but always it must be remembered that architectural fashions, to use a modern word, will prove but ephemeral unless they represent and grow out of the ideals of the people.

There is a tendency in modern criticism of matters artistic, and it would seem a wholly wise one, to trace cause and effect in the relation of artist and client and in their joint production. If there was any real recognition in the nineteenth century of the labourings which preceded the birth of a work of art, it took the form only of a feeling that matters artistic were quite incomprehensible and arrived at their maturity in some haphazard way. This

23.—SIDEBOARD AT DOLOBRAN, DESIGNED BY MR. CURTIS GREEN.

must all be admitted. Pictures were considered to be articles possessing certain wall-covering properties ; sculpture consisted of lay figures, invested with facial resemblance to leading statesmen, who being defunct were unable to protest against the proceedings ; and architecture—well, an architect was some sort of person who had to do with buildings, but what he really was no one knew. Foundation-stones were laid, and the buildings were duly opened, and the recognition accorded to ceremony and building exactly followed the illustriousness of the opener. As to furniture, there was a total lack of recognition that artistic work is only possible (geniuses excepted) when it reflects the desires and ideals

24.—RECESS MADE IN A ROOM TO FIT AN OLD SIDEBOARD.

of a period when Beauty is recognised. It cannot be ignored that each century has produced exactly the type of work which accords with all its other attributes. The houses built in the time of the Armada all seem worthy of having been inhabited by " English seamen of the sixteenth century," and still may be instanced as more truly English in type and plan and regard for convenience than any that have been produced since. The more rococo style of the seventeenth century is quite fittingly Caroline in character, and in the same way the eighteenth century architecture of Bath is the only possible background for the " School for Scandal." If this is so, it is only by recognising that artistic work is an outcome of the spirit of the times that we can reach safe ground. If the conditions are favourable, we may hope once again to do good work. If it is to appeal to us as a beautiful thing, it must have some human quality about it. It need not necessarily be made wholly by hand ; there may be some concession to cost of production, and there are many ways in which machinery helps in this direction ; but to feed wood in at one end of an insatiate monster and expect chefs d'œuvre at the other is but to court disillusionment.

The morning-room at Heathcote, Ilkley, was designed by Mr. Lutyens (Fig. 19). The room is conceived in a robust type of eighteenth century work ; it is in no sense a reproduction, but rather an acceptance of such a dignified base as a foothold for steps forward. Never was there such a misnomer as L'Art Nouveau ; always must there be tradition for a start, and without such basis results only eccentricity.

A bedroom fireplace in the same home is illustrated (Fig. 20). The two broad pilasters at the sides stop the panelled dado to the room, and carry the moulded capping of the china shelf. The ceiling of the

25.—CHINA CUPBOARD BY MR. LUTYENS.

26.—DINING-ROOM DRESSER AT SANDHOUSE.

ingle is lowered, as it should be for the sake of proportion, and there are two good boot cupboards at the side of the fireplace. Attention may be drawn to the ingenious arrangement of the hearth, taken right across the chimney, and the way that the white bands in it stop against the bases of the architrave to the fireplace and the side pilasters. Much painstaking care was necessary to make such a thing as this a success, and there must be a recognition, on the part of the public, that many things go to the successful production of a work of art or a period of good design.

The china cupboard designed by Mr. Lutyens (Fig. 25) shows a skilful use of a recess, and the glazed doors, behind which china is displayed, framed by the circular-headed architrave, make a dignified whole. The fitment gains in use, and does not lose in beauty, by the skilful way in which a heating radiator has been concealed behind the fret in the base.

Sir Robert Lorimer has also treated the problem of screening radiators in the anteroom of the dining-room at Lympne Castle. He was carrying out the reparation of a mediæval house, and consequently the panelling has the character of the period. Radiators are essential to modern dwellers in mediæval houses, and here is one contrived in artful fashion, again with china shelves over (Fig. 21).

The sideboard in the dining-room of The Homestead at Frinton-on-Sea was designed by Mr. Voysey (Fig. 22). The motif here was a holiday home, where all work might be reduced to the minimum, so far as domestic service and upkeep were concerned, and the angle treatment of the room arose out of a necessity of the plan. The dominant note of Mr. Voysey's work is its absolute sincerity and his adherence to the lines which he has marked out for himself as the right and proper ones. And it is a good creed this, to be content to work on a definite line, not following all the wayward caprices of fashion ; not being Queen Anne one year and Mary Anne the next. In the end it is so much the better for one's self and one's art, and the price once paid brings hope of Progress. One cannot serve both Beauty and Ugliness, and though expediency may be sometimes a necessity, it is rarely a virtue.

The sideboard at Dolobran, Chislehurst, designed by Mr. Curtis Green (Fig. 23), is an interesting piece of furniture made rather to fit into its resting-place than as an actual fitment. It seems to have been designed with more sympathy than has gone to its making ; while it is clearly an exceedingly well-made piece, it is a little hard in execution. The converse of fitting furniture to its place is shown in

27 —A BEDROOM "FITMENT," BY MR. VOYSEY.

another picture, which illustrates a room made to fit a sideboard of unusual shape. The house where it now is was being remodelled for a new owner, and the opportunity was taken to provide an alcove in which this beautiful piece could stand (Fig. 24).

In contrast to such work as that at Heathcote is the dresser in the dining-room at Sandhouse, Witley, designed by Mr. Troup (Fig. 26). Worked round the door in the centre, and under the covering arch, it is very charming in its simplicity and acceptance of the "joyned" school of English woodwork. It is doubtful, though, whether it will be long possible to carry out this sort of detail without the craftsman to give it the human touch it needs. It lingers here and there, but no rising generation is following to take its place, and the machine set to do such work fails, and that lamentably.

The "fitment" in the bedroom of a house at Frinton-on-Sea, designed by Mr. Voysey, would have gained if there had been some play of relief, in the way of panelling to the side or cupboard doors or some slight mouldings. It is hard in appearance—the top and drawer fronts look so rigid that they should have been in some way relieved (Fig. 27).

Another illustration is of a fireplace and wardrobe in a bedroom at Standen, designed by Mr. Philip Webb. At first sight the two parts may hardly seem to form a whole, and the inclusion of a mirror rather breaks up the unity of the surface. There may have been reasons for so doing with which one is not familiar, but a better practice is to place the mirror on the inside of the door, which can be hinged so as to open at the proper angle for use. As with all Mr. Webb's work, there are little refinements that give evidence of care ; but it is individual in design rather than execution.

An organ-case in the dining-room of New Place, Welwyn, is a better instance of Mr. Webb's design. The simple lines of its panelled framing, combined with the delicacy of the moulded architrave surrounding the upper

28.—IN A BEDROOM AT STANDEN.

grilles, all go to make up a very charming whole (Fig. 29). The layman may be inclined to think it bald, having in mind the walnut and gold of the American organ-case, but it is in this austerity that lies its charm. It is very difficult to indicate wherein lies the quality which gives Mr. Webb's work its distinctive character. Perhaps it is its peacefulness and lack of all vulgarity that pleases ; and, further, it must be remembered that its author is now living in retirement at the end of a life spent in good architectural work, and that he it was who influenced Morris in all his woodwork and designed most of his furniture. It is so much the simpler for us now that Morris and Webb did all this ; but what of their difficulty in preaching such a gospel to the nineteenth century machine tenders ? Just one word more, and that is the great hold Mr. Webb has over a very considerable section of his brother architects. Nearly always are there one or two artists who perhaps mean more to their brothers than the outside public, and in this case the tribute of their affection would certainly acclaim Mr. Webb as an architect's architect. Another interesting treatment on the same lines is shown in the organ-grille at Ewelme Down designed by Mr. Walter Cave (Fig. 30).

Finally, let it be emphasised that cheapness is not the sole end and aim of existence. The definite obligation, if we wish to have furniture that will equal that of the eighteenth century, is to find out more about it, and probe into the conditions of labour and craft that went to produce it.   One claims no standard of morality for Art ;   Benvenuto Cellini was a prodigious scoundrel but a great artist, and he could be the one and yet the other, because he recognised Beauty as an asset.   Our

29.—ORGAN-CASE BY MR. PHILIP WEBB.

30.—ORGAN-GRILLE BY MR. WALTER CAVE

civilisation appears to have neglected it, and so we suffer ; or do we think that ugliness is more respectable ?   C. H. B. QUENNELL.

FIREPLACES.

The Fire in the Mediæval Hall—Doubtful Virtues of Dog-grates and Hob-grates—Count Rumford's Invention—The Principles of Fireplace Design—Revival of Old Patterns—Mantel Registers—Causes of Fog—Anthracite Stoves and Their Uses.

THE ordinary house fireplace, as we know it to-day in its many and varied forms, is the lineal descendant of the open fire in the middle of the mediæval hall. In this position, though there could have been very little loss of radiant heat, and none went up the chimney, as there did not happen to be one, the smoke problem must have been an appalling one. The wind came eddying through the unglazed windows or through the screens at the end of the hall as doors were opened and hunting-parties returned to their supper. However, the hypersensitive nerves of to-day hardly afflicted the jovial knight and his squires; the smoke may have served as a useful deodoriser, but it is to be feared that they were a somewhat grubby lot. About the twelfth century the fireplace found its way to the wall, and it has stayed there ever since. There is an extremely interesting one at Castle Hedingham in Essex, which has all the characteristics that were to last right down to the eighteenth century—the open hearth on which the fire burnt, with a fine Norman arch across it, and then, instead of the familiar flue vanishing in a vertical direction to the chimney, it slants out at an angle of about 60deg. to the exterior wall, where the outlet is concealed behind one of the flat Norman buttresses. This must be quite one of the earliest fireplaces, and is, with its encircling castle, well worth a visit to anyone interested

31.—THE OPEN FIRE IN THE HALL.

in the subject. This type remained for many centuries, with all sorts of modifications to suit the varying styles of architecture, and it is one that is beloved of architects. The cavern of its recess, large enough for seats at either side of the fireplace, and the sudden leaps of flame which light up the eddies of smoke in their upward path, all go to make a picturesque whole. It is possible to give scale to such a treatment, and get a better effect than is possible with the ordinary modern grate, stuck in a hole in the wall, with a flat sort of mantel-piece for a surround. The unfortunate side of the business, though, is that the despised modern slow-combustion grate is much more efficient from the point of view of the consumption of bituminous coal and consequent production of heat. An illustration is given of a fireplace in one of Mr. Norman Shaw's houses (Fig. 34), which is an extremely satisfactory solution of the problem, excepting only that the dog-grate is one of the worst forms of stoves, a very large proportion of the heat going up the chimney. The design shows a fireplace within the ingle-nook, and it would now

32.—AT WHIXLEY HALL.

be quite possible to obtain a type of stove which could be used in the same design and give better heating results; but the dog-grate is an attractive type and looks better in the ingle-nook than the enclosed fire. In these days of hot-water radiators it is quite possible to combine appearance with comfort. A dog-grate can be fixed in appropriate surroundings, in the hall of the house, for instance, and its heating capabilities augmented with a few radiators. The hall fireplace at Whixley Hall, York, illustrated, is a beautiful example of an old dog-grate, and modern variations of the treatment are shown in the library at Little Thakeham, designed by Mr. Lutyens, and in the especially beautiful marble mantel-piece designed by Professor Lethaby for the drawing-room at Avon Tyrrell (Fig. 35).

The eighteenth century hob-grate, with the open fire and dog-grate, its immediate forerunners, were hopeless offenders from the point of view of smoke-production, as well as being extravagant in the way of fuel consumption, and wasteful so far as the heat generated was concerned, because this, or the bulk of it, went up the chimney. Designers, makers and users of fire-places had not yet begun to understand that a fireplace which was ideal from the point of view of burning wood was unsatisfactory for coal, and especially for the soft bituminous variety common to this country. An attempt to remedy matters was evidently made in the eighteenth century, and is instanced in the illustration of the old grate which has had the hobs enclosed by a semi-circular arched top (Fig. 38). It was

33.—IN THE LIBRARY AT LITTLE THAKEHAM.

not till quite the end of the eighteenth century that Count Rumford set about trying to design a proper fireplace for the burning of coal, and the principles which he enunciated, in a lecture before the Royal Institution, are those which obtain at the present day. Count Rumford was not successful in influencing public opinion ; here and there his principles were adopted, but not generally until 1886. Then in the same place another paper was read on the subject, by Dr. Pridgin Teale, who acknowledged how much he was indebted to the Count for his ideas, and from 1886 onwards these principles have been generally adopted, and may be set out as follows : 1.—A general contraction of the size of the fireplace. 2.—A use of brickwork and fireclay for the same instead of iron. 3.—Splayed sides to the fireplace and a sloping back. The first condition was an acknowledgment of the fact that coal instead of wood had become the staple fuel, and so less space was needed at the sides, and especially at the top ; as less smoke was to be produced, less room was needed for its escape. The second suggestion was a good one, as

36.—OLD CANOPIED FIREPLACE.

35.—AT AVON TYRRELL.

brickwork and fireclay are not good conductors of heat, which instead of being conducted and lost in the body of the surrounding wall, as was the case with the iron frame and cheeks to the hob-grate, was retained and radiated into the room. The temperature of the fire was raised in consequence, and in the result a more perfect consumption of the coal took place. The third condition helped to radiate heat into the room and again helped combustion. It must be remembered that the London fog is very largely caused by imperfect combustion, and many attempts have been made from time to time to remedy this ; there have been stoves which were fed from underneath, so that the products of combustion had to pass through the incandescent mass, and were thus largely freed from their deleterious components. Generally, however, such designs were either too intricate to be understood by the people or too costly to be put upon the market, and never, therefore, obtained any hold. Enough has been instanced to show that from the days when our forefathers sat on their heels around a fire made in a little pit in the ground, which made them quite cosy' in front, but very chilly behind, down to our own times, the tendency has been continually to reduce the size of the actual fireplace, until it became a sort of fireclay box in which coal could be raised to an incandescent heat.

These practical details must needs be emphasised if the development of the fireplace and its design is to be properly understood. This is especially true of the design, because the latter was wholly influenced by the question of how to consume the fuel of the moment economically, and in this way was parallel to the broader issues of architecture, which were evolved out of a series of constructional problems overcome, one by one, with resulting phases that we now dub Norman, Decorated, or Perpendicular, as the case may be. It is extremely interesting to note how long it took in the case of the design of fireplaces to drive into the heads of the builders the fact that a grate suitable for burning logs was utterly unsuitable for coal. As instancing how

37.—HEATHCOTE : IN THE DINING-ROOM.

a detail, started in the first case for a plainly utilitarian reason, may develop eventually into a recognisable architectural feature, an illustration is given of an old fireplace of canopied form. The primitive type was undoubtedly a simple timber-framed contrivance cantilevered from the wall on brackets, so placed to catch puffs of smoke from the fireplace under ; as time passed the frame was concealed in stone, and marble came to be the familiar type to be seen in many a French château. So the old builders when they came to the fireplace part of their houses did not say, here we will have an ingle-nook, here a dog-grate, here a hob-grate and so on, but fitted the type of fire that was in use at the period, with little more emotion than we in our time select a tap for the kitchen sink. They surrounded their fireplaces in a variety of ways, but always appropriately and with regard to their use. Not being very scientific people, they were content to waste a large proportion of the heat generated. That there is no need for us to follow their example is shown by an illustration of the dining-room at Heathcote, where Mr. Lutyens has fitted a modern grate into an extremely dignified surrounding fireplace. The stove, with its encircling marble slabs, looks small, and is perhaps not so satisfactory a centre for the design as an open fire ·

38.—HOBS ENCLOSED WITH ARCHED TOP.

but from the point of view of coal-consuming it is the proper treatment.   Simple panelled treatments for mantel-pieces are also illustrated—of a drawing-room at Standen, and another of a dining-room at Four Beeches.

Passing to the design of the actual grate, mention has already been made of the problems which confronted Count Rumford and Dr. Teale, and the solution of these fixed the form of the modern stove, that is, so far as the actual coal-consuming body of the stove was concerned; its architectural treatment was hopelessly vulgar and commonplace, and it remained for architects like Norman Shaw, Eden Nesfield (Fig. 43) and Philip Webb to remedy such a state of affairs. That they were able to find makers who

39.—FOUR BEECHES.

were willing to carry out their ideas is a matter for congratulation, so far as we are concerned.   Mr. Shaw especially produced many quite admirable designs for fireplaces (Fig. 42), and we are apt to forget the debt of gratitude we owe him.   It is comparatively easy nowa-days to find a well-designed grate ; in the heyday of his youth he had to design it and have it made, and the same applied to every detail in one of his buildings.   Pugin, again, was another giant in this way.

The " Cupid " design illustrated in Fig. 45 is interesting in that it is no mere reproduction of an eighteenth century grate, but is cast by a firm of makers from the original patterns which are still in their possession.   These were carved between 1780 and 1800 by Henry and William Haworth, who were both students at the Royal Academy in the time of Sir Joshua Reynolds.   Some of the delicacy of the modelling of the little god with the darts is lost in the process of reproduction, but the high character of the work is a tribute to the artistry of the carvers, and one wishes that twentieth century manufacturers

40.—STANDEN, EAST GRINSTEAD : DRAWING-ROOM FIREPLACE.

would always follow such a good example. It is very usual to find in all classes of work the most elaborate organisation for its production and distribution, and in many cases that could be instanced no expense is spared in these directions. When, however, it comes to the cost of the design, which is to be the inspiration for all this energy, stinginess often appears to be the rule, so far as the reward of the artist is concerned, with the result that the best men will have nothing to do with it. Here, then, is a concrete case of money well spent, and the good design has outlived generations of bad ones. In fact, it only needed the assistance of Mr. John Kinross, who remodelled this and other similar eighteenth century designs to suit modern requirements. to give them a new lease of life that may easily last till 2011. There are many embryo Haworths, one hopes, now at the Academy schools, and further comment is needless.

An illustration is given of a grate with enrichment modelled by Mr. Laurence Turner, quite admirable in its bold lusciousness, which well accords with modern principles in its sloped fireclay back and economiser underneath. Another polished steel fireplace is shown of the barless type (Fig. 46) ; the necessity of providing the fresh air inlets is well met by placing them in a step kept within the jambs of the fireplace, and not projecting into the room as a raised hearth, as is sometimes done.

41.—MODELLED BY MR. LAURENCE TURNER.

A further illustration (Fig. 44) is of that most useful article, the cast-iron mantel register, for use when economy is essential and when it is desired to avoid the expense of a separate grate, with tiles surrounding it and a wooden mantel. This one, designed by Mr. D. W. Kennedy, is very suitable for bedrooms and the like, and seems a practical fireplace. These notes would hardly be complete without mention of those most useful contrivances, anthracite stoves. Their main essential difference is that, instead of being a box of fire set in a wall, they have made a step out into

42.—A DESIGN BY MR. NORMAN SHAW.

43.—A DESIGN BY EDEN NESFIELD.

the room, and stand free but for the connecting flue-pipe linking them to the wall and chimney. This flue-pipe is the only means of escape for any heat ; though the stove stands in a tiled recess, it is open all round at the back, so the whole body of the latter serves its purpose and helps to heat the room. It follows, then, that as there is little loss of heat, it is not necessary to burn so much fuel, and that it will also be possible in such a stove to make less fuel do more work by raising it to a higher temperature. Incidentally, this means less smoke production and fewer fogs. As to the latter, it is undoubtedly the fireplaces and kitchen ranges of private houses that do the damage in London, while under the Public Health Act the factory can be brought to book. Of the damage caused by these nuisances of the metropolis there can be little doubt. It has been estimated that to every square mile of air in Chelsea there are six tons of

smuts, and Sir Frederick Treves states that " the lungs of an adult dweller in big cities are dingy thundercloud blue in colour, due absolutely to dirt and soot in the atmosphere," and, also, that "in London alone the fogs kill people, not by scores and hundreds, but by thousands." Which is a serious statement in all reason from a man eminent in his profession and in a position to

44.—A MANTEL REGISTER.

know. But, notwithstanding all this, the Englishman has remained wedded to the open fire, and has always condemned the enclosed fire as hideous, unhomelike and Continental. But it has its most distinct uses, and need not necessarily be fully enclosed. The illustrations show two types—the first wholly enclosed and suitable for halls, the second an open fire suitable for reception-rooms. So, starting with the hall type (Fig 48), the following details may be enumerated. It is made of plain rolled steel casing, is very simple and strong in its construction, and burns for twenty-four hours without attention. It is here shown in

45.—THE "CUPID" GRATE.

the hall of a very interesting house designed by Mr. E. J. May, and he is responsible for the polished brass screen, which is hinged to allow free access to the stove. This screen is a very

. 46.—BARLESS FIRE IN POLISHED STEEL.

practical notion, as it somewhat conceals the stove, which, though quite simple, is not yet a thing of beauty ; and it saves the chance of any small child burning inquisitive fingers. At the same time, it permits all the heat to radiate into the hall. Set as the stove is in a concave semi-circular tiled recess, with this convex screen in front, and surrounded by the pleasantly-moulded architrave of its mantel-piece, the whole effect is good. The hall, too, is an admirable place to have an economical continuous burning fire, for if the hall, staircase and corridors be kept warm in the cold weather it spells comfort generally, and especially saves that cold inrush of air which comes when doors are opened. The other illustration (Fig. 47) is of one for reception-

47.—A STOVE FOR RECEPTION-ROOMS.

rooms, and made as it is with a brass or copper body, it more closely resembles the ordinary open fireplace than is usually the case with anthracite stoves. This, by the way, is the fuel used in both the types illustrated, and they burn without attention for twenty-four hours. It is contended for this type of stove that it gives both an open fire and a smokeless one at the cost of one farthing an hour. The illustration shows it fixed in the room of a house of Mr. Gibson, the architect, which probably accounts for the pleasing tile surround and wooden mantel-piece. It is interesting here to see such a stove in its association with old furniture and china, and incongruous.

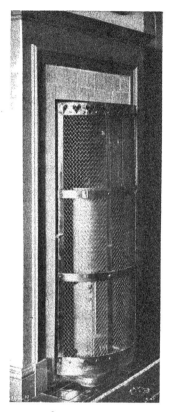

48.—A HALL STOVE

to note that it in no way appears

C. H. B. QUENNELL.

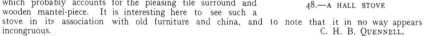

WOOD   CHIMNEY-PIECES.

*"The Small Thing" in Architecture—And the Architect's Care of It—Mr. Philip Webb's
Art—Evolution of the Chimney-piece—Legacies of the Salon.*

A FASHIONABLE architect of other times, entering his office one day and giving directions to
his chief assistant for a number of small and somewhat vexatious alterations to the scheme in
hand, wound up with the half apologetic remark, "The Duke of Blank is a man who judges
by small things." With this anecdote may be coupled another of a solemn conclave
of architects discussing the education of their successors, whereat an advocate of the grand
manner in architecture, declaiming against the attention given by the students to the design of small
subjects, tombstones and the like, was met by the remark from an able and well-known member. "Do
not you think it is precisely the small things that are so difficult to do? For myself, I am afraid of these
tombstones and the like; they give me so much trouble to work out." In the illustrations of
these charming mantel-pieces, those who have seen what Mr. Philip Webb can make of a country
house on a large scale will realise that the same ability can solve the problem of the small
thing with equal facility and success. Few clients probably realise that such designs as these are pure
gifts on the part of the architect, whose remuneration on the basis of cost can never repay the time and
thought bestowed on their artistic evolution. Probably one reason why in otherwise well-designed houses
we so often see such lamentable showroom chimney-pieces is that the architect has been discouraged, by
the attitude of the future inhabitants, from attempting any departure from the customary device—of
the stock pattern personally selected by the client. "What I like" is a formidable weapon, and as there
are few who can form any idea of the mantel-piece design, short of actual execution, it argues some
disinterested hardihood on the part of the architect to venture on so hazardous a field. Still, the time must come sooner or later when people will realise that the value of an interior designed by masters like Mr. Webb is a thing apart and beyond price.

In these instances of mantel-pieces quite economical in character there are elements of invention and graceful proportion and a reticence of features which will appeal at once to the cultivated taste. The individual note of Mr. Webb's work is most marked perhaps in the design (shown in Fig. 49) where the mantel-piece, though treated as part of the panelled walls, yet asserts itself by the bold combination of

49.—IN THE DINING-ROOM AT STANDEN.

the lozenge panels with the waving, arched line of the moulding below. We can quite imagine ladies exclaiming, " Oh, I should not like anything like that ! " It would be bordering on the unconventional, running the risk of a trespass on customary drawing-room decorums, if one may thus attempt to interpret the objection at the back of the mind of the speaker. It is precisely this sanctioned drawing-room convention that requires to be broken down, because, while it is not only negative towards fresh ideas, it is actually affirmative to many bad old ways which could not otherwise exist. Who really likes, if they come to question the existing order of things, either the boxed white marble legs and table top of the Early Victorian, or its successor, quite equal in enormity, the typical inglenook combination of the showroom, trumpery in construction and futile in design, that has superseded it in Fashion's graces ? How is it possible to obtain that note of grace, proportion and harmony that every interior, however simple, must possess unless the same mind that conceived the room as a whole also originates what is likely to be its centre point of interest ? Skill and care bestowed on windows, doors, ceiling and floor must not be jeopardised by some commonplace at the focus of the hearth.

How the Anglo-Saxon mind revolved round the fireplace was amusingly illustrated in the case of an aged

50.—CHIMNEY-PIECE AND PANELLING.

official, transplanted from his old quarters to one of those palatial edifices that recent Governments have erected in Whitehall. After a volley of complaints about his new quarters, he wound up by saying, ' and then there are those radiators, and no place where a man can knock out his pipe ! " This is to serve as a preface to the remark that there are other chimney-piece designs of a bolder character to be evolved for billiard-room, smoking-room and library, in which there should be some reflection of the character of the room and of its owner. The design of the fireplace really belongs to a long, continuous and most interesting development. We have arrived at a point where the actual grate has probably reached its minimum dimensions. From the old days of wide, cavernous openings, where whole logs could be burnt, the use of coal, as the conditions of its economical consumption have been worked out, has brought us to the tiny interior, one and a-half feet wide by two and a-half high, which yet gives a heat more constant while as powerful as the great fire of logs in an opening, say, six feet wide by four high.

As may be expected, modern designs still show traces of the original opening. " Surrounds," as they are called, of marble, stone and tiles are used to reduce the customary width to the new conditions, and the name of the grate itself—" an interior "—is also suggestive of the facts. The dog grate, so called from its original—the dogs on which the logs were piled—is a hazardous compromise. It is usually accompanied by the smoke trouble in an aggravated form, and it is not really a scientific way of consuming

51.—IN A BEDROOM.

coal fuel. As coal rises in price and legal disabilities fall on those who fail to consume their own smoke, we must expect more and more to have grates evolved on the lines of a fire-brick retort, small in size but powerful in radiant action. It falls, therefore, to the sensible architect to continue the manifest evolution of the mantel-piece and to work out his designs in accordance with the new conditions. Fancy, invention, grace and proportion are of all periods and will not die out, and the good architect will produce out of the treasure-house of his mind things old and new in admirable combination.

Much mischief has been done by the falsified scale of the mantel-shelf and the accompanying burden of ormolu and bronze that has accumulated thereon. This legacy of the great salon, with its furniture, heroic in scale, is very difficult to displace. It has been a hard battle to get a hearing for the small shelf up to six inches wide and perhaps four to five feet from the floor. Tenants have been known to decline architects' houses on such grounds, and to take their stand, morally and physically, as it were, on the wide, low shelf as a condition of occupancy.

We should be " still talking," like the hero of " Superman," if we continued on this fertile topic of chimney-piece design ; but this chapter will have served its purpose if it calls attention to the wide field afforded by the chimney-piece and interests the intending house-builder in the problem—to the end that he may encourage his architect to make special designs for these features.

Arthur T. Bolton.

52.—A DESIGN OF SIMPLE ELEMENTS.

THE BILLIARD-ROOM.

The Revolt Against the Ordinary Table—The Arrangements at the Billiards Control Club—Lighting Questions—A Stone Table—A Room with Raised Dais.

NOT least among the problems of the house is the equipment of the billiard-room. It must be admitted at once that most makers of billiard-tables have been content to repeat in thoughtless fashion the treatment which contented their predecessors of fifty years ago, when Early Victorian ideas were supreme. The worst parts of the ordinary table are the ugly and massive turned legs, which too long have kept their ascendancy. Sometimes variety has been secured by treating the top of the leg like the capital of a column with volutes of large projection ; but these not only offend by their borrowing of an unsuitable architectural element, but are apt to hit the legs of players. Of late, however, some thought has been directed to table design. Though there is still much to be done to bring the ordinary stock pattern into line with contemporary ideas, the examples illustrated show a good tendency. A few years ago considerable attention was given to this question by designers, who were captured by the superficial clevernesses of the New Art movement, and tables were produced with legs that seem to have been inspired by a guttering candle. No good purpose, however, would be served by illustrating examples which have no claim to interest, except in so far as they represent the outcome of a strained originality.

A billiard-table is from its very nature and use a massive thing. The slate top is heavy, and in order to secure an absolutely true surface, it is essential that the framework which supports the bed shall be entirely rigid and free from danger of warp or twist. To prevent sagging, not less than eight legs can safely be used. Nor is it enough that they should be strong enough in fact, for sufficient support could be secured by employing a stout iron tube. The decorative demand for strong things is that they should also look strong, and the legs must, therefore, be reasonably bulky. The table designed by Mr. Voysey shows how a simple thing, which lacks decorative adjunct, can yet be satisfactory (Fig. 57). There is nothing about the design which involves any expenditure above what is needful for a table fitted with the ugliest turned

53.—AT ARDKINGLAS.

legs. It shows an appreciation of the needs of a billiard-table, and expresses those needs in a straightforward way.

A more consciously d e c o r a t i v e   treatment characterises the equipment of the rooms at the Billiards Control Club. The tables, their marking cabinets and adjoining mantel-pieces form part of one scheme, devised by Mr. Wimperis. Though the frames of the tables are devised with a hint of Chippendale influence, there is nothing which stands out at all markedly. The club fulfils a valuable function in legislating for the most popular of indoor games. From such a body we are entitled to expect not only light and leading in the politics of the game, but also in those practical details which make for pleasure and comfort in playing. One or two practical notes about

54.—IN A FRENCH MANNER.

the equipment of the chief clubroom may, therefore, be instructive. On three sides there is a platform with low lounge seats, and this is raised seven inches above the general floor-level. The edge of the

55.—AT THE BILLIARDS CONTROL CLUB.

platform is four feet six inches from the outside line of the table itself. The lighting both of the table and of the room is an important feature. Above the table is a pleasantly-d e s i g n e d electrolier of the usual six lights, and each light is a cluster of three lamps of sixteen candle-power each. The intensity of electric light depends, of course, somewhat upon the pressure at the main; but unless this is below the average the amount of light thrown on the table may be regarded as ideal. Upon this point experts are likely to differ, but it is of interest that the B.C.C. has adopted about three hundred candle-power as a standard. The general lighting of the room is effected by a few short brackets on the walls, the lamps of which are veiled by green silk shades. The decorations help to ensure a restful effect. The walls are covered with a paper patterned in green and dim gold, and the furniture is upholstered in green. The clubrooms have no top lights for daylight play ; but even for billiard-rooms in country houses it is very doubtful whether lantern lights over the table are the best practice. There is always the danger that they may not be entirely water-tight, and the presence on the table of a spot or two, either of admitted rain or of water which has condensed on the glass, is a troublesome possibility. Moreover, it is to be remembered that the professional billiard player (who may be presumed to know something of the matter) never practises by daylight, because the light on the balls makes the angles appear different than when the table is lit by artificial light immediately above it. For the ordinary amateur, however, a billiard-room lit by daylight is naturally very desirable, particularly in the country, when outdoor pursuits are stopped by bad weather. It is doubtful whether architects are as alive as they might be to the advantages of attic billiard-rooms. Space in an attic is cheaper per cubic foot than the same space on the ground floor, and by carrying the roof a foot or two higher than would be needed if the attic is to contain only servants' bedrooms, an admirable billiard-room is often to be secured, the natural lighting of which by day through dormer windows is likely to be much superior to what would be secured in a ground-floor room. In the latter case it is very often difficult to secure lighting from more than one side ; but in an attic, dormer windows could sometimes with a little forethought be arranged on both sides of the room, with good results in the lighting of the table. It is necessary, however, for a billiard-table to rest on a substantial floor, and the joists beneath it would, therefore, need to be heavier than is usual in attic bedrooms.

56.—A STONE-BUILT TABLE.

In cases where a definite period has been adopted for the decorative treatment of a billiard-room, it is desirable that the table shall be in accord with it. Figure 54 shows a room with admirable French furniture, and the billiard-table has been ornamented in harmony with the prevailing feeling. Attention may be drawn to the simple and reasonable arrangement of the lights, which hang singly from the ceiling without any electrolier. This strikes quite the right note. The lighting of rooms of the period was by candles, and for the general illumination in this case wall sconces are provided. Any attempt to carry out the same rich motive in so large a fitting as a billiard-table light would have meant something gorgeous to the point of vulgarity, and the decision to meet the needs of the case on simple utilitarian lines shows decorative wisdom. Period decoration has its limitations for historical reasons which ought to be obvious, but seem too often to be overlooked.

Figure 56 shows a billiard-table of singular originality and interest, designed by Mr. E. L. Lutyens for Marsh Court. Any question as to the treatment of table legs has been magnificently swept away by setting the table on a masonry base, which gives it an air of supreme solidity. A treatment such as this must, of course, be regarded as a counsel of perfection, as it need scarcely be pointed out that so fine a conception cannot be materialised at a cost within the reach of the ordinary householder. Another interesting feature of the room is the very beautiful wooden electrolier. For such a purpose wood is an ideal material, and one could wish that it were more frequently employed instead of the restless confectionery in polished brass or hammered black iron which so often disfigures billiard-rooms otherwise well equipped.

The point of view in the first illustration of this chapter (Fig. 53) was chosen rather to show the planning of the room itself than the design of the table, though the latter is of a robust and simple sort. It is at Ardkinglas, and the architect, Sir Robert Lorimer, has treated the room in an interesting and practical way. It serves, as in so many cases, not only for billiards, but as a general smoking lounge for the men of the house. One end of it, therefore, has been treated as a raised dais, where there are writing-tables, and steps lead down to the billiard-room proper. The players are thus saved from the distraction of having people walking about on the same level near the table, and spectators can draw up chairs to the railing that guards the edge of the raised floor and look down on to the table. A plan of this type is not always possible, as it depends naturally on the disposition of the other rooms; but where it can be contrived it makes a pleasant and convenient room.   L. W

57.—A SIMPLE DESIGN BY MR. VOYSEY.

LIBRARIES AND BOOKCASES.

Early History of the Care of Books—Four Main Systems of Housing Them—The Pepys Bookcases—The Problem of Doors—Decorative Treatment of Libraries—Good Dimensions for Bookshelves.

THERE is perhaps no room in a house which may be expected to reveal the character of its owner more markedly than does the library. It is a place where one meets silent friends, and it is seemly, therefore, that the decorations should be restrained and subordinate to the main purpose, the care of books. They may be housed either in separate bookcases, or on shelves which form part of the architectural treatment of the room. Both methods will be discussed in this chapter. The history of bookcases is an interesting one, and necessarily bound up with the whole arrangement of libraries. As in the case of all other furniture, their study is helped by some knowledge of the requirements arising out of the care of books. This subject has been admirably dealt with by the late John Willis Clark, whose " Care of Books " is a mine of information to which one naturally turns. His researches, however, were carried no later than the end of the eighteenth century, while the subject-matter of this chapter will include some interesting modern examples. Bookcases may be divided into four main types: 1. Chests, presses and cupboards. 2. The lectern system. 3. The stall system. 4. The wall system. The evolution wrapped up in these four types must be considered, even if it involves delving into habits of antiquity.

Perhaps the first reference to a library is that in the Book of Ezra, where we may assume that the " House of the Records " was the repository of inscribed clay tablets. For the latter, the thoughtful Mesopotamian provided slate shelves. There seems no doubt that shelving was also provided in the magnificent library at Pergamon, extending to about two hundred thousand volumes, which Mark Antony gave to Cleopatra. In the days of Imperial Rome there were no fewer than twenty-six public libraries, the chief contents of which were rolls kept in presses. Plutarch mentions Lucullus as a collector of fine books, whose examples set a fashion in Rome. Seneca, who was more interested in the insides of books than their outsides, wrote with an entertaining savageness about those who regarded books as ornaments rather than tools for the mind. He tilts, moreover, at the folk who liked handsome bookcases, " why should you excuse a man who wishes to possess book presses inlaid with *arbor-vitæ* wood or ivory ? " In his annoyance, however, he gives us some useful facts. Bookcases were built as high as the ceiling, and, it would appear, against the wall. The presses found at Herculaneum seem to be very much like the modern bookcase with cornices at the top, but, of course, deeper from back to front, because they accommodated rolls more than flat books, though the latter type, called Codex, was in use as early as the beginning of the third century. Most Roman bookcases, however, seem to have been built up of pigeon-holes rather than with shelves, except in the case of bedside books, which the younger Pliny kept in a press let into the wall, and holding books " not merely to be read, but read over and over again."

We may roughly assume, then, that the classical librarian resorted chiefly to bookcases of our first type. consisting of presses arranged pigeon-hole fashion, with some employment of the wall system for the flat books or codices. This does not mean, of course, that shelves were not used in presses, for there is a mosaic representation of a fifth century cupboard with a pair of doors and two shelves on which books he flat-wise. The next stage in the development was in the direction of the lectern. Books were so valuable in the Middle Ages that they had to be handled carefully, and as, moreover, they were heavy, the best method was to read them as they lay on a sloping desk, to which they were brought from cupboards, such as the great " almeries of wainscot " which stood in the Cloister at Durham. In monastic houses reading was generally done in carrells, which were little bays in one or more of the Cloister walks. As the number of books grew, presses were scattered in odd spaces about the monastic buildings, and it was only in rare cases, such as at Christ's Church, Canterbury, where separate libraries were provided to house them.

The lectern system reached its most characteristic form in such libraries as that of Trinity Hall (Fig. 59), Cambridge, where the sloping desks were set back to back. In some such cases the books were chained to a top rail. We are brought into intimate touch with this arrangement through a sketch by Michelangelo himself for the lectern type of bookcase which he fitted in the Medicean Library at Florence. This shows a figure sitting in front of the bookcase, and indicates that he was considering what height would be most convenient for the reader. Beneath the sloping lectern are shelves on which additional books lie flat. As books became less rare, the system of chaining them to lecterns broke down, and the next step in the evolution was the arrival of the stall system, devised to obviate waste of space. The earliest surviving seems to be at Corpus Christi College, Oxford.   The main idea was to separate the two halves of the sloping desk by a broad shelf with one or more shelves fixed above it.   The desk, however, was still an important feature in the scheme, and the great innovation of omitting it came at the beginning of the seventeenth century.   The Library of St. John's College, Cambridge, finished in 1628, furnishes an admirable example, where the bookcases run out into the room from the wall spaces between each pair of windows, and loose stools only were provided for the use of readers.

Another interesting variant is to be seen in the Library of Peterhouse, Cambridge, illustrated in Fig. 62.   The carved wings once masked the ends of readers' seats.   We come now to the fourth type, which is the most common to-day, the bookcase set against the wall, though, as far as the absence of the reader's desk is concerned, it was practically contemporary with the stall system.   It is, of course, impossible to say when the wall case was first introduced, but a very interesting example is to be found in the Library of the Escorial in Spain, built between 1563 and 1584.   Though there is no doubt that small shelves on the walls were often used in earlier times for the accommodation of a few books, the Escorial example seems to be the first where the whole of the walls of a great room were covered with bookcases. They seem to have been adopted in England at the Bodleian Library, completed in 1612, and from that time on held their own either alone or in conjunction with bookcases running out from the wall toward the middle of the room.   In the housing of books, as in everything else architectural, Sir Christopher Wren's influence was great. His first library was built at Lincoln Cathedral in 1674, and other notable examples by him were at Trinity College, Cambridge, and —perhaps the best known of all—at St. Paul's Cathedral. In the latter case he relied entirely upon wall book-cases, which run up to the point from which the stone arching springs, and are divided halfway by a gallery running round the room.

It may be well at this point to make a practical suggestion to those who have a diffi-culty in providing book room, nor are they few

58.—LORD HALDANE'S LIBRARY.

in these days when everyone is a book buyer.   In several small houses which the writer has recently visited the architect has provided wall bookcases in hall or passage.   A fine example of this is to be seen on a large scale at Shirburn Castle, where the Earl of Macclesfield preserves the splendid library bequeathed to him by book-loving ancestors.   The main library is far too small to house this historic collection, and the big corridor shown in Fig. 60, and now named "The North Library," has been pressed into service, with what pleasing results may easily be seen.

So far we have dealt entirely with general types governing the arrangement of libraries.   Most of these involve questions of architectural treatment, rather than the design of individual bookcases, to which attention must now be drawn.   It seems unlikely that much attention was given to bookcases, considered as free standing pieces of furniture, until the latter part of the seventeenth century.   Wren was too busy a man to devote much time to furniture design, but it seems quite likely that the famous bookcases made for Samuel Pepys, and bequeathed by him with his library to Magdalene College, Cambridge, were actually designed by the great architect.   Pepys was an intimate friend of Wren, for whom he had the greatest admiration, as appears often enough in the Diary.   He was, moreover, a most discerning and enthusiastic collector of books, differing, however, from the modern bibliophile in one marked characteristic, viz., that when a new edition of a book came out he made haste to discard the first edition in its favour.   Whether the Pepys bookcases, one of which is shown in Fig. 61, were designed by Wren or not, they exhibit a very clear understanding of the problems involved.   The lower parts of the cases have a larger projection than the upper sections, and were so arranged to take the great folios

in which the seventeenth century delighted. It is worth noting that there is a bookcase at Cuckfield Park so like the Pepys example as to suggest it was made by the same hand.

It was not until the eighteenth century, however, that the free standing bookcase came into its own, and was the subject of infinite trouble in design. One of the debts we owe to the group of academic architects who worked under the patronage of the great Earl of Burlington is the definite architectural character which they imparted to furniture design. This is nowhere more apparent than in the very handsome bookcase, now illustrated, which was designed by William Kent (Fig. 63). The base is treated as a panelled cupboard, and

60.—AT SHIRBURN CASTLE.

the upper part turned into an architectural composition of considerable charm with its broken pediment surmounted by an antique bust, and its middle opening finished with a round arch.

Mr. H. B. Wheatley is the fortunate possessor of a singularly fine bookcase which it seems safe to attribute to the great Hepplewhite himself (Fig. 64). Its practical merit consists in the ingenious way that it is made to suit both big and little books. The middle part is of considerable projection, and the lines of the vertical beading, which holds the glass, mask the vertical partitions on which the shelves rest. Between these uprights in the middle are two shelves provided to take the largest tomes. Right and left of them are shelves set more closely which take small folios and quartos, while the curved wings are devoted to still smaller volumes.

Book-lovers will always differ in opinion on the question of bookcase doors. There are some early mediæval examples of doors filled with a large wire mesh, which protects from theft, but unless curtains are hung behind, it does not deliver the books from dust. Perhaps, on the whole, doors glazed with clear glass are the best way out. Sometimes, however, as in a very interesting example at Devonshire House (Fig. 65), the doors are filled with mirrors, a device certainly not to be imitated, except in a great *salon*, and even then only after grave thought.

The old examples so far illustrated show that for all practical purposes the designers of the eighteenth century had grasped all there was to be learnt about the care of books. In the equipment of great public libraries, modern invention has evolved various devices for the saving of space, such as the

61.—ONE OF PEPYS' BOOKCASES.

hanging bookstacks on overhead runners which are so marked a feature of the British Museum Library. They do not, however, give any hints for the equipment of the library of an ordinary private house, and need not, therefore, be discussed. Practically the only recent innovation which need be mentioned is the unit system of bookcases, by which they are built up of sections of standard size, and are thus capable of indefinite expansion. Though this American idea is practical enough, so far no care has gone to the design of the units or of the stock pattern cornices which surmount them; and though useful for offices, they can hardly be regarded as pleasant features in a library claiming any artistic merit. While the first and most important point to be considered is the practical necessity of housing books in a convenient fashion, a library is a poor place if no æsthetic judgment has gone to its equipment.

In a bookcase designed by Sir Robert Lorimer for Lympne Castle (Fig. 66) the cupboards which form the lower section have been treated with linenfold panelling, which carries on the general Gothic tradition of the Castle, while it is yet in every way a

63.—BY WILLIAM KENT.

practical place for books. An interesting type of wall bookcase is that designed by Mr. Philip Webb for Standen (Fig. 67). Though treated as a definite part of the room, it is equally applicable to a free standing bookcase. In order to accommodate the larger tomes, the lower part has been brought forward in its middle bay, which gives as well an interesting break in outline, and provides a shelf space not only for the clock, but also to receive a casual book. The tall bookcase designed by Mr. Lutyens (Fig. 69) marks his affection for treating glazed doors of furniture, as well as windows, with the heavy sash-bars that we associate chiefly with the architecture of William and Mary. The lower cupboards are practically contrived. Their doors are hinged at the bottom instead of at the sides, and when opened are kept at the horizontal by jointed arms. They serve thus as shelves on which books and papers may be laid temporarily, instead of on the floor.

From the first half of the eighteenth century onwards designers were much attached to the combination of bureau with bookcase. Most often the bookcase was simply the width of the bureau and sat upon it, but sometimes the middle compartment of a long range of bookcase would be fitted as a bureau. This is an obviously convenient arrangement, as the writer is thus surrounded by his books. Among modern variants of the old bureau with sloping hinged front or with drawer front that opens down with

64 —BY HEPPLEWHITE.

quadrant arms to support it, the most convenient and the most unpleasant in appearance is the American roll-top desk. Its proportions are invariably ill-conceived, and the curve of the roll top is usually the most ugly possible. Nevertheless, its practical merits are not to be denied, and Fig. 70 shows an ingenious attempt by Mr. Arthur T. Bolton to mask its native ugliness by surrounding it with a mahogany bookcase. The side wings are of·· the ordinary type with projecting cupboards below. The middle section is made of larger projection, so that it overhangs the top of the desk a little and incidentally provides space in its two glazed cupboards for the largest folio volumes. Between them is room for an old clock and for a row of books of moderate size. By treating desk and bookcase as a whole, the unhappy proportions of the former have been masked, while its practical virtues remain unimpaired.

65.—AT DEVONSHIRE HOUSE.

So far we have dealt chiefly with the bookcase itself. We come now to the important question of the relation of case or shelves to the general architectural treatment of the library. There is certainly nothing which furnishes a room in so ripe and satisfying a fashion as a great tapestry made up

66.—AT LYMPNE CASTLE.

of volumes clothed in the divers fashions that mark the history of the bookbinder's art. Of pictures in the library one demands but few, and they should be alive with literary or historical associations, and rather seem to illustrate the books themselves than stand out abruptly as claiming attention in their own right. Fig. 71 illustrates this aspect of the question. It shows a library fitted some years ago to the designs of Sir Robert Lorimer at Fettercairn, Forfarshire, one of the homes of Lord Clinton. The house is old, but has suffered considerable alterations during a period careless of architectural wisdom. A large library was wanted, and two rooms were thrown into one, making an apartment about forty feet long. Bookcases were run along the entire side of the room, and the frieze was brought out to the face of the bookcases at the top. In this frieze were set a number of family portraits, which thus appear flush with the bookcases, while the coats-of-arms of the various families that have been connected with the house were carved on the

67 —AT STANDEN.

intervening panels, and family badges on the frames of the pictures themselves. · One can hardly imagine a more suitable way of displaying family portraits, so markedly superior is it to the usual scattering of them on the walls in gilt frames of diverse types. Where portraits find their natural place elsewhere, however, it is desirable that the library should be adorned with canvases of a more markedly decorative character rather than with those which may be described as easel pictures. In this respect a room designed by Mr. Lutyens for Lady Horner at 16, Lower Berkeley Street, strikes exactly the right note. It is panelled in basswood left untouched from the tool, and on the plain wooden filling above the books on one side of

the room are three charming pictures of amorini, painted by Mr. T. M. Rooke. The long panel in the middle shows them playing among the flowers, while in the octagonal panels at the sides they gracefully act as supporters of coats-of-arms. Altogether it would be difficult to find a room treated in a fashion more graceful and scholarly than is this (Figs. 68 and 72).

The general treatment of a library with respect to its bookshelves is a topic upon which few book-lovers can be got to agree. The principal difficulty is caused by the majestic folios which the *dilettanti* of the eighteenth century delighted to produce. The fondness for great books has decreased, but there are still some subjects, notably great works on architecture, which demand a large page for their illustration. Some learned societies, too, have the habit of producing at long intervals slim mono-

68.—LADY HORNER'S LIBRARY.

graphs printed on sheets of enormous size, which so trouble their recipients with the difficulty of storing them that it is feared they do not always escape an early grave in the waste-paper basket. A similar problem of storage faces the owners

69.—BY MR. LUTYENS.

of portfolios of drawings and prints, and, still more, of maps. Except in large collections of books, these abnormal volumes are generally few in number, which increases the difficulty of housing them. If folios are placed on an ordinary bookshelf which they do not completely fill, they are apt to lean against each other, with consequent damage to the binding through buckling, and defacement of the pages through the admission of dust. Undoubtedly, the ideal method is to provide a separate shelf for each great book on which it may be laid flat ; but not only does this involve costly shelving, but it is so inelastic that there is no space to take additional books of the same size. A good plan, therefore, is to legislate for the volumes standing upright, but to provide thin, removable vertical partitions, between each pair of which can be placed, say, two to five books, according to their thickness.

70.—BOOKCASE BUILT ROUND AMERICAN DESK.

With reference to the proportions of space which should be allotted to small and large books, it may be borne in mind that three-quarters of the contents of a normal library will not exceed ten inches in height, and this size will cover most of the books in what are known as "library editions." Most novels and reprints will go into a space eight inches high, and though probably the prevailing tendency of publishers now is to make their books smaller and smaller, it is unwise to provide in the shelving a space less than eight inches. The present writer has never ceased regretting a bookcase he had made for a large series of dainty little reprints, which later had to be moved to other shelves in another room, and they left their old home derelict because it would not serve the purpose of the ordinary novel. With regard to the general question of height, it will usually be found that seven feet six inches to the under side of the cornice is as high as can be compassed conveniently without a library ladder, a piece of furniture very apt to get in the way, and the level of the top shelf should certainly not be more than six feet six inches from the ground. It is a mistake to put the bottom shelf too near the floor ; four inches is certainly the minimum amount it should be raised. It is much more

71.—AT FETTERCAIRN.

comfortable if the lower stage of the bookcase is taken up by cupboards, which are always useful for the storage of loose portfolios of drawings, unbound proceedings of learned societies, albums of photographs, and other stray elements of a library which look untidy if set on open shelves. This arrangement has been followed in the case of some shelves designed by Mr. Lutyens for Viscount Haldane and shown in Fig. 58. Each of the lower cupboards has a door of a single panel hinged at the bottom and falling towards the floor.

When it comes to the spacing of the

72.—AT 16, LOWER BERKELEY STREET.

shelves themselves, the first and invariable rule should be to make the shelves adjustable. There are various devices obtainable to secure this, of which perhaps the simplest and cheapest is known as Tonks' bookcase strip, furnished with little metal studs, adjustable at intervals of about an inch, on which the shelves rest. Another method is to groove the sides of the framing, which gives an equally elastic adjustment. With regard to the depth of the shelves from back to front, eight inches will accommodate practically all books below the size of quarto ; but here, again, it is unwise to cut down the width of the shelves unduly.

The general question of glazed doors or no glazed doors has already arisen in connection with the mirrored doors of the Devonshire House bookcase. It will always provide differences of opinion. In favour of them, there is the protection which they afford against dust. Against them is the bother of opening them continually, the fact that books grow musty in them if the library is rarely used, and last, but not least, is their cost. Moreover, there is the sentimental feeling that the glass seems to shut one

73.—DESIGNED BY SIR ROBERT LORIMER.

from the books ; that they do not invite the reader to take them down and browse ; to get an old
from its accustomed shelf becomes in some sort a formal proceeding. In some cases it may be
nient to provide, as Mr. Lutyens has done in Lady Horner's charming little panelled room, half
ir, half library, a small part of the shelving with glazed doors sliding in three leaves, and reserve it
e choicer elements of the collection. When we come to the general treatment of those parts of the
which are not ablaze with the books themselves, there can be no doubt that panelling is the ideal
es a unity to the whole room which is particularly restful. In this connection it may be added that
·d Haldane's room the shelves and panelling are in unpolished cedar, which has retained its thin
nce.

The last illustration (Fig. 73) shows the interesting treatment by Sir Robert Lorimer of the library
Burrell's house at Glasgow. The work is markedly Gothic in feeling, and attention may be drawn
neat curtain provided to cover the unattractive paraphernalia of the telephone. L. W.

THE CHILDREN'S ATTIC.

*The Attic in the Ideal House—Robert Louis Stevenson and Toy Soldiers—The Cost of Fitting
Up an Attic for Children—Practical Suggestions—Indoor Cricket.*

THE discriminating lover of Robert Louis Stevenson is bound to confess to some small twinge
of disappointment with his essay on "The Ideal House." The title promises much ; we expect
something from that wise and nimble mind that will give new food for architectural thought,
but outside he shows us only an ideal site, and within only the arrangements that make for
comfort and pleasant living. For the subject of this chapter, however, he provides a happy
text: "The whole loft of the house from end to end makes one undivided chamber; here
are set forth tables on which to model imaginary or actual countries in putty or plaster, with tools and
hardy pigments ; a carpenter's bench ; and a spare corner for photography, while at the far end a space
is kept clear for playing soldiers."

It is clear, from the precise instructions that follow about the two armies of five hundred horse and
foot and the use of footrules and chalk, that these military occupations are as much for children of a
larger growth as for the real juniors. One of the players, too, is to take up the pen of the army correspon-
dent and write a report of the operations every day or so, and we may imagine that some of the warlike
doings in Stevenson's
novels were conceived
with just such aids. For
the present purpose it is
enough, however, that
the support of so power-
ful a pen is given to
establish the consecration
of the attic to the plea-
sures of the younger
generation. The elders
will not always give it
up. There is a great loft,
in the house of a student
of sociology, which is
known as the "thinking
room." Its owner believes
in the principle of *solvitur
ambulando*, and can best
collect his thoughts by
tramping up and down
his long attic. Generally,
however, it is the lighter
moments that can best
be spent in the space
beneath the tiles. In

74.—AT LARKSCLIFF, BIRCHINGTON.

another chapter it is suggested that where billiards are impossible on the ground floor it would often be
possible to use attic space for a billiard-room, and this has often been carried out with success. The present
illustrations, however, are devoted to attics where the first thought has been for the games of smaller
folk. The present state of Mr. Quennell's loft at The Four Beeches, Bickley, was bred by a wholesome
spirit of emulation. "It was COUNTRY LIFE," he writes, "that landed me, by illustrating the playroom
in Mr. Bolton's house, Larkscliff, Birchington." That picture is now reproduced. It shows an ideal
playroom, which is lined throughout with fireproof slabs, and the arching over the chimney flues forms
a natural proscenium for juvenile drama.

To anyone who may contemplate making valuable use of wasted roof space, The Four Beeches
attic is particularly interesting, because the cost of the change is available—eighty pounds. It is,
perhaps, in one way hardly a fair example, because when the house was built the future utilisation of

the attic was not contemplated. Only a small part of its area was fitted with a floor, to take empty boxes, and it was reached only by a trap-door. In consequence, the joists, though provided of ample strength for their original purpose, viz., of carrying the ceiling below, were not stout enough to support a floor on which children might safely romp, and particular care was needed to prevent disturbance of the plasterwork of the ceiling during the substitution of stronger timbers. But for this strengthening of joists the cost would not have exceeded fifty pounds. The vertical parts of the walls are match-boarded, so that—

75.—AT FOUR BEECHES.

note the paternal caution expressed in a phrase set down *verbatim*—" the kids can hack into it without damage," and the slopes and ceiling are covered with patent slabs. These are excellent non-conductors of heat and cold; they save the cost of lathing, and are stronger than ordinary plaster. Access was provided by the sacrifice of a large cupboard on the first floor, which yielded space for a staircase up to the attic. The picture itself explains the rest. Not only the big table at the far end, but the little one with its fixed benches in the tiny bay formed by the dormer, are sanctuaries where the solemnities of nursery teas may duly be performed.

Beyond the fireplace on the left is a nook, where rests the baby's playground. Here it is out of the way of those disasters which involve the youngest-born in damage irretrievable, when his elders pursue the fierce joys of trick roller-skating without due regard to the rights of minorities. The person mostly concerned with the use of this children's paradise named it at first sight the Twopenny Tube, but this title can be given with even more reason to a cricketer's attic, which is also illustrated. It is rare that adequate room can be found for the larger games, but this loft belongs to a large house, and the needful length of pitch is available. The careful housewife may perhaps be affrighted by visions of broken glass; but all the windows are set in dormers of large projection, as is clearly shown by the photograph. Only those nearest to the batsman are, therefore, endangered, and they can easily be protected by wirework. Needless to say, a soft ball is desirable rather than an ordinary cricket ball, which would soon wreck the plaster of the ceiling. The playroom at Sandhouse, Witley, brings us to the moving pleasures of see-saw and rocking-horse (Fig. 77). The attic here differs from

76.—BIG ENOUGH FOR CRICKET.

those already described in that it is entirely in the sloping roof and has no vertical wall. Moreover, it boasts no other finish than the boarding to which the tiles are fixed. While the effective floor space is much less than in those cases where the wall is perpendicular for a few feet, it affords sufficient room for the purposes of chivalry. After all, extensive headroom is not a marked necessity where very small mortals pursue such studies in Biblical and natural history as

77.—THE GLORY OF MOTION.

78.—PLAN OF LAVEROCKDALE ATTIC.

occupy the time of the queen regnant at Littleholme. The stature of Noah and his family and flocks is not a serious difficulty in any attic, but in this well-lighted and spacious room the varied company condemned to travel two by two for ever have ample room for any evolutions, however complex. At Laverockdale, near Edinburgh, Sir Robert Lorimer has treated the whole attic floor as the children's domain. The day and night nurseries, pantry, etc., are grouped round a central playroom, which is fitted as a gymnasium with swing trapeze and monkey rope. It is altogether a particularly happy piece of nursery planning, and can be studied not only in the photograph of the playroom, but in the plan of the whole floor now reproduced. There is in France an admirable society which offers great prizes every year for the best ways to utilise waste products. In very many houses to-day the attic is for all practical purposes a waste product of architecture, and there must be ten thousand children who would yield their parents a welcome prize in rosier cheeks if use were made of

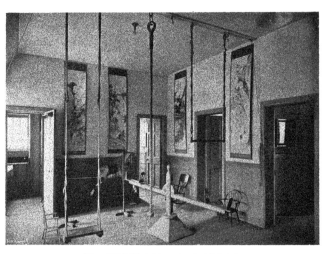

79.—ATTIC PLAYROOM LAVEROCKDALE.

the acres of potential playrooms that now lie fallow. There is, moreover, a selfish reason which may appeal to elder folk in these days of tender nerves. They will be free from the sound of feet, ' which heard at times as they totter along floors overhead " (to use De Quincey's phrase) reveal the pursuit of great adventure, while the children will find a happy employment for those hours that must perforce be spent indoors.   L. W.

80.— A PAGEANT OF THE ARK AT LITTLEHOLME.

THE CASE FOR MODERN FURNITURE.

The Impulses that Re-created Furniture Design—Influence and Work of William Morris—The Arts and Crafts Society—The Work of Mr. Ernest Gimson, Professor Lethaby, Mr. Ambrose Heal and Others—Reproductions of " Antiques" versus Modern Design.

W E are all users of furniture, many of us owners of some, and to most there comes the time when fancy lightly turns to thoughts of furnishing. At this springtime even the man of commerce is wont to wish that he could trace beauty to its source ; he feels vaguely that his home should be pretty, but it must be cheap. He would not think of buying a cheap motor-car, but for some inscrutable reason has no objection to cheap chairs. The latter half of the nineteenth century was undoubtedly the *cheap* age, and certainly nasty, so far as furniture was concerned. It is difficult to trace how this all came about ; but until recently it was general.

Now it is only by a few degrees less so, and we find houses furnished throughout with chairs, carpets and curtains which indignant housewives of three generations back would have thrown away as rubbish. Is the modern man less virtuous or more foolish than his forbears ? Does he really think a Chippendale chair (with apologies to the great cabinet-maker) can be made and sold for a pound ? It is want of thought, not heart ; our man of commerce, if he will but think, must realise that his chairs are but poor sweated imitations, and as such should find no place in his home. Better things are expected of him, no less than that he should seek for furniture produced in other ways— perhaps as Morris used to hope, by " an art made by the people, and for the people, as a happiness to the maker and user."

To write of Morris brings to memory the good story told about him when taken as a youth to the Great Exhibition of 1851. He sat down on a seat near the entrance and refused to go any further, declaring that it was all " wonderfully ugly." If we judge by illustrations that remain of some of the exhibits, it was a just criticism. Nothing was too silly or too ugly to be included, and this is true especially of the furniture. Yet less than a century before, from Chippendale, Sheraton and Hepplewhite had come the wonderful furniture that made their names famous. The following gem, from an illustrated encyclopædia, describes an oak niche at the exhibition : " The great peculiarity of this niche consists in its being designed after the old principle, to suit the material in which it has been executed.' Open confession is good for the soul, and here we get to the kernel of the whole matter—the commercialist of 1851 had 'no principles or scruples ; his one idea was to set his machine going, and if it would not make a thing in wood, then it was stamped out in papier-mâché.

81.—AN OAK CHEST OF DRAWERS.

The wave of commercialism which flowed over the country as a result of the exhibition left men no time or inclination to carry on the traditions of the Arts and Crafts ; rather was it the fashion to depart violently from them. But if the exhibition served no other useful purpose, it set Morris to work to institute sounder principles. Born in 1834, he was articled to Street, the architect, in 1856, and though he speedily tired of the routine of the office, one likes to remember these tee-square days ; architecture, as the mother of the Arts, never fostered a healthier babe. He was married in 1859, and the difficulty of furnishing his house drove him to the useful end of founding the firm of Morris, Marshall, Falkner and Co.

To all the architects of this period, and especially to those who started in Street's office, the· great exemplar was Augustus Welby Pugin. Born in 1812, he died in 1852, and one of his last works must have been the arranging of the Mediæval Court at the 1851 exhibition. The illustrations of this show fonts, candlesticks, altars and railings · that look curiously like those in a church furnisher's catalogue of to-day, and are evidence of how little progress has been made in the interval. Pugin, though,·was a great genius, and the work he did at the Houses of Parliament was a source of inspiration to men of the Nesfield school. This work may have been somewhat imitative, but withal his buildings had that nameless something

82.—BY MR. SYDNEY BARNSLEY.

which makes them living works of art. To the Gothic Revival, then, must be given the credit for the forward movement which, in the end, administered the death-blow to Early Victorian taste in furniture, and Morris ably carried on the work started by Pugin. It would be difficult to find in any century any two such men working on the same lines and possessed of the same super-abundant energy. The average man is content to keep to one craft, and feels happy if in this one he can rise above mediocrity. Morris mastered the secrets of dozens, and, treated in the first instance by the professionals as an absurd amateur, had a way of speedily reversing such judgment and of being able to teach tradesmen their trade.

Stained glass, colour printing, fabrics and furniture, printing and embroidery and tiles may be mentioned as some of the crafts he revolutionised. The small dining-room at the South Kensington Museum is one of Morris' earliest works, and is familiar to most people ; it was carried out in 1866, and excited much comment at the time. Another and very considerable factor which has had great influence in the decorative arts and crafts should be instanced in the Arts and Crafts Society, which had its first show in the autumn of 1888. Since then its doors have always been open to examples of good craftsmanship and sound design. Reproduction has been wisely banned, and craftsmen have been encouraged instead to carry on the traditions of their art and suit the same to modern needs. With so much by way of preface, attention must now be drawn to some examples of modern furniture which show that modern design has large claims on our regard.

An oak chest designed by Mr. Gimson will probably, at first sight, impress the reader as being a singularly bald piece of work. Yet our complaint against it is that it is too sophisticated, and that a cabinet-maker should have been able to make it without an architect's assistance. It should not be necessary for a man who can build fine houses to design cottage chests of drawers. So this piece is an exotic, rather than a real wild flower. But as it is a sound thing, it is a pity that there are not more like it. The settle by Mr. Sydney Barnsley (Fig. 82) belongs to

83.—A FUMED ASH CHAIR.

8*d*.—A FOLDING WALNUT TABLE.

the same school of design as the oak chest of Mr. Gimson, and the same things can be said for and against it. Its motif is the chamfer to be found on the country waggon, and its inspiration the art of the peasant. It would be pleasant to live with if it could be found as part of the furniture of one of the delightful stone-built houses Mr. Barnsley knows so well how to build; but it must be made by hand, and the machine can play no part in its manufacture. It is, therefore, an aggravating piece of furniture, because it seems to mock at the industrial system. If settles could talk it would say: "Here I am, and know not the meaning of compromise; I must be made as once all settles were made; if you attempt to standardise my parts and make me by machinery, I shall at once become so hideously ugly that you will be appalled. I am human in that men have made me." Which is all very interesting, but does not solve the problem of how the twentieth century is going to wed Utility, being the machine, to Beauty, being the craftsman. So we get no " forrarder," but, nevertheless, we like the settle.

The turned ash chair (Fig. 83), is quite admirable and of a sort to be commended to anyone wanting a cheap chair, for it is a far finer thing than any reproduction of Louis This or Louis That or a sort of hotch-potch of Chippendale, Sheraton and Hepplewhite. It is surely much better to eschew such vanities, if economy is essential, and to furnish the home with furniture on the lines of this chair designed by Mr. Gimson, which looks what it really is—a very beautiful and simple bit of craftsmanship, on good lines and withal honest. The " Dryad " chair (Fig. 85) is the practical outcome of a class started at the Leicester School of Art, to train workmen to design as well as to make. The possibilities of the idea

85.—A " DRYAD " CHAIR.

are endless and may contain the solution of the problem mentioned in a preceding paragraph, and if cane furniture can be produced on these lines, why not other sorts? The abuse of machinery must lead in the long run to the extinction of the craftsman as such, and the substitution instead of a mere machine-tender, dull of spirit and hopeless. The chair illustrated is to be commended as one showing appreciation of the material in which it is made, which the design admirably suits, and is, in addition, a graceful piece of work.

The folding table made in English walnut (Fig. 84) is also from the design of Ernest W. Gimson. It is a thousand pities that English walnut is not more used. The wood is of great beauty, with markings varying from grey-brown to tawny yellow, and capable of being highly finished as in the case of this table. It is admirably designed and constructed with numberless little refinements of softened arrises which are not at first apparent.

The Italian walnut secretaire illustrated in Fig. 86, and inlaid with various woods, was designed by W. A. S. Benson. It is a well-proportioned piece made on

86 —A WALNUT SECRETAIRE

sound lines with nothing of *l'art nouveau* about it, but with much proper feeling for the use of material and evidence of a knowledge of what has gone before.

The inlaid mahogany wardrobe (Fig. 87) is a very stately piece of furniture, depending for a good deal of its effect on the pleasant grain of its veneers, which, by the way, are not so pronounced in effect in the piece as in the photograph. Though obviously inspired by late eighteenth century furniture, it is not in any way a reproduction; rather does it very successfully carry on the traditions of that time, and is thus suitable for smarter folk than would use the oak chest of Mr. Gimson.

The inlaid oak wardrobe (Fig. 88) is very satisfactory and well-proportioned. The two spacious hanging cupboards on either side serve to frame up the smaller partitions of drawers and cupboard; the articulation of the panelling is framed on proper lines, and, these structural necessities being recognised, there are

87.—AN INLAID MAHOGANY WARDROBE.

added touches of inlaid ornament that give interest. The designer could not be offended by the statement that it is twentieth century in feeling, because doubtless his ideal is to create furniture suitable to his own time. Fig. 89 shows a very fine cabinet in ebony and satinwood. The photograph gives little, if any, idea of the beauty of the grain of the wood; but the designer has wisely recognised that when dealing with a precious wood it is not necessary to fret it by a super-abundance of intricate mouldings. So in this cabinet we have simple surfaces and good proportions. There is again evidence of abundant knowledge of style, but the designer, while keeping to the traditions of his craft, has expressed his own individuality.

The music cabinet (Fig. 90) is another interesting piece, made in satinwood and ebony. Very wisely, the grain of the wood is allowed to show its beauty without being fretted with mouldings, and the inlays used seem to be just in the right place. The mahogany cabinet on a black stand, shown in Fig. 91, is also satisfactory. It serves to show that proportion rather than ornamentation is essential, for here is a piece that has little about it but its fine shape, and the result is very dignified. It is, perhaps, hardly necessary to explain that the little treasure cabinet, standing on the top of the lower piece, is a separate piece.

88.—INLAID WARDROBE IN OAK.

The walnut cabinet designed by Professor Lethaby and illustrated in Fig. 92 is probably the most important piece of furniture illustrated in this chapter. The illustration can only show its shape, and all the beauty of surface and graining of wood is lost. But it stands as an exemplar of the right direction for furniture-designers to take if they would found a school and leave behind them household equipment that may afterwards be recognised as twentieth century, and as such bear comparison with that of the preceding centuries. At a time when there is hardly a peasant left in England, it is not logical to design furniture for him ; and to adapt it for the use of the more sophisticated is but to re-create the sentiment of poor Marie Antoinette's hamlet at the Petit Trianon ; it was playing at being a peasant, and its only interest remains in the personality of the player. The

89.—OF EBONY AND SATINWOOD.

hamlet is poor stuff architecturally and by way of a joke. In just the same way it would seem that, if we are to be real, there must be some quality of complexity in the design of our furniture, and it must take its place with us. Cannot we get some of the wonderfulness of a high-grade motor-car into artistic designs? Machinery is wonderful in itself, and only fails when it attempts to produce things; there is much Art, though, in a fine engine.

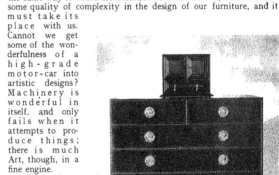

The bookcase illustrated in Fig. 93 and designed by Ambrose

90.—A MUSIC CABINET.

Heal, jun., is interesting in that it has been made in a new Australian wood called "black . bean." It is a very charming grey-brown colour, with cream and dark brown figure, and has been left without any kind of polish. The inlay work is of mother-of-pearl, with lines and bands of brown ebony and boxwood and ebony star inlays. There are two slides in the bottom carcase for placing books upon. It can very truly be said that Mr. Heal has revolutionised the design and production of furniture on a commercial basis ; and the fact must never be lost sight of that Chippendale himself was first and foremost a man desirous of

91.—A MAHOGANY CABINET

producing good furniture and selling it at a profit. Work made under these conditions has more chance of enduring than the isolated attempts of the dilettante working under artificial conditions.

The semi-circular oak washstand (Fig. 94) is a useful little piece, again designed by Mr. Heal, the absence of angles making it very suitable for a small room. It is not Jacobean or Georgian, Elizabethan or Adam. The designer thought that a semi-circular front might make it useful, and planned it so. Washstands are like men—they want legs to stand on ; so this one was given four at the proper place to take the weight put on them. It was felt that, as one sometimes blows like a grampus when washing the face, a hanging that would save the wall-paper and be removable for washing was a good idea, and this embroidered one is very dainty and

92.—DESIGNED BY PROF. LETHABY.

charming. But if this washstand is of no dated style, it has the merits of those mentioned. It has been designed to suit its purpose.

That modern furniture has not held its own is clearly proved by the way in which antique chairs, tables and all the furnishings of the home have been collected. Begun in the first place by connoisseurs, it has become a habit reaching into Suburbia, and so one finds that there is an apparently unending supply of "genuine antiques" to suit all purses.

The writer has a very real love for old furniture, and is among the first to acclaim its beauty ; but the time seems ripe to urge that we should no longer continue to fill our homes with a medley of indifferent antiques, or machine-made reproductions of the same. The reader may protest that he or she has little alternative. On the one hand is the furniture of commerce, honest only in that it looks commercial, on the other remain the wild imaginings of *l'art nouveau*. So the purchaser buys simple old stuff, or reproductions of it. If this procedure is not retrograde, it is just as certainly not progressive, so that we must at once admit that invention has reached its limit, and no new types or forms are possible ; or, putting this aside as sluggish, must push our way on, helped forward by what has been done. It is, perhaps, the youthful way not to esteem too highly what has been done, buoyed up by the hope that one may do better ; and it would needs be a very youthful, and perhaps impertinent, cabinet-maker who to-day said that he intended to do better than Chippendale. The impertinence could be put up with, if it was coupled with a little of the magnificent assurance the great cabinet-maker possessed. His book does not

93.—BOOKCASE IN " BLACK BEAN."

need reading very long to find that here was a man who believed in himself and his work ; who had what our engineers have to-day, tremendous enthusiasm, and who would have no more willingly designed a " Jacobean " chair than a motor-designer would revert to the types of engines of ten years ago. Before this atmosphere can be re-created the user of furniture must bring to bear something of the same knowledge that the eighteenth century connoisseur possessed ; he must be as much interested in his home and its fittings as he is in his car and its accessories. If he will only do this, be interested, it can safely be prophesied that he will speedily obtain just what he deserves, which, after all, is what has always happened. This chapter does not profess to do more than suggest to the reader that modern furniture is a serious branch of the applied arts, and to show a few good examples. It would need a separate book to illustrate the work of the many men who have re-established furniture design as a serious art.

C. H. B. QUENNELL.

94.—A SIMPLE OAK WASHSTAND.

THE DESIGN OF GRAND PIANOS.

*Piano, Elephant and Toad—Ancestry of the Piano—A Sheraton Design—Painted Pianos—
Recent Designs with Stout Under-frames.*

A FEW years ago, Mr. Halsey Ricardo, when writing of the attempts to accommodate the grand piano to ordinary rooms by shortening its tail, pointed out that this agony of effort tended increasingly to disfigure its appearance. " It gets lumpier," he said ; " it has the size without the handiness of an African elephant and the elegance of a mammoth toad." This is a poignant accusation, but a true one, and there is reason in his demand that, if no home is to be complete without a piano, we shall at least have a presentable tyrant instead of an awkward monster. ' Awkward" is a fair and moderate instalment of abuse for the ordinary piano of commerce ; but before some examples of successful effort in the direction of artistic treatment are considered, a sketch of its history may be given. Though we are not now concerned with the various mechanisms of the piano or of its predecessors, a brief reference to them will help to the understanding of the decorative problems presented, which they necessarily have influenced greatly. It may, moreover, remove some current misconceptions.

The earliest mediæval instrument in which the strings were struck by the pressing of keys was the clavichord, in which a short, faint note was made by the upward blow of a " tangent." It never secured a strong hold on the affections of British musicians, and even as early as the fifteenth century the plucking action, whereby the strings were sounded by a quill or strip of leather, entered the lists

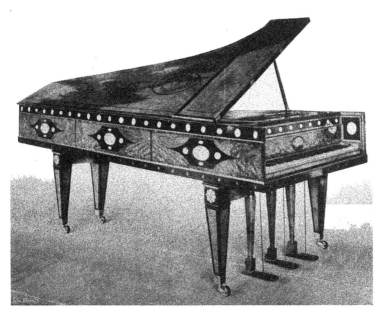

95 —DESIGNED BY SHERATON FOR GODOY.

A .carving in Manchester Cathedral shows the earliest form adopted, the clavi-cymbal ; and here we get at once in touch with our main subject, because the outline of its shape was, roughly, that of the modern grand pianoforte. Later modifications produced the virginal, the spinet and the harpsichord, all with plucked strings. The true virginal was of oblong box shape. In its early history its stand was generally separate, and the instrument in consequence was easily portable. This stand was a framed structure, and the attachment of legs to the instrument itself marks a later stage of development. . The spinet was of a form variously described as 'pentagonal, trapeze-shaped or wing-shaped, *i.e.*, in general outline like a modern. grand piano. The harpsichord usually followed the same shape, and at its latest stage of development was treated almost exactly as the modern grand piano, except that it had two keyboards and that the pedals were attached to the under·framing. The example known as the " Empress " harpsichord was made for the Empress Maria Theresa in 1773 by Shudi and Broadwood, and though the narrowness of the keyboard gives the instrument a grace of proportion impossible of reproduction in a modern grand piano, the decorative problem presented by the latter is not markedly different. We

96.—ORPHEUS PIANO, DESIGNED BY SIR EDWARD BURNE-JONES.

come now to the piano, which differs in essence from all the instruments so far named in that its strings are struck by falling hammers. The history of its invention ·is wrapped in some mystery. The first piano has been attributed to Father Wood, an English monk at Rome ; but this must be dismissed as a suggestion of patriotism. It is probably the fact that one Bartolomeo Cristofori (or Cristofali), a harpsichord-maker of Padua, made the first piano in 1711. If so, the year 1911 marks the two hundredth anniversary of a discovery that has not only profoundly changed the possibilities of music, but has enormously increased its popularity among the masses. Germany claims the invention for Schroter in 1717. One Silbermann is supposed to have stolen Schroter's idea ; in any case, he markedly improved the piano, and, more important still, won for it the approval of Sebastian Bach.

The first piano made by Silbermann in 1745.followed the later forms of harpsichord in being the shape of the modern grand. ·In 1760 twelve piano-makers came from Germany to this country, and were hailed as the twelve apostles to convert England to the new instrument. Zumpé, the best-known of them, made his pianos oblong. Though very small and wiry in tone, they became popular, and fixed the rectangular shape as the favourite one until the end of the eighteenth century. Meanwhile the harpsichord was not as yet losing its hold on public favour, and in 1765 Burckhardt Tschudi (*Anglice* Burkat Shudi) was at the top of his fame as a maker, and took into partnership, five years later, one John Broadwood. The latter had been in his employ since 1751, had married his master's daughter and succeeded him in the business. The piano, however, gained ground so rapidly that the last harpsichord was made in 1793, and it was never played in public after 1794. Until the early years of the nineteenth century the piano retained its oblong shape, and the present writer has a charming example, cased in satinwood delicately inlaid, made by Muzio Clementi of Cheapside about 1805. Instruments of this type are comparatively common, and very charming they are with their tapering legs and the maker's name engrossed in flourishing letters between painted bunches of roses or wreaths of sweet peas. They are nearly always vaguely described as spinets, which is altogether incorrect.

So much for the history of the genesis of the pianoforte; but one point may be emphasised before passing to

97.—DESIGNED BY SIR ROBERT LORIMER—

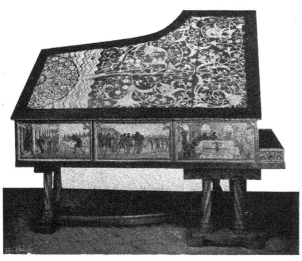

98.—AND PAINTED BY MRS. TRAQUAIR.

the grand piano as we know it. Many of the great makers of harpsichords, notably the Rückers, at work in Antwerp for nearly one hundred and fifty years, were accomplished artists, who made the cases of their instruments beautiful with their paintings and mottoes. It is noteworthy, too, that Sebastian Erard, who made his first piano in 1772, ascribed his success to his early training in architecture and design. In those days, at all events, beauty of appearance was thought as important as beauty of tone. The first illustration brings us into touch with a great name in decorative art, that of Sheraton. It has long been known that he designed a grand piano for Godoy, " Prince of the Peace," who presented it

ın 1798 to the Queen of Spain. Broadwood made it, and the case is of satinwood, superbly decorated with inlay
and with Wedgwood and Tassie medallions in gilt frames (Fig. 95). It is now in
a London drawing-room, but the portrait
of Godoy, by Alexander Taylor, which
was fixed where the maker's name is
usually written, has, unhappily, disappeared. Its peculiar interest lies
in the fact that Sheraton made the
innovation, doubtless startling to the
makers of those days, of putting the
body on separate legs instead of on a
frame connected by stretchers—an
unhappy departure from which the
treatment of pianos is only now beginning to recover. An unfortunate
feature of the design is the presence of
three pendants, to which the pedals
were attached. For these Sheraton
was probably not responsible, and they
show the perpetual conflict between
the practical needs of the instrument
and its artistic treatment. The discovery that this was the piano made
from Sheraton's design is due to the
acumen and research of Mr. William
Dale, F.S.A., to whom everyone concerned with the history of the piano
and its predecessors is heavily in debt.
The need for longer strings, the increase

99.—DESIGNED BY MR LUTYENS.

ın compass and the growing weight of the instrument, due to the introduction of heavy iron frames,
when added to the general depravity of Victorian art, reduced the piano to a melancholy level of
ugliness. Like the
billiard - table, it
was subjected to
the tyranny of
hideous turned
legs, and all
attempts to
beautify the case
were abandoned.

In 1880,
however, Sir
Edward (then Mr.)
Burne-Jones could
bear the existing
horror of the
average piano no
longer. He de-
signed not only the
famous Orpheus
example (Fig. 96),
but one of the
same form for
himself in oak,
but perfectly plain
and stained a
bright green, and
a third for Mr. Muir

100.—DESIGNED BY MR. FORSYTH.

Mackenzie which was decorated all over in gesso. Two years earlier Sir Lawrence (then Mr.) Alma Tadema had designed for himself a grand piano of great merit, made beautiful by inlay and carving of Byzantine feeling, but the ordinary form was retained. The qualities of the Burne-Jones pianos, which mark them as re-creating old and fine traditions, were, first, the rejection of the three-legged principle and the return to a six-legged under-frame connected by stretchers, and, secondly, the return to a pleasant line for the curve of the bent side. This Burne-Jones drew out full size and free-hand, and by a singular coincidence the proportions of the curve proved to be identical with those employed by the eighteenth century makers of harpsichords. Of the splendid paintings on both sides of the lid and on the circular medallions it is not needful to write,

IOI.—IN THE CHIPPENDALE MANNER.

for the illustration tells its own story. The piano designed by Sir Robert Lorimer and decorated by Mrs. Traquair (Figs. 97 and 98) is in some sort the lineal descendant of the Burne-Jones instrument. Sir Robert has reverted to the idea which inspired the early makers of keyed instruments by treating the piano itself and its supports as separate things, *i.e.*, by making it a painted box upon a trestle stand. It was made for Lympne Castle, Kent, and in order that the woodwork might be in character with the linen-fold panelling of the Great Hall there, the mouldings of the case have the touch of domestic Gothic work. The outside of the lid has been covered by Mrs. Traquair with a freely-treated Arabesque tree, rising from a world full of flowers, with Cupid sleeping in the centre. Among the branches of the tree are fauns' angels, centaurs, dragons and birds, while behind the world is a sea full of fishes. All these delightful conceits are depicted in transparent oil-colours on a ground of gilt toned to a greenish tint, the natural wood not showing anywhere. It is a form of technique which demands great certainty of touch, because the work is finished as done, and it is impossible to make any alteration without a fresh ground.

The decoration of the piano is so well worked out in idea as well as execution that space must be spared for a description of it. On the inside of the lid is a large picture of Psyche meeting Pan, who symbolises the music of Nature. The god is seated on the round green world, surrounded by water, on which Psyche stands, looking at him with a gaze instinct with wonder. Pan, however, is absorbed in the music of his pipes and does not observe her; but Eros with his bow surveys them both. Round the outside of the case on its vertical surfaces is a series of nine panels which illustrate the greatest of songs—the Song of Solomon. In the first scene (which begins at the treble end of the instrument) the Shulamite is brought before Solomon, who sits in the porch of his palace. In the second panel (which does not appear in the photographs) she is with the King in his banqueting-hall. Next follows the picture of her in the Women's Rooms, with the shepherd stretching his hands through the bars of the windows, while an attendant plays

102.—A SIMPLE AND INEXPENSIVE DESIGN.

the lyre.   In the adjoining panel the Shulamite is asleep, and her dream is represented in the encircled corner picture.   The fifth and sixth show Solomon returning from war, and pressing his suit with the Shulamite.   These two panels are on the end of the instrument, and the remaining three on the straight side show the return of the shepherd lover, the release of the Shulamite and her return with him, and, finally, the wedding feast.   This notable sequence of pictures incorporates, in a naive and delightful way, various features of Scottish scenery, and the progression of events is marked by the changes from dawn to midday, and through night to the brightness of another day.   One feature only remains to be noted—the long panel over the keyboard, whereon are represented three subjects taken from Rossetti's Sonnets, " I sat with Love beside the wayside well."   Altogether the treatment of the instrument, both in its woodwork and in its painting, emphasises the fact that a piano can be made a thing of beauty.

Among other notable designs on a less ambitious decorative scale those by Mr. Forsyth (Fig. 100) and Mr. Lutyens (Fig. 96) can be considered together, for they also revert in principle to the old harpsichord manner, in that the weight is distributed over a well-knit frame, which rests on many legs.   They have, however, one notable difference.   That by Mr. Forsyth is based on the idea that the instrument is one thing and its means of support another, and the legs are not directly framed into the body of the piano.   This is an echo of the virginal, which was generally quite separate from its frame.   In Mr. Lutyens' design the instrument and its frame are treated as a unit.   One may note, too, the skilful way in which the pedals are mounted on light and graceful metal supports, a far remove from the hideous lyre-shaped object which usually carries them.   These are, of course, costly things, with their delightful panelling and intricate framing, by comparison with the ordinary piano ; but Fig. 102 shows a type that costs, and need cost, no more than the usual monument of ugliness with which people are content to distress the eye.   By the use of severe lines and the substitution of an under frame of six simple taper legs for the usual corpulent three, an attractive result is secured without increased expense or sacrifice of the musical qualities of the instrument.   Such a design, paying no homage to any historical style, but succeeding by reason of its simple reasonableness, looks well in any surroundings.   Where, however, any definite period of decoration governs the treatment of a room, it is often desirable to bring the piano into accord with the prevailing feeling, and of success in this direction the mahogany case designed in the Chippendale manner is a good example (Fig. 101).

Reviewing the progress made in the last twenty years by the firms who are producing pianos made to admirable copyright designs, such as the four last mentioned, there is reason to hope that the ugliness too long associated with the instrument will die a natural death.   It is, of course, very difficult to give an attractive outline to a very small piano.   Some are made as short as five feet from tip to tip to meet the needs of those who live in small rooms.   This fashion is unlikely to persist, however, because anything less than six feet means unduly shortened strings and a reduction in the sounding-board, which cannot fail to prejudice the tone.   In any case, the piano, in Halévy's words, " forces every door . . . a rare, discreet friend who only speaks when a question is asked, and can at once be silent."   Such a friend deserves to appear before us in gracious guise, so that it may faithfully symbolise when it is silent the beauty it creates when its voice is heard.   KATHLEEN PURCELL.

HOW TO CHOOSE OLD FURNITURE.

A Warning Against French Polish—Monk's Benches and Gate-leg Tables—Old Pieces with Added Carving—
Spurious Satinwood—Lacquered Pieces—The Need for Watchfulness—Some Typical Genuine Specimens.

TO those of us who have been brought up from childhood surrounded by the furniture of our fore-fathers the buying of old furniture does not present many difficulties; but everyone, expert and amateur, ought to examine with the greatest care the elaborately carved and inlaid pieces which run into high figures. Speaking broadly of English furniture, oak was used from the earliest times until about the middle of the seventeenth century, when the use of walnut became general and the carving found on oak was replaced by the saw-cut veneer of walnut, with its beautiful "figure" and rich tone. Authorities differ as to the date when mahogany was introduced into this country; but it was probably extensively utilised as early as 1730, and has continued in use ever since. Lacquered furniture was introduced from China and Japan in the last half of the seventeenth century, and was soon copied by English, Dutch and Spanish workmen. The European copies are easily distinguished by the untruthful representations of the Oriental figures and their surroundings. Satinwood, with its attendant inlays of king, hair, tulip and other woods, came into vogue in the third quarter of the eighteenth century. At this time furniture was gilded and painted under the influence of the brothers Adam. Walnut and mahogany enriched by gilding were also very popular from 1720 to 1740, and were often used on the furniture designed by Kent. Rosewood was employed at quite the end of the eighteenth century, though it has been used for the purpose of inlay since the days of the Tudors. The novice, if he wishes to make a fine collection, should first of all go to museums and houses where he knows he can find undoubted examples of old furniture, until he gradually acquires the intuition of knowing the genuine thing from the forgery, as well as the general appearance of pieces of different dates and origins. On the other hand, if he merely wishes to furnish his house with old things, he should put himself into the hands of a reputable and honest dealer. We

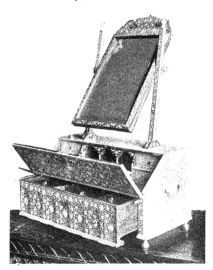

103.—INLAID WITH MOTHER-OF-PEARL.

think that the first thing to guard against is the specimen which is French polished; that is to say, covered with the red, sticky, treacly medium which one finds smeared over furniture of all woods and periods, to the obliteration of the grain and natural colour of the wood. This treatment was intro-duced in the middle of the last century. It is very difficult to know whether the piece is genuine unless this is removed, which should be insisted upon, and it must be remembered that when the polish is removed the wood appears dull and lifeless; however, if the piece proves to be an old one, a great deal of its original beauty of colour and grain can be brought back by simply oiling and waxing and repeated polishings with a soft cloth. Many collectors will reject any piece of furniture, however genuine, unless it possesses its original patina and colour, which only age and constant attention can give it. The most difficult thing to detect is what is called "made up" furniture; that is to say, pieces made up of old wood. For instance, old panelling and carved fronts of oak chests, worth a few pounds, are converted into oak buffets or cupboards, for which one is asked fifty pounds or more, according to their importance. The carcases of these pieces should always be examined very carefully, and the presence in unusual places of nail-holes or signs where locks or hinges have once been should be regarded with great suspicion.   The general decoration and construction should be studied ; unless the carving has been added when the piece was " made up," one will often find odd bits of carving inserted that have no relation to each other, and which, if looked at with a critical eye, will impress one as being obviously out of place.   The dates on oak furniture should always be disregarded until the genuineness of the piece has been proved by its internal evidence of construction, condition and carving.

Table-chairs or monks' benches, the back working on a hinge or wood-peg to form a table, are frequently made up from an ordinary old oak armchair or bench and a table top, in consequence of the rarity of the genuine article.   The ordinary plain but genuine oak gate-leg table with plain turned legs can be bought very cheaply, but the example with spiral legs, and especially those with spiral under stretchers, fetch a great deal more money owing to their scarcity.   The genuine spirals were done with

a hand lathe, and had sometimes two and three separate spirals, which are somewhat uneven and show the individual hand of the workman, whereas the modern ones display all the hard regularity of the machine.   Moreover, a close scrutiny will also show the rough stain of the freshly-cut wood, unless it has been hidden under some thick colouring matter.   The surface of the carving on both oak and mahogany should show the same colour and wear as the rest of the piece ; and though the forger takes the greatest care to rub down the edges of his new work and to colour in his tool marks, he is, after all, only mortal, and a careful examination will show a rough edge which would have been worn down, or a chip of newly-cut wood which would never have remained so light in colour during the course of two or three centuries.

It is curious how comparatively few plain mahogany tripod tables one comes across, the reason being that they are eagerly bought up by the forger for a few pounds, and emerge again carved and glorified at ten or twenty times the original value.   Certainly eighty per cent. of the tripod tables and rectangular "silver-tables" with spindle or fret galleries or richly-carved edges which the writer has seen lately have been forgeries.   In judging these tables, one should first of all see that the balance of the table is correct.   The addition of a gallery or the reduction of the size of the top by carving may make it too clumsy or too light, as the case may be, for the size of the legs.   Next, the pillar or the points of the toes may have been carved away, which will at once give the table an appearance of insecurity.   Again, the fret or gallery and top must be examined for any sign of colouring matter, and absence of original surface and fine marks of sand-paper are an almost infallible proof that it has been through the hands of the restorer.

A tripod table was recently offered to the writer, which at first sight appeared to be a very rare example of Chippendale's finest work.   The top had a very richly carved and shaped border ; the pillar and legs were noble in proportion and also very finely carved.   But, looking at the table from a constructional point of view, the proportions of the lower part seemed a trifle heavy for the top.   On examining the carving, parts here and there showed traces of having been recently rubbed down, and there was a difference in the " skin " at the top next the carved edge compared with the centre, which was of rich and beautiful colour and in an untouched condition.   On looking at the underneath part of the top, the ends of both supports, which were used to strengthen the table, had been undoubtedly shortened, and the screws appeared too close to the end.   The problem now became interesting, and on carefully examining the outer edge below the carving two minute holes at each end were found carefully filled with new soft putty.   The case was now proved, because the tell-tale holes had originally contained the points of the old screws, the shaping of the top having necessitated their removal.   The table had been a fine old Spanish mahogany piece of about 1750, with probably a plain top and a heavy pillar, massive legs and club feet, a type which is a veritable find for the " faker," who can work to his heart's content on its

virgin simplicity. Tripod tables with what are termed
" pie-crust " or ' ribbon " edges should be carefully
scrutinised in a strong light. Genuine examples of
the eighteenth century are invariably cut out of a
solid piece of wood, with top and rim all in one ; but
those that are " faked" have the pie-crust or ribbon
added to the original top, though when the whole of
the top is new it is often carved out of the solid piece
as of old.

There is a great deal of spurious satinwood furniture on the market, but this is more easily detected
than mahogany, owing to the light colour of the wood
and the difficulty of concealing the new colouring
matter. Let it be borne in mind that all satinwood
in its original state is white, but the beautiful mellow
honey colour of old satinwood is due more to age than
to artificial colouring. New satinwood is hard and
vulgar in its garishness, while the old is soft and quiet
in tone. Genuine bureau bookcases in satinwood are
rare and expensive, and the writer has seen old pieces
from which the original mahogany veneer has been
stripped and replaced by new satinwood—a forgery
which, if success-
ful, would
more than
double their
value.

Care must be
taken when
choosing
inlaid
pieces
that one
buys the

105.—GEORGE I.

English examples, and not the Dutch, as both these
countries were occupied in producing thém at the same
periods. Our own workmanship is far superior both in
construction, cabinet-making and inlaying. Many Dutch
artists in marquetry came to England towards the end
of 'the seventeenth century, and it is difficult to decide
whether the work of that date was done by a Dutch or an
English hand ; but the marquetry which is well and
carefully done and is reserved and quiet in decoration, is
generally accepted as having been done in England. The
revival of inlaid work which took place in England about
one hundred years later is in every way superior to that
done in Holland at the ' same time, and when once a
comparison has been made between the delicate inlay
added to the most perfect cabinet-making produced at
that period in England and the rough, coarse articles made
by our neighbours over the water, the collector will never
hesitate in making the right choice.

By the term " old furniture," nothing later than
that of the eighteenth century is usually implied, though
good work was done in the early years of the last century
as far as actual workmanship is concerned. Taste gradually,

106.—QUEEN ANNE.

however, became worse and worse, until the most ghastly horrors were perpetrated in the way of design, though still well made and of good material. It is perhaps as well to make a rule, to which, however, exceptions must be allowed, to buy nothing later than that of eighteenth century date if the purchaser wants to surround himself with things which will be always pleasant to live with.

Old lacquered furniture of the seventeenth and early eighteenth centuries, whether it be Oriental or European, blends harmoniously with all Old English furniture except the lighter and more delicate products of the end of the eighteenth century. The most prized and by far the most beautiful is the work of the Chinese and Japanese of the seventeenth and early eighteenth centuries. The incised cabinets and screens of the former, decorated with the most beautiful pigments and gold, provide a feast of colour for the eye. The early work of the Japanese is usually found in cabinets, and the scheme of decoration is black and gold, and, though sombre, is beautiful, the gold work being of the utmost delicacy and refinement. The European work is very coarse compared with the Oriental, but is pleasing and harmonious in tone. The market abounds with imitations, most of which are crude and garish, but have to be examined carefully, because they are apt to pass muster at a distance. The real old red lacquer is most beautiful in colour, rich but not glaring, and genuine pieces are very rare. Many spurious pieces are being offered for sale, and old black lacquer cabinets have reappeared with a red coat; but the modern red lacquer is dull and lifeless. Black and gold japanned furniture, some of which was pretty and graceful, appeared for a short time in the early years of the nineteenth century. It is generally most suitable for bedrooms, and the chairs are cane-seated. When offered " long " sets of dining-room chairs, one should examine each one, because sets of twelve or more of the same date are rare. Original sets were often divided among members of the family, who subsequently had them copied, perhaps many years ago. Likewise, armchairs should be carefully chosen, as, being of more value, the arms are often added to single chairs by dishonest dealers. An armchair should always be rejected if the arm covers the carving of the back, for the workman of former days would never do that. The carving should be finished off immediately above and below the join of the arm.

As to price, the ordinary plain old furniture can be bought at present at the same figure as, or less than, the modern article, and the value is very much greater from all points of view; but prices are going up, old things are becoming more scarce and, to a much greater extent than people think, are being exported both to France and to the Colonies. America for long has been annually draining the country of large quantities; but since the duty of sixty per cent. has been taken off and everything over one hundred years old is allowed in duty free, enormous quantities of Old English furniture of every kind, and also silver, Sheffield plate, china and glass, have left the country never to return. For rare and beautiful specimens very large prices are obtained, and unless the purchaser is sure of his own judgment he should get expert opinion, and always a guarantee from the seller. Forgeries are done by such skilled and highly-paid workmen that a table will perhaps cost in actual work-sheet wages fifty pounds to make, and the seller reckons to get for it two or three hundred pounds. Auction sales, particularly in private houses, often prove dangerous pitfalls, and unless the would-be purchaser has his own or somebody else's expert knowledge upon which he can rely, he had far better buy from a dealer, when he can examine the piece at his leisure, and, if necessary, return it in the event of both the dealer and himself having been taken in.

Though the trend of this chapter has been to warn the would-be buyer against worthless imitations, it must not be supposed that there are no honest dealers. There are many such who are continually refusing things offered them by the professional " faker "; but the tendency is, except among the few, to take the piece for granted so long as it passes a cursory examination, and not to know too much about it for fear of finding out that it is not all that it purports to be. Therefore it is important to deal not only with the man who has the knowledge, but with one who, at the same time, honestly examines every piece before he offers it for sale. When all is said, the buyer of furniture has to rely largely on his own judgment, which will mature as the result of careful study of authentic pieces and their pictures. The illustrations here shown are all of notable specimens, and should be examined in the light of the descriptions which follow :

In Fig. 108 is shown an inlaid mahogany bookcase, with a classical cornice consisting of a broken pediment flanked by a spindle gallery with urns; the cupboards and drawers below are bow-shaped, divided by round fluted columns. These latter, with the half-round panels of the glazed lattice doors of the upper part, in which appear the Prince of Wales' feathers, place this cabinet in the last quarter of the eighteenth century. Figure 106, on page 69, shows a high-back single chair with embossed leather back and seat, which is very Dutch in character; the pillars are carved and the elaborate cresting is surmounted by a shell, which appears also on the lower rail of the back and again on the seat rail; the legs are slightly cabriole and have splayed feet, which have a suggestion of the hoof foot so often found in Dutch furniture. The stretcher joins those at the side and lies back from the front legs. The date is about 1680. Figure 105 is a photograph of an armchair showing the development of the Queen Anne type, with the round top rail and the openwork wood back made by Chippendale. The back, front rail and cabriole legs are carved in relief; the latter are hocked and finish in rounded toes. This chair was

107.— AN OAK BEDSTEAD AT SPEKE HALL.

probably made during the reign of George I. On page 68 is shown a richly-carved high-back single chair; the centre splat and rails, consisting of elaborate scrolls, are supported by two carved pillars. The serpentine stretchers, with milled cups on the legs and bun feet, date this chair early in the reign of William and Mary. Fig. 103 illustrates a dressing-mirror inlaid with mother-of-pearl; the stand, containing drawers and pigeon-holes, resembles a miniature writing bureau; below is a drawer with shaped front containing boxes—brushes and combs—which was in fashion at the end of the seventeenth century. The photograph on page 71 shows an oak four-post bed with panelled tester and an open frieze of leaf and scroll decoration. The back is richly carved with arched panels and amorini on either side; beneath, in the centre, is a medallion portrait of a monk or saint suspended by ribbons; the tester rests on carved columns springing from a cup-shaped support with spreading foot, which stands on a four-legged pedestal with owls' masks at the corners protecting a flaming lamp. It is English of the seventeenth century.   BASIL OXENDEN.

108.—A SHERATON BOOKCASE.

FLOOR COVERINGS.

Carpets and Their History—Influence of Oriental Rugs at the 1851 Exhibition—Morris Gives New Life to Carpet Design—Floor-staining and Its Difficulties—Parquetry and Its History—Notes on Its Laying—Linoleum.

CARPETS, so far as England is concerned, are a comparatively modern luxury. The rush-strewn floor of the Norman hall remained for many a year, and carpets, if any, and these only of the most homely sort, were for the ladies' chamber. So much was this the case that they became an attribute of luxury and effeminacy, and in the sixteenth century it was still the reverse of polite to call a man a knight of the carpet. In the seventeenth century, though, they became a necessary article of furniture for the wealthy ; but Macaulay has an interesting note on the subject, when he refers in his History to the state of lodging-houses of Bath when " the floors of the dining-room were uncarpeted, and were coloured brown with a wash made of soot and small beer, in order to hide the dirt." This, of course, was the city before the Woods took it in hand and turned it into something very much like the Bath of to-day, fit background for the smart eighteenth century folk of Sheridan and his contemporaries. If the fare was good in those days, the accommodation could hardly have been described as cleanly, for Pepys, who was on his way to Bath, tells us in his Diary that on June 12th, 1668, staying at an inn, he got up one morning, " finding our beds good but lousy ; which made us merry." Clearly he was a philosopher. Dryden, a few years later, was to talk of " Persian carpets spread the imperial way," and the reference is interesting as showing a knowledge of these beautiful fabrics.

Carpets remained, though, the luxuries of the wealthy, and there may have been beside the very practical reason that uncarpeted rooms, stone flagged or oak flanked, were more readily cleansed of the mud and dirt which was ever present in those days. When Prince George of Denmark visited Petworth in the winter, he was six hours in going nine miles, with body-guards of peasants on each side of his coach to prop it up. And if the country roads were like this in the seventeenth century, in the towns they were, in addition, open sewers, and there was some point in giving or taking the wall, so that one might be as far removed as possible from the splashing of the road traffic. After Pepys' confession of mirth, one is a little doubtful whether it can be urged that cleanliness prevented the housewives of the times carpeting their rooms ; but it is certain that had they done so they would have soon been caked with liberal layers of mud. So that it is probable that they were used only for the parlours, as in the farmhouses of to-day, and the outer rooms, being brick or stone paved, could easily be swilled down with a pail of water.

It should be borne in mind that in very early times the Monkish Latin word " Carpita " meant a kind of thickish cloth, or a garment made of the same. Murray gives a note of the Carmelites at the end of the thirteenth century, who wore " a carpet which is the distinctive dress of our order, not sowed together of pieces (or patches) but woven together " ; and in another inventory, taken in 1527, of Sir W. Guildford's goods, there was included " a carpet of green cloth for a lytill foulding table." It is as well to remember that carpets were not always what we now understand them to be.

Early in the nineteenth century carpets were imported from Flanders and France, and were as well, of course, largely manufactured at home. An interesting sidelight on this subject is given in a letter written to *The Times* in 1845, in which the writer points out that " There are many kinds of carpets made of cotton in India—stout, serviceable, handsome things ; generally they are termed *serrigee*," and goes on to say that he wonders they are not imported to England. This state of things was remedied at the '51 Exhibition, where many Indian carpets were shown, which probably started the trade with which we are now familiar. Talking of Eastern carpets shown at the Exhibition, a paper of the day waves the good old flag, still possessed by the halfpenny Press of to-day, and shouts of progress. They say that they view these carpets with much interest, " Yet they evidence no progress ; whilst those in the English portion of the Exhibition show that the day is not far distant when the far North will supply the East." Which, being very tall talk, makes one turn up with great interest the English exhibits in this section, only to find illustrations of the sort of thing one was familiar with in one's bedroom as a boy, after it had served a hard apprenticeship on the lower floors, slowly yielding place, room by room, through successive spring cleanings. This train of thought hardly agrees with present-day ideas, when the Persian rug reigns nearly supreme. One carpet shown at the Exhibition, a French one, by the way, had the Royal arms as a centre, surrounded by devices of typical and emblematical character. In the corners were representations of Europe, Asia, Africa and America ; in the borders, Poetry and Sculpture,

Music and Painting, Commerce and Industry, and a few pictures of towns. No wonder the Persian rug looked a little old-fashioned beside such a wonder. Morris, on whom this Exhibition acted as a healthy stimulant, determined to remedy matters so hideously ugly. He had such an appreciation of Oriental carpet-weaving that he half doubted whether we had any business to make carpets at all, and knowing that we were very unlikely to beat the Persians, with their centuries of tradition in the craft, thought the endeavour should be made " to get enough of form and meaning into it to justify our making it at all." He started by designing cheap Kidderminster, Brussels and Wilton piles, which for want of another term might be called " Morrisey " in pattern, and the flowing lines of which were spoiled by translation into the fabric itself. He then followed on with weaving real Axminsters of a close soft pile, all in one piece in the Eastern way, and these he called the " Hammersmith " carpets. It is very doubtful if anything better than these have been done, either before or since, in England. The design is not too obviously founded on Eastern patterns, yet in it is the same appreciation that a carpet is in reality a mosaic of small *squares* of wool, and the lines are definitely subordinated to those squares. As well Morris realised that, as a carpet may be seen from any side, it should either have an all-over pattern or follow the Persian model, with a central figure filled in all round.

Of Eastern types, so much could be said that the limit of these notes would be reached in a recapitulation of the different sorts alone ; it can only be stated, then, that fine work is met with throughout the East ; and so unprogressive, according to the '51 standard, are these people, that it is still nearly impossible

109.—PART OF A MODERN PERSIAN RUG.

to find any uninteresting work, so obstinately do they cling to their ideals of colour and beauty. For the same reason of space their history cannot even be indicated, as it is probable that they were being made, on much the same lines that they now are, when we were more concerned with ornamenting our bodies rather than dyeing our carpets with woad. Beautiful as Persian carpets and rugs undoubtedly are, it yet remains doubtful if they are thoroughly suitable for Western schemes of decoration ; a glowing Eastern rug, littered all over with " occasional " tables and chairs, and fringed around with cabinets and revolving bookcases, seems always to call for space in which it can be seen, and sunlight—real hot glowing sun— to show its intricate beauties. In very much the same way, the marbles and mosaics of Ravenna and Venice need the Italian atmosphere, and lose all their beauty in our murkiness. So that it would seem well, in any scheme of decoration, when using fine Persian carpets, in some measure to subordinate them to their surroundings, or in the case of the smaller rugs, to use them only here and there, as jewels on a plain under-carpet.

One need not recapitulate all the sorts of carpets made—they can be found in any house-furnishing list ; but, instead, carpet buyers may be reminded of a few essentials we all know and yet sometimes forget. The carpet is the foundation of one's colour scheme ; here one starts, and if a bad start is made, we can never regain our hold on harmony. It should always be remembered that colour is wiped out in some measure by sunshine or shadow. The painter prefers a grey day, because then he sees colour in the half-tones, midway between the extremes noted. For this reason the Italian peasant can wear coloured dresses that would be garish in our grey isle, and the blue and yellow macaw is not nearly so vivid a little bird personality in British Guiana as he is at the Zoo. It is not meant by this that we should rush into greys and disconsolate drabs ; but a certain discrimination must be used in introducing vivid colourings into our homes. They need more sun than we have. If we look about and see what Nature has attempted with us, we shall hardly find a marble or rock, stone or slate, bird or beast, that has not been coloured on sober lines, though in joyous mood she sometimes stains the granite rock with golden lichen or lets the gorse flame across the common. So that if we do not get that riot, that ecstasy of colouring, of the tropics as a whole, there is no reason why we should not occasionally let ourselves break loose in detail.

One of the finest pieces of writing in " The Stones of Venice " concerns itself with a comparison between an English cathedral, " grey, and grisly with heads of dragons and mocking fiends, worn by the rain and swirling winds," and St. Mark's at Venice, all " set in pillars of variegated stones, jasper and porphyry, and deep-green serpentine spotted with flakes of snow, and marbles, that half refuse and half yield to the sunshine, Cleopatra-like, ' their bluest veins to kiss,' " which may not have very much to do with carpets, yet is well worth remarking, in so far as it touches on the colour characteristics of North and South. It may be as well to touch also on the necessity of restraint not only in colouring, but in pattern. Assuming that there is much elaborate detail in the carpet, then chair coverings, curtains and the like may be allowed in simple colours ; or, *vice versâ*, a plain under-carpet, with rugs displayed thereon, should form a good background for chintz coverings to chairs and the like material for curtains. To have instead patterns on floors, coverings, curtains, walls and ceilings, is the certain way to rob the home of that feeling of quietude and peace that is a necessity in these stirring times of hustle and rush, if we are to preserve our sanity.

We come now to colder forms of floor covering, such as parquetry and linoleum. If parquetry is the more stately of the two, reminding one of Versailles, for instance, linoleum has its uses, its most distinct uses, and it must be considered. It is a humble brother, but offers one solution of that most difficult problem—what to do with the floor. An architect was described in a recent novel as " a man who quarrelled with women about their kitchen sinks," which, if a little undignified, at least shows interest in that important fitment, and is more thinkable than the other one, in Mr. Galsworthy's "Man of Property," who makes love to his client's wife. This is quite unbelievable, and of the two we prefer the one who, shall we say, had the temerity to maintain his views about the sink. But to leave sinks and to return to floor treatment. If the client's wife quarrelled with the architect because he had views about sinks, it is with considerable trepidation that the present subject is approached, as it can be safely affirmed that every woman has her own idea and recipe about staining floors and the way to do it. To suggest, then, that such ideas and methods are antiquated is to risk rebuke. Yet so it is, and the writer has had his experiences with the homely permanganate of potash and other equally ineffective remedies for those signs of wear that will appear at the doorways.

The staining of floors probably started about the time of the nineteenth century Gothic revival ; in the better work the floors were, of course, of oak, with rugs displayed thereon, and so the fashion of cutting the carpet close all around the walls went out in some measure. From the artistic, as well as the hygienic, point of view, the square or oblong carpet that is a complete piece of design in its own borders does not suffer from the mutilation of its pattern in the irritating way that the cut carpet does, and has the great advantage that it can be readily taken up to be

110.—A MORRIS CARPET.

cleaned, and not only cleaned, but thoroughly sweetened by being put out on a sunny lawn. Floor-staining, then, has filled its useful purpose, but does not do its work so satisfactorily as parquetry or linoleum. As to the history of the former, it seems to have been first used in France during the sixteenth century, and since that time the very general way it has been employed suggests that the French housewives find it so economical in the long run that they do not mind spending the additional money that is required at the outset. Certain it is that in France the floors of palace, house, or hotel seem invariably to be of parquet. It is probably this question of upkeep that holds the solution to the problem. We have already touched on the difficulties encountered with stained floors, and the like holds good of painted margins. Assuming that, instead of being stained, the margins are felted, there is a certain expenditure necessary, and felt is the most difficult material to keep clean. Matting, again, soon wears, and the fitted carpet now is seldom seen outside a dressmaker's showroom. So the French parquetted floors, which give such a finish to the rooms, may in the long run prove the best of bargains to the economical French housewife.

French parquetry is generally thicker than English, being seldom less than one inch thick, prepared in squares that form the multiples of the design, and once laid they undoubtedly make a very permanent floor. Any other woods which may be introduced are usually inlaid with the oak. The oak used is Austrian, but cut for straight grain, rather than figure, as with us. Many of the French floors are very beautiful examples of design and workmanship; but such elaboration does not seem necessary for the living-rooms of a house which are to have their due complement of carpets, rugs, chairs, tables and so on. In a ballroom, though, where the floor is to be displayed, some of these beautiful designs seem very appropriate, and in the old days such work was not thought below the dignity of an artist, though even in Vasari's time the production of the often useless painted picture was esteemed the real criterion. It is probable that the early French craftsmen were influenced by the intarsia work of Italy, and some of the elaborate floors are inlaid as beautifully as a fine cabinet. So far as English parquetry is concerned, it has not had a life of much more than about sixty years, or from the time of the Great Exhibition. A Russian floor was shown there which excited comment at the time; the craft was, of course, known, but, as has been stated, the almost universal method of carpeting all over the floors did away with any necessity of making the floor itself beautiful. Evelyn quotes in his Diary for August 23rd, 1678, "The rooms are wainscoted, and some of them parquetted with cedar, yew, cypress, etc." In 1816 Murray gives a quotation for parquetry as a name "given to boards of fir intersected by pieces of walnut tree, or disposed in compartments of which the walnut tree forms the frame or border." This must evidently have been for a floor, inlaid in much the same way that the Swiss inlay their pine panelling, and is so distinct from the French and Italian method of inlaying in a hard wood. Evelyn's quotation takes us back to the heyday of Sir Christopher Wren's work. He had been to Paris to escape the Plague in 1665, and was thus familiar with the colossal works Louis XIV. had in hand. It may be that the floor Evelyn saw was a French innovation introduced by Wren.

III.—CORNER OF AN ENGLISH CARPET OF 1604.

Leaving the historical side of the subject, one may turn to the present-day uses of parquetry and the method of its application to new and existing floors. Just as it is essential that the floor should be bone-dry before linoleum is laid down, so is it very necessary to take the same precaution with parquetry. In the case of new work it should be left till the last possible moment before it is fixed, because, even assuming that the house is quite dry, if it is left unoccupied for any time without windows being opened and so on, the dry wood will absorb any moisture there may be in the air, and, instead of shrinking, will swell up in unsightly blisters. In England, a quarter of an inch and half an inch are the thicknesses generally used, and the floor is veneered with these, being glued and bradded, and the tiny nail-holes stopped before polishing. The simplest form of parquetry is the plain herring-bone pattern, and it is possible to obtain this in oak a quarter of an inch thick and have it laid for eightpence-halfpenny per foot super. Another form is long battens, three inches wide and a quarter of an inch thick, laid the reverse way to the floor-boards under, and the effect is simpler and perhaps better than the herring-bone. If this sort of parquetry is used in a long room with windows at the end, the battens should run the long way of the room, and it is not necessary to have more than a one-inch deal flooring under it. This type costs rather more than the herring-bone, as longer lengths of stuff have to be used. If properly laid, the parquetry should be quite solidly attached to the under floor, without any suggestion of springing or creakiness in it. The half-inch thicknesses make a better job, but there is endless wear in the quarter-inch.

For dining-rooms, or where a large carpet covers the central area, there is no need to parquet more than the borders, and the cost being kept down in this way, the one initial expense settles the problem once and for all, and in the long run proves more economical than even staining or painting. It is, as well, quite possible to apply it to staircases, but a solid oak nosing must be inset, so that the parquetry has something to step against. Where it is applied to old floors, all traces of any varnish or paint must be planed off, so that the glue may obtain a good key. As an example of its cost, assuming that it was desired to parquet a three-feet border round a dining-room twenty feet long by fifteen feet wide, this would mean that there would be one hundred and seventy-four feet super, which at eightpence-halfpenny per foot, if plain herring-bone pattern were used, would cost six pounds three shillings and threepence, with some small extra charges over this for cutting round the hearth and doors, and for a border if one were desired. This, of course, is quite the cheapest type there is, and prices run up to fifty shillings a foot for the more intricate patterns.

So far as linoleum is concerned, there has of late been a distinct improvement, and the plain-coloured cork carpets may be instanced as being very useful floor coverings, gaining immensely from the fact that they do not pretend to be other than they are. Just as in the early days railways were like stage-coaches, and then motor-cars at first like the latter, so oilcloth has had to pass through a preliminary stage, when it pretended to be either tiles, parquetry or most gorgeous Brussels carpet. This is most extraordinary, because never was there a material with fewer limitations, so far as its manufacture is concerned. In carpets the designer has to recognise that the knot of wool makes it in reality a mosaic of small woollen squares ; in tiles the difficulties of baking go against very intricate shapes, which may twist or crack in the process. With linoleum one cannot but feel that, if the makers had in the first place founded their designs on the principles of enamels, filled with separate *cloisons*, they would have been on safer lines, and the craft would have gained in interest and have developed characteristics of its own instead of having entered into a variety of other disguises. Certainly whenever pattern is applied the colours of the same should go right through the fabric of the linoleum, or signs of wear will speedily appear if it is only a surface decoration. Another point to be remembered is that it is very unsafe to put down linoleum on to a new floor and close cut it all round the skirting ; some space should be left for ventilation, and many cases of dry rot in buildings have been traced to a neglect of this precaution. Linoleum, then, has a great future before it. It is cheap and very hygienic, in that it can be easily washed Cork carpets are nice to walk about on, and infants can sit on them without chilly discomfort resulting. But a lot remains to be done when we come to the patterned sorts, and salvation here seems to lie in forgetting as speedily as possible that there are such materials as carpets, tiles, or parquetry. To use material aright is the keynote of all successful work, and this is not attained by trying to make one thing look like another. C. H. B. QUENNELL.

WATER SUPPLY FOR COUNTRY HOUSES

Geological Basis of the Problem—The Mischievous ' Dug'" Well—Outputs of Typical Tube-wells—
The Question of Pumping—Various Methods Contrasted—Cost of Wells—Quality of Water
Supplied.

HOW common it is to find the provision of water for a new house to be the last item to enter into a man's calculations ! And yet how very costly may be such a provision. A whole village may be amply supplied from the smallest well it is possible to put down in a given district. Less than this one well cannot be made to serve a single house. Thus it is that the expense of supplying water for ten people may be as great as of that required to supply two hundred. Clearly, water supply deserves special attention. It should form the first study when a new house is proposed. When a house already exists, there is nothing to do but to make the best of existing conditions. All water comes from the clouds. How may it best be conserved ? Is reliance to be placed on natural or on artificial springs—an artificial spring being a well which may or may not yield a supply that will overflow the surface ? The question of water supply is closely connected with that of geology, and a study of geology is essential to a sound practice in supplying water. The rocks which form the crust of the earth appear to have been deposited in water as sand or mud or mixed gravel and clay, in an approximately horizontal plane. These different materials have become hardened by pressure, and ultimately, by reason of shrinkage or movements of the earth's crust, they have been thrown into inclined positions, bent, and variously contorted as shown in Fig. 108, so that to-day we walk over the edges of many rocks of very different ages, and by constant study we are able to unravel the torn and crumpled pages of the book of Nature. Thus we know by study and knowledge of the rocks that, if we dig a well at W into the

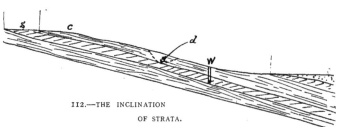

112.—THE INCLINATION
OF STRATA.

clay C, we shall find water in the sandstone rock S, which geology tells us lies next below this clay C. We know that the exposed edge of the rock S lies higher than the site of the well. A map of the elevations of the country-side shows us no exposed surface of the rock S at a lower elevation than is the earth's surface at the site of the well W. From this we argue that rain which falls on the surface at S will sink into the porous rock and make its way under the clay rock above, and will fill up the whole of the rock S unless there is some escape for it. From all this comes confidence that a well put down at W will overflow the surface, or, if the conditions are somewhat different, and copious springs are found issuing from the sand rock at some spot not too far removed from W, then we may know that the water in the well will not rise much above the level of that drainage point. Such a lower drainage point might be furnished by some lateral valley extending through the stratum C and draining off the water down to the level *d*. This is a simple case. In practice much more complication is usually encountered ; but each case must stand by itself and is only to be solved by local study.

Generally in England the surface consists of alternate outcroppings of sandy or " clayey " rocks, into or through which a well may be bored to obtain water. There are three ordinary types of well : first, the old-fashioned dug well, often dangerous by reason of dirty surface water which may get into it from polluted surface soils, the drainage of which creeps down behind the lining of the well and finally enters it. Animals, like rats, may fall into a well. A user may employ a dirty pail in which to draw water from a well, and a well-cover is sometimes a favourite roosting-place for fowls. *The dug well is named so that it may be condemned.* It should never be employed if it is possible to avoid doing so. In many localities the surface earth is largely composed of beds of sand or gravel. These deposits are frequently glacial. They are good water-bearing beds, and if not too near dwellings, and away from the influence of cesspools

and farmyards, these may be relied upon to furnish a fair supply of good water.   Such a bed may be tested by driving down a perforated pointed " driven well," and if this test-well shows that the water is within pump-suction reach of the surface, a number of these wells may be driven at 20ft. or 30ft. intervals along a given line and all coupled to one suction pipe.   Such single wells, only 2in. diameter, will often yield sufficient water for a large house, and may be pumped by wind or by petrol engine or by suction-gas plant and engine.   When the water-bearing rock is deeper, a bored tube-well must be drilled.   These vary in this country from 50ft. to 1,200ft. in depth, a usual depth being 100ft. to 300ft.   The smallest practical size is 3in., but about 4in. is a better minimum diameter.   A 4in. well will contain a 2¾in. diameter pump capable of raising 300gal. to 400gal. per hour, and so may be quite sufficient for a large house. Should the boring prove " artesian " or the water rise over the surface, a 4in. bore-hole into a freely yielding rock will yield a flow of as much as 12,000gal. per hour from a depth of 150ft., with a very few feet of head of overflow.   With a 10ft. head a 6in. bore-hole 170ft. deep has been known to yield 30,000gal. per hour. However, the question of well-sinking is of less importance than that of pumping, for the pumps will always be an expense, and a well-made bore-hole has a long life.   Lucky is the man whose bore-hole overflows. He can lead the water into a tank and control the flow by a ball-valve, and he can employ the simplest form of pump to raise a supply to the house cisterns.   If the water rises nearly to the surface, an ordinary pump will draw it, down to, say, 20ft., easily.   If much water is required and the depth is beyond pump-suction, the fullest possible yield of a well can be secured by means of the compressed air-lift pump.   This is more costly in power than an ordinary pump, and is rarely to be advised for any country house, for it will usually give so very much more water than is required.   To save wear and tear and trouble, it is most desirable that a pump should be run slowly.   A speed of twenty rotations per minute is ample for country house work, with a stroke of 18in.   Especially is this the case where the water-level is far down the bore-hole and must be reached by a long single-barrel pump.   Sometimes these pumps reach to 200ft. from the surface.   If a house possesses its own electric-light plant, the well pump, whether a mere surface pump or a deep pump, may be driven by an electric motor supplied with current from the dynamo or the storage batteries.   Such a pump may be placed a long way distant from the source of power, and may be started and stopped by a switch in the power-house.   The power required, allowing liberally for friction, will be one sixteen hundredth of the gallons per minute multiplied by the total height to which the water is raised.   Thus, if ten gallons per minute are to be raised from 100ft. below the surface to a tank 50ft. up in a tower, the brake horse-power required is less than one.   Where electricity is not available, an oil engine may be usefully employed.   Such an engine will use crude petroleum, or the cheap forms of lamp oil, and even the drainings of heavy residual petrol from the carburettor of the motor-car.   The oil engine is self- contained, easily attended to and will run for hours without attention.   It may be used also for other purposes, such as those of the farm.   Perhaps there is no better system of connecting the engine to the pump than by a leather belt and the usual fast-and-loose pulleys.
     In cheapness of fuel probably nothing exceeds the gas engine drawing its gas supply from a suction-gas producer.   In this case the fuel is anthracite or broken gas coke, and, with an automatic fuel-feed to the producer, very little attention is required.   Perhaps the chief difficulty with motive power by gas or oil is that usually the power required by the pump is much less than the smallest really satisfactory gas producer or oil engine will give.   Thus a 5 h.p. oil engine will work a deep well-pump for quite a large public institution and still be too large for its work.   This raises the question of windmills.   These machines do not give very much power, nor are they very regular in their attendance to duty, being dependent on the more or less capricious wind.   But on an average they will work about eight hours per day ; and if winds are so capricious that at any season there may be sometimes three days without wind sufficient to turn the mill, then the tank ought to have at least four days' capacity, so as to tide over the idle periods.   Considering the very small power required to pump water for even a large house, the economy of fuel is by no means to be accounted of the first consideration.   Very small suction-gas plants are apt to be troublesome.   Where a public supply of gas is available it is generally cheaper for private work to use that gas in an engine than to manufacture producer gas.   A small gas engine will run for 20 cubic feet of ordinary lighting gas per hour per horse-power.   The gas engine to use such gas can be bought to work well down to sizes of half a horse-power, and no time is wasted in lighting up.   Let the advantages and disadvantages of each motive power be summed up.   They are as follows :
     The Oil Engine.—Advantages : Self-contained in small space. Fuel purchasable everywhere if cheap lamp oils are used.   Disadvantages : Time required to start. Small engines not easy to obtain. Makers apt to push upon buyers engines much larger than the power actually needed ; therefore, waste of fuel. Small engines not very satisfactory.
     Suction Gas.—Advantages : Very cheap in fuel per horse-power hour, and fuel usually easy to obtain.   Producer durable and engine works quietly with producer gas.   Expense not great.   Can be used for other purposes of farm, etc. Disadvantages : Time required to light up. Small power plants not very satisfactory.   More or less constant attention needed to producer unless automatic feeder employed.   Space required much greater than with oil engine.   A certain danger exists owing to the

poisonous nature of the gas; hence, special care required to ventilate power-room, and producer is best placed out of doors with only a roof over.   Producers for small sizes not very satisfactory.

Public Gas.—Advantages: No expense except when running engine.   Easily and promptly started. No plant but engine required.   A minimum of first cost.   Will run well on small powers. Disadvantages: Public gas often expensive,·but usually cheaper than a lamp oil engine.

Electricity.—Advantages: Fairly cheap if made on premises for lighting.   Motor started any time and from any distance.   No cost when standing.   Disadvantages: The high speed requires special gear for reduction.   Current apt to be expensive if purchased from an outside supply.

Water.—Advantages: Costs nothing for motive power.   Disadvantages: May dry up in summer or freeze in winter.   May cost a considerable amount to build dam or other head works.

Wind.—Advantages: Costs nothing for motive power.   Disadvantages: Mill expensive.   Power intermittent; large storage capacity necessary.

In Fig. 113 is shown an approximate section north and south through London, in order to illustrate how the rain falls on the high ground of Hampstead Heath at H and sinks down until it is

stopped by the London clay C, which lies below the capping of Bagshot sands which form the gravelly Heath. The water thus caught on the clay travels along the junction until it issues at S in the

113.—SECTION OF LONDON SOIL.

form of the springs which produce the ponds in Parliament Fields and issue finally as the river Fleet, which flows into the Thames, T, at Blackfriars Bridge when in flood only.

Now there are many parts of the country where no water can be got from wells of any reasonable depth.   This is the case over large areas of "clayey" Essex.   A house may, however, produce its own imitation of Hampstead Heath.   Every acre of ground receives 100 tons of water annually for each inch of rainfall.   Taking a household of ten persons at 20gal. each per day, this amounts to 326 tons annually. Allowing it to be possible to save 14in. of the rainfall of Essex, which amounts to 24in. annually or thereabouts, then one-fourth of an acre would yield 350 tons per year.   That is to say, the household named could be supplied from an area of ground 40yds. by 30yds. Selecting this at the highest point, the ground would be stripped and levelled and covered with a layer of concrete suitably channelled to a central channel of half tiles.   The whole area would be covered as deeply as expense would allow with clean sand, or gravel, fenced round to keep off animals, and a suitable tank would be sunk in the ground to contain the water which would filter through the sand.   There are many localities where such a scheme could

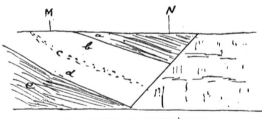

114.—SECTION AT BENNETS' END.

be easily arranged, and if low cost is a consideration and rough water for rough purposes is available, the pure water-collecting area may be reduced to that necessary for potable water only, or for that for the toilet. Such a plan is at least well worth consideration in localities where, as over so much of Essex, a well must pierce a great thickness of London clay to reach the chalk, and the water-level may then be far down. Such a bored well may be very expensive.   No underground water-level in its natural condition can ever be so far below the surface as the sea-level.   All the fissures of the earth's crust must be full of water to that level.   By prolonged pumping, however, the level may be reduced, as it has been in London, where the artesian water-level is now far below sea-level.   Were not the chalk outcrop under the sea well puddled over with clay, there would long ago have been an influx of the sea into the chalk below London. This is a risk to which these low-pumped London-bored wells stand constantly exposed.

It will naturally be suggested to the mind that any pumped water supply will require some amount of storage capacity, for it is not desirable to work a pump continuously, and storage sufficient to tide over small repairs or other stoppages will be necessary. For medium houses a water-tank in the roof will often be quite sufficient and satisfactory. For larger establishments a more pretentious water-tower may be erected into which the well pump discharges, and from which a supply is taken in pipes to the various house and farm tanks fitted with ball-valve control. Where the water is hard, a softening plant may be contained in the tower. Towers are sometimes placed at a considerable elevation on an adjoining eminence, so as to afford ample pressure for fire purposes without the aid of any special fire pump. All this is a question to be decided by the expenditure it may be agreeable to incur or the degree of pride felt in the water undertaking by the house-owner. Various circumstances enter into the determination of the expenditure. It may be necessary to place a water-tower in an exposed situation, so that a well-designed stone tower might be justified with an enclosed tank ; or the tower may be hidden in a wood, when a very plain, simple affair may suffice.

As regards the cost of boring wells, this may be set down at about £1 per foot for diameters of 6in. to 8½in. in London. This cost would include the lining tubes necessary. A well of 100ft. and 4in. to 5in. diameter would cost, including lining, perhaps 7s. to 12s. per foot. Above 400ft. the cost begins to increase considerably. The cost of pumping will vary from ¼d. to 1d. per 1,000gal., according to quantity pumped and height raised. It is obviously impossible to give exact figures to fit every case. But wells have been bored and set to work with pumps that have recouped the outlay in saved water-rate in a year's time ; and the writer once bored a well, about 200ft. deep, near London which paid its cost in three months, the water standing within suction reach of the pump. There is, of course, a great difference between what can be effected at different places. At one place, for example, a single-driven 2in. well, costing, perhaps, £6, will give an ample supply for a large house. At New Lodge, Windsor, the writer engineered a well bored into the lower greensand to a depth of 1,243ft. A small supply of soft, pure water rose to a height of nearly 8ft. above the surface, and was piped through glass-lined pipes to the first floor of the house. The cost was, of course, great ; but there was no subsequent pumping cost for the main supply, and the quality was excellent. The ex- istence of this bored well would no doubt add to the value of the house if ever sold, much more than the cost of the boring. A safe bored tube well will sell a house which would now be barely saleable

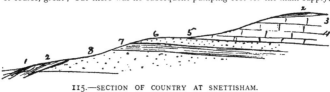

115.—SECTION OF COUNTRY AT SNETTISHAM.

1. ALLUVIUM.	4. HARD CHALK.	6. CAR STONE. ⎫
2. BOULDER CLAY.	5. RED CHALK.	7. CLAY. ⎬ LOWER GREENSAND.
3. CHALK AND FLINT.		8. SAND. ⎭

with a contaminated or risky dug well. This point should always be taken into account when considering rival schemes. There yet remains to be considered the impossible site for boring of a house perhaps high on a hill, with a stream in the valley below. If there is even a low fall possible by construction of a dam, a small water wheel may be used to pump up rough water, the better supply being obtained from rainfall collected as described ; or the rough water may be forced up by a hydraulic ram, when no dam is needed, the water being piped from a higher point of the stream to the ram placed further down. A very low fall may thus serve to ram water up to a house at a considerable elevation. But usually the stream will not be pure enough for potable purposes.

Quality of Supply.—The hardness or softness of a water supply is determined by the nature of the surface from which the water is gathered or of the rocks into which a well is bored. From sand rocks the water is soft ; from clays it is often found to be charged with soluble salts, such as sulphate of soda, sulphate of magnesia and common salt ; from chalk or from other limestones or calcareous rocks generally hard waters are obtained, the hardness being of that quality known as temporary, that is to say, it is removable by boiling. Certain marls, such as the Keuper marls, contain gypsum and yield small supplies of water, often of considerable hardness of the so-called permanent variety which is not removable by ordinary boiling. Thus in Newark town hard water may be obtained from borings of moderate depth. If soft water be demanded at Newark, it would be easy to obtain it at the expense of boring several hundred feet so as to enter the new red sandstone which underlies the marls. In England especially the sequence of the geological strata is generally such that some water is usually to be obtained, either from the surface stratum or that next below. Even in one of the worst parts of Essex water enough for a large house has been obtained at less than 800ft. Artesian boring is now much less costly than it was twenty years ago, and the hardest granite rock may be bored at the rate of several feet per day. Bad localities for water are usually those, such as so much of the County of Essex, over which there is a thick layer of clay. Essex is an area of London clay, and there is practically no water in London clay. It must be pierced to the chalk beneath. Deep chalk is often comparatively waterless. But the term waterless has not so much significance when a single house supply is involved, for it is a poor supply indeed that will not find water for a large house in a day of eight hours' pumping. Often a careful examination of a district will show some peculiarity, such as a geological fault, which renders a successful well possible only a few yards distant from an undesirable situation. An example of a geological fault is shown in Fig. 114 on the right, where, as recorded by Mr. Whitaker, the chalk is faulted upwards so as to abut against the basement bed of the London clay. The beds a, b, c, d are the

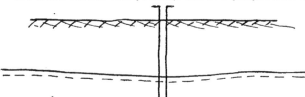

116.—GENTLE DEPRESSION   CAUSED BY EASY PUMPING.

London clay, and e is the chalk, and such faulting may between a well at N and one water. That at M would need the success might be greater local conditions. Fig. 115 from "Woodward's Geology of" Reading clay. Here at Bennets' End they are level with the make all the difference between early success or failure, as at M, for that at N would soon reach chalk and might obtain to go much deeper to reach the chalk, but when it did do so than in the case of boring at N, depending, of course, on other shows a characteristic section across country at Snettisham England and Wales." When any well is bored records should be carefully kept of the material passed through and the distance from the surface. In time such records accumulate evidence that may solve some hidden mystery in geological science. Every bore-hole not so recorded has failed to be of the fullest possible service to the country generally.

In conclusion, it may be repeated that the maximum of safety and the minimum of cost are usually to be obtained with a bored tube well. The elaboration and greater magnificence of the dug well is only obtained at a greatly-enhanced cost and a serious risk of pollution. There is, of course, no very imminent risk if a dug well be made in clay simply to enable a pump to be placed within reach of the water in a bore-hole put down at the bottom of the well. In such cases the bore-hole is to be hermetically sealed to the pump suction, and the dug well is merely a dry pump chamber, the bottom of which is proofed with concrete and the sides are clay behind the lining. Serious cases of pollution have, however, occurred where a well, bored in the bottom of a dug well, has been left with its lining pipe standing up open in the dug well. Water has entered the dug well and risen over the open top of the tube. The tube should therefore always be closed and directly connected to the pumps, so that, even if water should collect in the dug well, none of it can be drawn by the pumps. Pumps in dug wells ought never to be drowned, that is,

117.—HEAVY DEPRESSION   CAUSED BY PUMPING HARD.

should never be exposed to be covered with water collected be had it may pollute the pump water by its contact with water is almost invariably safe, because it has been well earth's surface. Plant roots seem to have much influence doubt also that water becomes thoroughly oxidised in earth. Every change of the barometer causes influx or efflux of the pores of the rocks. But, strange to say, living artesian wells. This has occurred in France and once in country, where a well was bored on a hill to the depth were hard, blocky and much fissured, and the water to in the dug well, for if such water the pump glands and rods. Artesian filtered in its passage through the in this direction, and there is no passing downwards through the of vast volumes of air into or out creatures have been brought up from the writer's experience in this of the nearest valley. The rocks the bore-hole had doubtless travelled. Though such cases from the valley stream horizontally to the boring through the wide fissures. Though such cases will be rare, it is always desirable to remember their possibility. It is probable that in the instance named a deeper boring would have obtained water free from life, for living creatures would not descend far. Even where there is much pollution of the surface water this need not be feared to extend deeply below the water surface in the strata.   And this leads up to an important consideration.   Where there is any risk, heavy pumping at any one point is inadvisable.   A heavy draught at one point creates a depression round the well if the supply is meagre, and the impure top layers of water may be drawn into that depression, as in Fig. 116.   In such conditions pumping must be moderate, so as not to produce serious lowering about the well.   If the dotted line represents the less pure upper layer of water, it is clear from the diagrams how this may or may not be drawn into the pumps according as these are worked beyond or within the fair yield capacity of the rocks.   The extent of this so-called cone of depression depends upon the amount of water in the strata and upon the freedom with which it can flow to any pumped centre.   Speaking generally, the yield of a well will vary with the square root of the depth lowered.   Thus, if a pumping rate of 10gal. per minute causes the water to lower 1ft., a supply of 20gal. per minute would lower it 4ft., and 30gal. would demand 9ft. of lowering.   This shows how a heavy demand may produce a very depressed cone. Usually this matter is not important, but it may become important in certain hydrogeological conditions, and it is always desirable when undertaking a water supply to have the aid of an independent expert. Practical well-borers are sometimes tempted to bore much further than is necessary.   On the other hand, the practical man who is carrying out the work may also hesitate to advise boring deeper when he really should do so, for his advice may appear interested.   The independent expert can restrain undue expenditure, and can advise additional expenditure as the true wants of a case demand.   W. H. Booth.

SEWAGE DISPOSAL.

Arrangements for Disposal—Detritus Tanks—Septic Tanks—Treatment of Effluent—Costs.

I T is only during the last few years that this important subject has been seriously considered generally by property-owners. It has usually been sufficient for them to hope that all was well so long as the house itself was not apparently inconvenienced. Sanitary science has made tremendous strides, but it is to be hoped that in ten years' time some existing methods will be looked upon as out of date.

Better consideration should be given to the position of the sanitary arrangements within a house. It would be ideal to adopt for houses the planning usual in modern hospital buildings, and place the baths, w.c.'s and sinks in a separate block cut off from the main part of the house by a thoroughly cross-ventilated lobby. However, the ordinary arrangements of to-day, so long as they last, must be made as free as possible from danger, and the shortest length of waste-pipes fixed inside the house will help to achieve this. All pipes so fixed should be exposed, so that frequent and easy examination is possible. All w.c.'s and slop sinks should be trapped at the nearest point to the receiving receptacle, and should have a flushing cistern of not less capacity than three gallons where the water companies will permit. Most companies, however, will only allow two gallons, which is certainly not sufficient. It is important that the " waste " dealt with should be conveyed and disposed of with the least possible risk of contamination. It must, therefore, be removed as quickly as possible and treated in the most efficient manner compatible with reasonable capital outlay and a low maintenance cost. Details of the arrangement of pipes, gulleys and traps are too technical to be dealt with usefully within the limits of this article, which is concerned rather with methods of disposal.

The selection of a site for disposal works depends to some extent on the system to be installed, for some require a greater fall in the ground than others. The important fact must be borne in mind that with any system there may be a slight " earthy odour " near the tanks, which, however, can be reduced to a minimum if the system is properly designed and trees are planted close to the tanks. In deciding upon the system to be employed, four principal factors should be taken into consideration · 1. Possible position of the site, together with its levels and nature of subsoil. 2. Possible outlet and discharge for resultant effluent. 3. Quantity and quality of sewage to be dealt with. 4. Cost, both of installation and of maintenance. The site should be as far as possible from the house consistent with a reasonable length of drain. Provided the tanks are fairly closed in by high vegetation and are not in the direct line of the prevailing winds, a distance of about one hundred yards is ample. They are often placed much nearer, without disagreeable results. Bacteria beds should not be in a too exposed position, as the bacterial action is somewhat reduced during cold weather. A site giving the most fall or greatest difference in levels is preferable, as it will allow of a good " fall " in the tanks without resort to pumping or other form of lifting. It is important that a good outlet for the effluent should be at hand, either in the form of a natural watercourse or an arrangement whereby it·can be economically distributed or utilised in the garden. Where this form of use is possible, it is against economy to allow the effluent to run to waste. Quality and quantity of sewage per person varies greatly, the quantity being from fifteen to eighty gallons per head, depending a good deal upon the source of water supply and extent of garages, stabling and home-farm property, and also on whether the rain-water is discharged into the drain. For ordinary purposes, however, twenty-five gallons per head per twenty-four hours can generally be safely reckoned upon. The initial cost depends upon the falls obtainable, the quality and quantity of the sewage, and upon the degree of purity of the effluent required, which again depends upon the nature of the ultimate disposal of the effluent. Cost and maintenance depend upon the system installed, the quality of materials and workmanship employed, and the care given to the installation from the first day it is in operation. It must be remembered that no disposal works are absolutely automatic, and that regular and careful attention is therefore required.

The object of a disposal works is to liquefy the solids and obtain an effluent free from solid matter and practically free from solids in suspension. It depends somewhat upon the nature of the outlet available for the ultimate discharge of the effluent as to whether a good chemical or good bacteriological result is desired. The first operation necessary in all systems is to free the sewage from " foreign matter," such as rags and scrubbing-brushes ; in fact, from all matter that will pass through to the various tanks and beds and not liquefy in a reasonable time. This is generally achieved by discharging the sewage into a sump chamber, or detritus tank, fitted with a fairly large mesh screen, so that the sewage will pass through with a minimum amount of resistance. There are various ways of obtaining the purification of sewage, and some of the reasonable methods suitable for private property will be reviewed.

The old system of discharging the whole of the sewage into a cesspool, or midden, and allowing the liquid to gradually filter into the adjoining land, though a convenient form of " disposal," is hardly such as will be accepted to-day, and the more modern local bye-laws now compel all cesspools to be water-tight without an overflow. This has rendered the cesspool system very costly and inconvenient, owing to the continual necessity of cleansing and emptying. Many people still contend that the old open cesspits should be allowed where it is not reasonably probable for wells to become contaminated. It should be remembered, however, that liquids percolate and travel to a vast distance, and the health of the community at large must be considered. When it is taken into account that bacilli (such as that of typhoid) will not be rendered harmless by any amount of ordinary filtration, every endeavour should be made to conduct the effluent into the most harmless channel. All sewage, then, should be treated to obtain a reasonably high standard of purity, and the sludge and effluent disposed of in the safest manner.

Though the open cesspool or pit is not to be recommended, a modification of it may, in certain circumstances, be allowable. This consists of an ordinary water-tight tank, into which the crude sewage is discharged and the overflow conducted to bacteria beds, as described later ; it should, however, only be adopted as a temporary measure. Present knowledge indicates that the septic tank, which has had a long trial, gives general results which have proved satisfactory. The system has many advantages, and is undoubtedly the most convenient form. The method of treating sewage chemically by adding iron and lime, and thus causing precipitation, is not one which can be cordially recommended for private houses ; the labour and consequent cost and trouble are such as to render it undesirable. Moreover, the effluent from chemically-treated sewage is not so satisfactory as that obtained from properly-designed septic tanks and bacteria beds, and the comparatively large proportion of sludge resulting from the chemical process has to be cleared out and disposed of. The general lay-out of a septic system consists of three main divisions—(a) preliminary chamber or detritus tank, (b) septic tanks, (c) bacteria beds (often misnamed filters). The detritus tank should be arranged to retain all foreign matter, including, as far as possible, sand and grit. Screens should be inserted so that the sewage has a path with the least possible resistance. Where the rain-water is discharged into the sewage system, an overflow pipe should be connected to this chamber, so that a sudden rush of water will not unduly disturb the septic tanks. The connection from this preliminary chamber to the septic tank should be so arranged as to allow a free flow, but at the same time to cause as little disturbance as possible. In order to obtain this result, the inlet may be brought in at the top of the tank, but discharged about six inches above the bottom. Septic tanks are plain chambers without any filling, and with outlets taken from the top, though the pipe dips to about six inches from the floor, and they remain full. During the course of putrefaction the gases cause a thick scum to form on the top, which should not be disturbed ; hence the arrangement of inlet and outlet as described. Provided that the septic action is not interfered with, there will be practically no sediment or sludge in the septic tanks.

The preliminary, or detritus, tank will require cleaning out at certain periods, but the septic tanks should not require this. The action in the septic, or anaërobic, tanks should reduce the organic solids by about eighty-five to ninety per cent. To ensure this result it is better to have about three septic tanks together, as a better and surer result will be obtained with three small tanks than with one large one. They should be of sufficient capacity to take not less than thirty-six hours' discharge. No such tank or tanks will give an effluent of sufficient purity to be discharged without further treatment ; therefore bacteria beds (or so-called filters) are used. These beds are open to the atmosphere, whereas the septic tanks are closed (with the exception of small safety-valves to relieve undue pressure formed by the gases). For private installations these bacteria beds should be of such a size that not more than fifty gallons is passed through the beds for every yard superficial per day of twenty-four hours, and the beds should be not less than four feet deep.

To ensure proper action in the bacteria bed, which is essentially aërobic, the filling material must be of such a nature as to allow free and easy circulation of air, and material which gives the greatest surface in contact with the air reduces the size of the beds, and is thus the most economical. Such material, however, should not be one that easily clogs or in any way disintegrates. Of the many that are in use, coke probably gives the best results. The percentage of voids in coke beds varies according to the size of material used, but an average of about thirty-five per cent. may be safely taken, and coke will absorb water up to about fourteen per cent. of its own weight. There is thus a large surface free to the air, and experiments show that large porosity and power of reabsorbing atmospheric oxygen are necessary. In all aërobic beds it is essential that periodical and proper periods be allowed for "rest," so that they may become thoroughly aerated. The time allowed varies according to circumstances ; but for private installations, if two aërobic beds are in use, one bed would be filling for twenty-four hours, and should then be allowed to stand full for, say, three hours. If then emptied, twenty-one hours are allowed for aerating. Provided coke bacteria beds are allowed proper time for aeration, they do not become choked. If by any accident, as in the case of excessive storms, the tops of the beds become charged with sewage before proper treatment in the septic tanks, the top layer of coke requires raking over or possibly renewing, but the material can be used again after " resting " several days. It is important that the effluent from the septic tanks be properly distributed over the bacteria beds. To secure this a small collecting chamber is made between the last septic tank and the bacteria bed, fitted with a siphon, which discharges the liquid, about forty gallons at a time, and distributes it over the bed by means of perforated wooden troughs. Where the purity of effluent, either from the chemical or bacteriological point of view, does not reach a sufficiently high standard after contact with a single bacteria bed, a second bed should be installed. The first bed is called the primary and the second the secondary bed, and the secondary contact produces a great improvement. It can be reasonably assumed that the primary bacteria bed will reduce the number of bacilli contained in the crude sewage up to twenty-five per cent., and the secondary contact up to sixty per cent.

There remains the question of the ultimate disposal of the effluent. In this matter each individual case requires to be considered on its merits, as local circumstances have an important bearing, and the ultimate means of disposal has a direct influence upon the design and construction of the bacteria beds. The effluent has excellent fertilising properties, and provided it is possible to utilise it in the garden, beneficial results will accrue. It is desirable, however, that the liquid should be spread over the ground by means of movable troughs or other suitable arrangements, as if discharged for any long period in one place the ground will become sodden and sour. If consideration be given to other ways of nourishing gardens, any prejudice against the utilisation of the effluent for garden purposes will be quickly dispelled. The liquid should be utilised in a fresh condition, without resort to storage, except in exceptional circumstances. Whether the effluent is discharged over the garden or into a ditch or other channel, it is necessary that the course should be kept clear of vegetable matter, such as fallen leaves, etc. Ditches need to be kept quite clean, and all bacteria beds should be covered with small-mesh galvanised wire movable screens.

No matter what the method of disposal of the effluent, it is necessary, after passing through the bacteria beds, that it should be given the maximum opportunity to aerate properly. This can be secured by separating the fluid, by passing it over steps with " baffles " inserted, and if the installation is of sufficient size, a small apparatus for spraying may be installed. It is beneficial if a portion of the conduct channel is paved with hard bricks or other similar material. Undoubtedly aërobic action continues in the effluent after its discharge, this either being helped or retarded according to the manner of its disposal. There are certain other fittings not mentioned in detail, which should always be of the simplest kind, of strong make, and such as can be easily replaced if necessary.

As previously mentioned, no sewage disposal works are absolutely automatic ; but with a little systematic and intelligent attention the cost of maintenance of a septic system with its necessary bacteria beds is trifling. The system known as " broad irrigation " has not been dealt with here, as it seems an impossible method for private works. As can be readily understood from the foregoing, the cost of a suitable septic tank and bacteria bed installation depends a very great deal upon the circumstances of each case ; but assuming the disposal works have to provide for a population of sixty, with reasonable requirements, the cost would be from forty pounds to one hundred and thirty pounds. The cost of all maintenance, including labour for attention, for such an installation should not exceed four pounds to fifteen pounds per annum.   A. ALBAN H. SCOTT.

KITCHENS AND SCULLERIES.

Relation of Domestic Offices to the General Plan—A Short Historical Survey of the Kitchen—The Problem of the Scullery—Danger of Over-specialised Equipment—Various Types of Kitchen Ranges.

IN the well-regulated household, which it is the ambition of all housewives to maintain, the smooth running of the domestic machinery must depend on the efficiency of those offices, which, hidden away behind the baize-covered doors of the service passage, are not visible to the eyes of the visitor. The drawing-room may be upholstered and furnished in the very best of taste ; the rooms may be all, or even more than, the neighbours can boast, and yet excite ridicule rather than envy, if not backed up by the more solid qualities of a business-like disposition of these offices, which stand in the same relation to the house as the heart does to the body. In the same way the offices, even if perfect in themselves, will fail. if their inter-relation to the other parts of the house is not harmonious. There needs must, then, be some small digression to trace the relation of kitchen and dining-room if any useful purpose is to be served. It is quite possible to have a perfect kitchen so arranged or planned that even in conjunction with an equally admirable dining-room the result is yet quite unsatisfactory.

So far as the chapters in this book are concerned, various parts of the house have been considered separately ; but the most urgent insistence is necessary that good architecture is that which blends all the parts into one harmonious whole, and the very best architecture of all is that which gives consideration to the practicalities of existence. If our houses are afterwards to be "readable," they must make apparent the life that has been lived in them, and must be carefully designed to fill its every need, which would seem to be asking much of the architect ; yet a reference to the types of plans of, say, the last one thousand

118.—KITCHEN AT GLEMHAM.

years will show that the same are quite readable, and
that they were designed, or evolved, to suit the needs
of the people of the times in which they were built.
This can easily be verified by conjuring up an idea of
any particular epoch, by what we know of it from
history, and then taking a house of the same period
and seeing how well it agrees with the life that must
have been led in it; and all this is quite possible to
us if, instead of designing houses in a spirit of eclectic
dilettantism, we endeavour instead to build them around
our own definite requirements.   We are at the moment
an extraordinarily mechanical people; think of the number
of amateurs who have an excellent knowledge of the
working of an internal-combustion engine and its detail
of ignition.   The matter interests them because the
subject is one of efficiency; our houses, then, must
be efficient, and that in more ways than slavish imitation
of bygone types of ornamentation on the exterior.   The
planning of the kitchen and its offices may be said to
have proceeded on eminently rational lines until the
Palladian period of architecture.

In Saxon and Norman times the first necessity
of a house was that it should be easily defended, and
we find that the cooking arrangements were primitive,
and consisted of sheds without the fortified keep.   The
methods of cooking were probably elementary, and the
large roasted joint could be depended to retain its heat,
by reason of its size, during the passage from kitchen to
hall.   The most rational type of planning of the domestic
offices we have ever had was that which followed on
Norman times, and had its inception in the granges,

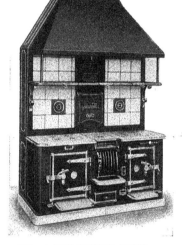

119.—A FREE-STANDING RANGE.

which the abbots built for their accommodation when travelling to view distant farms and
estates.   These buildings were an adaptation of the monastic type of plan grouped around a
cloister.   The monks took the parts which were necessary to form a home, so that we find these
early granges had a central hall with screens at one end and a raised dais at the other; at the dais end of
the hall were the private rooms for the abbot; at the screen end came the buttery and kitchen.   The
type remains with us in the guise of collegiate buildings, and it was universal down to the end of the
sixteenth century.   During this period the English gentleman lived almost entirely on his land,
and unless he happened to be a great personage of political importance his visits abroad or

120.—A RANGE FOR LARGE HOUSES.

to London were very few and far
between.   The type of plan that
was evolved was admirably suited
to the requirements of the household,
and was wholly English in its conception and evolution.   The houses
were not adapted for ceremonial,
but rather for comfort.   At the end
of the sixteenth century, however,
a great change set in, until we find
in the Palladian period that comfort
had been almost wholly given up for
ceremonial; and whereas in the sixteenth century the kitchens were
always arranged so that meals could
be served into the hall quickly, in
the eighteenth century they were
placed in such a position that only
by a miracle could food reach the
dining-room before it was quite
cold, the kitchen being placed in
the basement, or far away in a wing

planned symmetrically to balance one on the other side, that might, perhaps, contain the stables.

If we think, then, of a " School for Scandal " set of folk, we find, looking at the plans of their houses, that what they required was a fine suite of rooms for entertaining purposes, little care ·being · given to the kitchen and its offices. They were daintier feeders, though, and would probably have . turned up their noses and stigmatised as gross such a dinner as was given by the Earl of Hertford to Queen Elizabeth. The roasting fires were retained, but, in addition, it is usual to find in kitchens of this period provision made for cooking by charcoal. A sort of brick table was built up on a series of arches which served to store the charcoal in, and on the table enclosed in metal rings charcoal fires were made and cooking was done over these in small pots.

A singularly interesting old kitchen at Glemham is illustrated—it has been given a new lease of life by the introduction of the modern hot-plate and ovens for stewing

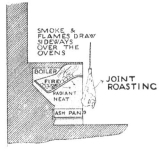

121.—SECTION THROUGH FIRE
OF NEW RANGE.

and baking ; but the old roasting fire is still shown with a bird trussed and spitted in front. The spit-rack can be seen attached to the front of the range, and the method of turning the spit with the smoke-jack. There are trivets at the sides of the fire, on one of which a kettle is standing. The screen in front of the fire serves to keep the cook from being grilled as well as the bird, and is also used for plate-warming. On the side of the screen are basting ladles. There are as well many fine old pots and pans, and the clock is such a beauty that serving meals to time by its aid must be a pleasure. Passing to the details of the modern kitchen, first consideration must be given to the size of the house and the number of servants to be accommodated. If there is to be a highly paid specialist in charge of the cooking department, with attendant kitchen-maids, the accepted plan of kitchen and sculleries; servants' hall, butler's pantry and housekeeper's room solves the difficulty, and if care is taken that the suite of offices are arranged like a modern factory, so that from the moment when the food is delivered like raw material at the tradesman's door it will pass along until it is delivered as the finished product into the dining-room, and make steady progression during

122.—RANGE WITH ROASTING FIRE AND NEW TYPE BATH BOILER

its journey, then it can be safely predicted that the domestic machinery will work smoothly.   In any case, it is clearly impossible within the space of these notes to do more than indicate the various types.   It may be taken as a rule, though, that the larger the house the easier it is in one way to plan it.   Space can be afforded for each of the departments.   Laundries will be separate buildings, with their own staff of maids, and one has not to provide offices for composite purposes.

In smaller houses, where only one class of servant will be kept, it seems a good plan to adopt the North Country practice and dispense with the scullery, and have, instead, a living and working kitchen. The latter contains the range and sink for preparing vegetables and washing-up purposes ; the floor and walls are tiled where all the necessary part of the work is done.   The floor has rounded angles where it joins the wall, and the whole idea is that the place should be cool and clean.   The living kitchen is for the maids to have their meals and see their friends in.   Their photographs can here be displayed and the amenities of existence enjoyed.   Such arrangement is very suitable for a house run with a cook-general, house-parlourmaid, and nurse for the children. Unless the cook has a kitchen-maid it is difficult to see the use of a scullery. It is dreadfully easy to plan a house with the range at one end of the kitchen and the sink at the other end of the scullery ; assuming the kitchen be eighteen feet long and the scullery twelve feet, the cook will have to walk sixty feet every time she leaves the range to go to the sink and come back again, which conjures up horrid visions of hot cooks walking unnecessary miles in the course of a week.   It is eminently desirable that the two fittings should be in close relation, but if it is desired to banish the sink from the kitchen, it can be placed

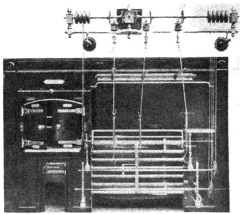

123.—ROASTING RANGE, WITH JACK.

in a recess with a screen in front.   It is, perhaps, safer to keep to the common-sense principles which should guide in the planning of kitchens, rather than give lengthy descriptions of details which must vary considerably to suit the varied needs of different households.   Too intricate a specialisation of the fittings should be avoided.   Cooks are a conservative race, and a place for everything, and everything in its place, is a rule more honoured in the breach than the observance. As a race, they are prone to untidiness in their work, with a grand clear up at its conclusion, and much time and money is often expended in providing separate little compartments for each thing, with a result that they are never used for such purpose at all.   The simpler the arrangements can be the better. Some illustrations are given of ranges, and these have their racks for plate-warming.   Dressers should be provided of ample size with good drawers and pot-board accommodation.   There should, as well, be cupboards.   Sinks must be of good size, and preferably white coralled porcelain.   Draining-boards should be of a hard wood like teak, and the secure fixing of taps is worth consideration.   If these are fitted with gun-metal pad plate bosses, screwed to plugs in the wall, it will be found much better than the usual method of clips, which very shortly become loose.

Aspect should be considered.   It is a very usual practice to place kitchens to the north of the house when they are not put in a basement, an arrangement which the Palladian architects found so useful in getting them out of a difficulty.   There can be no doubt that this northern aspect for a kitchen constitutes real cruelty to cooks and deserves the attention of the Humanitarian League.   To be condemned to labour in a room into which no gleam of sun shall ever find its way is awful.   So then the kitchen should be planned that some early morning sun can find its way in and give the day's work a cheerful start.   Needless to say, the full blaze of the south or the level glare of the west would constitute an inferno.   If, though, one has a large north window and a small eastern one, this is avoided ; furthermore, the two windows give a chance of cross ventilation and help to keep the kitchen cool.   Ventilation should be also provided by means of a flue in the chimney-stack.   The range should be so placed that it is lighted from the left-hand side.   It seems hardly necessary to mention such details, yet the common way in which they are disregarded is, perhaps, sufficient excuse. It is usual to place the range in a recessed fireplace, and if this is tiled out it is quite possible to light the hot-plate adequately ; on the other hand, when the covings are black iron, it is, perhaps, a little gloomy. The range illustrated in Fig. 119 strikes one as an extremely well-designed fitting, and, standing against a flat wall without any recess at all, should give an excellently-lighted hot-plate. In all other respects it follows the proper range lines, and has a rising fire, which can be open or closed. The dampers are regulated from the front of the plate-rack, and the oven doors can be opened by pressing a lever with the foot.

The kitchen must be arranged so that there is ready access to the dining-room. In a large house there should be a service corridor leading to the latter, on which the domestic offices all open. In small houses, where, for reasons of economy, the service corridor has to be dispensed with, and the kitchen becomes a passage room, it should always be managed that the way through is kept, if possible, in one corner, or across the end. Kitchens are often planned with the two doors at diagonally opposite corners, which at once turns the room into a glorified lobby. The consequent dislocation of the cook's temper is apparent. She is by way of being a personage, and should be accorded certain state, and it is not fit, right or proper that her subordinates should have free run of her domain. If we cheer her up with a glimpse of the sun at the start of the day, her temper must not be ruffled after. A very frequent source of trouble is the provision of hot water for baths, and in quite large houses it is often found that there may be more than one bath, and yet the boiler at the back of the kitchen range is expected to supply not only baths, but scullery and pantry, sinks and so on. It is quite a moot point whether it is not better, even where there is only one bath, to have an independent boiler ; it can be safely stated, though, that where

there is more than one, most certainly the range should not be depended upon. Many people seem to think that they have only to instal a range, and that, this done, it should cook their food, heat the water and the house as well. The standard type has a fire which can be regulated, as a rule, by a lifting bottom, and there are ovens on each side ; fines are taken across the tops of the ovens, down the sides, under the bottoms and up the backs, with a reversing damper, so that heat can be taken to the bottom of the pastry oven. The boiler is set at the back of the fire, and has an arched flue under it and up the back—so that here we have three flues into which we can direct the heat by means of dampers. It is obvious that if we pull out the boiler damper and shut in the others, we can have hot baths but not bake our cakes. It is extraordinary what a number of cooks will not take the trouble to use the dampers properly, and especially is the new cook an offender who comes to a different style of range from the one to which she has been accustomed. She makes an onslaught in the morning and wakes the entire household long before the

124.—STANDARD TYPE WITH LIFTING FIRE.

cup of tea comes, and it has been a source of wonder to the writer what a volume of sound quite a small cook can get out of the largest range if she is really enraged.

This difficulty, which the range in a small house has, of serving the dual purpose of heating water and cooking, has led to a new design in ranges shown in Figs. 121 and 122, and it is claimed that the trouble has been overcome. A section is given which shows that the hot-water boiler is so constructed that its body comes directly over the actual fire, and there is no separate boiler flue which serves to divert the heat from the ovens. As soon as the fire is lighted, the boiler must be heated by reason of its position, and the heat then passes through the oven flues. Another point is that air is admitted from underneath the fire, and cannot get to the oven flues except by passing through the fire. The form of the latter lends itself to roasting joints, a form of cooking preferred by many to baking in the oven.

In large houses it is better to keep cooking and heating separate, and to instal an independent boiler for the latter. Fig 120 shows such an arrangement. The range illustrated has a very adequate hot-plate, with good ovens and a fire which is thoroughly practical for roasting, and at the side is shown an independent boiler with cylinder over. In the summer months, for instance, when one may be having cold dishes, it is quite possible to dispense with the range fire altogether and depend on the boiler for hot water for sinks and baths. A fire will last for twenty-four hours in the boiler, and so one is ensured hot baths in the early morning. Also the boilers are economical from the point of view of fuel, and though they will not subsist on potato-peelings, as some cooks expect them to, they will burn coke and cinder with a little small coal.

Fig. 123 shows a good roasting range, and to such as prefer roast to baked meat here is a fitting that will appeal. The spits can be turned by a smoke-jack or electrically, and the way it is done is so clearly shown here that there can be no need of further explanation. The fire has a winding check and trivet, and at the side is a pastry-making oven. The range, while being thoroughly modern, is yet pleasingly mediæval in appearance and would give interest to the kitchen of a large house. As touching on this, it should be noted that, while the majority of the ranges illustrated are suitable for moderate-sized houses, in larger ones they would need to be enlarged, the principle being the same, though, whether there are two ovens or four, whether the fittings stand against a wall or in the middle of the room like an hotel range. The range in a large house would be used for baking only, with a roasting fire in addition, as here illustrated, and perhaps a grilling stove. Ranges can be used in a more architectural fashion by dispensing with the tiled covings and plate-rack and setting the hot-plate and fire and ovens in a white glazed brick arch with the flues and dampers in a brick back. It makes a pleasing treatment. if somewhat an unusual one.   C. H. B. QUENNELL.

REFRIGERATION

*Main Uses of Refrigerating Plant—Ice-making—Cold Storage for Food—Compression System —
Description of Plant and Insulation.*

AREFRIGERATING machine is a thing which owners of country houses, perhaps, seldom consider as being suitable to their own special requirements, yet there are certainly a very large number of houses in the country in which such a plant would be a most valuable adjunct. It may be said that in practically every house a considerable quantity of ice is employed in one way or another for preserving provisions and icing drinks. The fact that ice is used demonstrates the necessity of producing " cold " by some means or other ; and once this fact is established, it only remains to point out the great superiority of mechanical refrigeration over cooling by means of ice. Where ice is used for preserving provisions, it is difficult to keep them fresh and at the same time dry for any length of time, as the atmosphere created in the ice safe, or refrigerator, is extremely damp and the temperature cannot be controlled. With mechanical refrigeration, on the other hand, eatables, such as meat, poultry, game, vegetables, fruit, dairy produce and the like, may be maintained at any desired temperature, and thus preserved dry and in perfectly good condition for practically any period ; and the house is entirely independent of any outside source of supply for ice, the result being a very considerable saving of expense.

What ice is required for placing in butter-dishes, cooling drinks and other purposes can be made with the same machine. In this connection a question of health is very often also involved. The ice is made from the water used for the regular drinking supply of the house, whereas the origin of bought ice is unknown. One of the large London hospitals, indeed, lately was sufficiently interested to analyse some ice which had been bought, and the result of the examination caused the authorities to congratulate themselves on the possession of a refrigerating machine by means of which they were able to produce their own ice.

There are three main uses to which mechanical refrigeration may be put in a country house : First, there is cold storage for use in connection with the house larder where various classes of food can be kept and sufficient ice made to meet the demands of the house—for this purpose some sort of cold must be employed, and where there is no refrigerating machine ice is used ; secondly, there is the storage of game, where mechanical refrigeration is the only feasible method, as a store containing the bag of a large shoot cannot be maintained at a sufficiently low temperature for long storage by means of ice. A store of this sort on a sporting estate can be used both for holding over the bag of a shoot till it is convenient to dispose of it, and for the long storage of game to be used in the house itself. The third use to which refrigeration can be put on a country estate, namely, in dairy-work, is a subject by itself. Here refrigeration is not only used for the storage of milk, but also for cooling it when the milk is pasteurised or treated in some such way. When one considers all these advantages of mechanical refrigeration over the use of ice, and the many purposes for which it can be used, it may seem curious that this class of machinery is not more often installed in country houses. The reason probably is that people are apt to think of cold storage by means of mechanical refrigeration as something to be done on a large scale only, as they are familiar with large cold-storage establishments with powerful refrigerating machines, or with the large installations on board first-class liners. Refrigerating machines, however, are also made in quite small sizes entirely suitable for the needs of the country house, and can be worked by a small electric motor wherever electric power is available, or by a small gas, oil or petrol engine. Such machinery requires very little attention, and can be looked after by a person who has other duties to perform ; for instance, one plant in a certain country house has been for two years run and looked after by the laundress. It is only necessary when the machine is working to look at it quite occasionally to see that all is going well, and the stores required are very few and extremely cheap.

Another objection which may also arise is, perhaps, the thought that it may be necessary to erect a special building to contain the cold stores and the machinery ; but any space or unused rooms in the house can be easily converted into a cold store, and, indeed, a plan is given of a plant installed at Moreton Hall in Warwickshire, showing how conveniently a plant can be arranged in three existing rooms. Any refrigerating machine can be used for each of the three purposes mentioned, the only variation being in the design of the machine and the manner in which the cold produced is applied.

Practically all the machines of this size work on what is called the compression system ; that is to say, by alternately compressing and allowing to expand some gas which can be easily liquefied. The system of operation is as follows : The gas is first compressed in the compressor ; it then passes, still under a high pressure, through a coil of piping known as the condenser, where the heat, generated by compression, is removed by means of water flowing over the coils. When the temperature of the gas is reduced to somewhere near that of the water, being both cool and at the same time under pressure, it becomes a liquid. This liquid is passed through a valve and allowed to evaporate into a gas, which causes it to become intensely cold. In this state it is passed through another coil called the evaporator, which is surrounded by brine, which, in its turn, is made cold, but by its nature cannot freeze. The gas is then drawn back to the compressor and the operation begins afresh, the same charge of gas being used over and over again. The brine which is cooled in this way can be used for making ice and for reducing the temperature of the cold store, being pumped to the point where the cold is required by means of a small pump in the engine-room.

For making ice the brine is contained in a tank in which galvanised steel moulds are suspended. These moulds are filled with water, which is frozen by the cold brine surrounding them. The length of time that it takes to freeze a block solid depends on the size of the block ; the most convenient form for the size of plant under consideration is about twenty - eight pounds in weight, which would freeze solid in approximately eight hours.

The cold chamber is formed by insulating some room or larder, as described later. The cooling appliances are fixed in the chamber and vary slightly in their design. These sometimes take the form of piping bent into grid shape, the grids being suspended on the ceiling

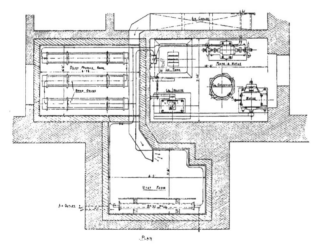

125.—PLAN OF REFRIGERATING PLANT.

and sides of the chamber. When it is desired to maintain an even temperature, it is usual to place what are termed brine drums in the chamber. These are practically large pipes, about nine inches in diameter, and as they contain a large volume of brine, the cooling effect is continued for some time after the machine itself has stopped working. In a small chamber a brine wall is sometimes used to produce the same effect; this is a flat steel tank containing brine, which is placed at one side of the chamber. When it is desired to keep the atmosphere in the chamber sweet and fresh, an air cooler is used. This is usually formed of grid piping similar to the grids already described ; but they are closely nested together and are put in an insulated casing, which is often placed outside the chamber itself. A fan blows air over these grids, which contain cold brine, and any moisture is deposited in the casing, the air in the chamber itself being perfectly dry. The gases most commonly used as a refrigerant are carbon dioxide (CO_2), ammonia, sulphurous acid and ether. Each of these requires a special compressor to suit its special properties. The CO_2 machine is by far the most suitable for this class of work ; the gas used is the same as that which causes the aeration in aerated waters and wines ; so that it is absolutely safe to use these machines whatever may happen, whereas the occurrence of a serious leak in the other machines would cause danger to life. Besides this advantage, the CO_2 system is fully as efficient as any other and the compressor is very much smaller, so that the machine occupies less space.

Figure 126 shows a convenient plant where it is not possible to insulate a separate room. On the left is seen the compressor of the machine, which can be driven by a small electric motor or engine. The circular cast-iron casing on which this compressor is mounted contains the condenser coils, the ends of which can be seen projecting ; through this casing the cooling water is passed. The two gauges show the pressure of the gas under the full compression and the pressure when the gas evaporates from the liquid to the gaseous state in what is called the evaporator coil. The evaporator coil in this case is contained in the ice tank itself, seen in the centre. This tank, it will be seen, is covered by boarding, which contains the insulating material, so that no heat passes into the brine. There are two moulds in this tank, and the lugs for lifting them can be seen projecting. On the right of the illustration is an insulated cabinet divided into three parts. The two partitions are formed by flat tanks extending from

126.—-PLANT WHERE SPACE MUST BE ECONOMISED.

top to bottom of the cupboard. The brine cooled by the evaporator coil in the ice tank is circulated through these tanks and causes the temperature in the cabinet to fall.

The particular cabinet illustrated was designed for hanging meat, poultry and game in the centre compartment, dairy produce in the left-hand compartment, and wine and fruit in the two right-hand compartments. The shelves are made of perforated zinc and are all removable. The pipes are not connected up, as the plant was merely arranged for photographing.

In the plan of the plant illustrated in Fig. 125 the engine-room is situated in the basement underneath the front hall ; it will be noticed that the compressor is driven by a belt from an electric motor with the condenser close by. The ice tank in the left-hand corner of the room is fitted with an apparatus for producing clear ice ; the moulds are swung to and fro during the process of freezing. If this were not done, cloudy, opaque ice would be produced unless distilled water were used. If it is required to make clear ice from ordinary water, as in this instance, some such method as this must be adopted. Sometimes paddles are used for agitating the water ; but rocking gear is preferable, as the paddles sometimes get frozen into the ice. Near the motor driving the compressor are placed the two pumps driven by an electric motor. One of these pumps circulates the cooling water through the condenser, and the other circulates the brine cooled in the ice tank through the various cooling appliances. The brine drums are clearly shown in the dairy produce room, the meat-room being cooled by a brine wall, while outside the engine-room is placed the air cooler immediately underneath the ceiling. The air is led to the chamber by wooden ducts.

This plant, therefore, illustrates three separate methods of applying the cold produced by the machine besides ice-making. The plan also gives a good idea of the insulation which is required. This is a most important point in connection with cold-storage plants. The object of the insulation is to prevent any outside heat from passing into the chamber. If this were not done, it would be necessary for the machine to remove not only the heat from the goods placed in the chamber, but also the heat passing through the walls. Several materials can be used for this purpose, those most commonly used being silicate cotton, cork, charcoal and sawdust. When insulating a room already in existence, if the walls are dry the material to be used can be placed against them. The method of construction in this case would be to place wooden battens six inches to eight inches broad against walls, floor and ceiling, and nail boarding to these, the six-inch space between the boarding and the walls being filled in with insulating material. If it is wished to give a very good finish, the boarding can then be covered with white tiles, which give an extremely clean and fresh appearance to the chamber. Insulation such as described can always be carried out by a local carpenter at a very small cost.

For use in connection with the storage of game, the plant would be similar to the one already described, except that the chamber would probably be considerably larger. The best cooling appliances to use in this case would be brine drums on the ceiling worked in conjunction with an air cooler. When the chamber was filled up with fresh game, the air cooler would be used to reduce the temperature and to freeze the contents of the chamber ; the brine drums would then be used for maintaining the temperature which had been reached. It must be borne in mind that the more perfect the insulation of the chamber is made, the less work has to be done by the refrigerating machine.

Dairy-work, as before noted, is rather a subject by itself. The cold store to be used in connection with a dairy is constructed on the same lines as the dairy-room shown in Fig. 125. Besides this there would be the cooling of the milk, which is carried out by passing it in a thin film over a special milk cooler. Coils of piping, through which brine is circulated, are also sometimes placed in railway churns containing the milk, so that the temperature may be rapidly reduced.   DUDLEY G. GORDON.

AN UP-TO-DATE GAME-LARDER.

The Practicability of Small Cooling Plants—Description of the Machine—Notes on Insulation—Air-locks—Cost of Installations.

WHERE do all. the grouse come from which are eaten in London on " The Twelfth " at lunch and dinner ? Quantities of birds are offered for sale early in the morning, and all of these cannot possibly have been shot even on the moors nearest to London that same day. The solution of the problem, of course, is ' cold storage." In the last chapter were described refrigerating installations suitable for supplying the necessary cold-storage accommodation for a country house, and therein was mentioned incidentally that one of the most useful purposes for which such a plant could be employed was in connection with the game-larder. The object of the present chapter is to offer some further remarks on this branch of the subject. The birds referred to above are supplied usually from public cold stores, where they have been kept in a frozen state for some considerable time ; but this same cold storage can, of course, be used for keeping any sort of game for shorter periods to be eaten out of season, or to be held in store during a portion of the season, and used if there is a temporary shortness in the supply.

To the majority of people this appears to be the end of the matter, and hitherto it has not been usual to have a private cold store as part of the establishment on a sporting estate. Such stores, however, have been erected in several cases, and they have been proved so convenient and satisfactory in working that they have come

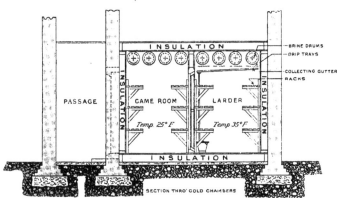

127.—DIAGRAM OF STOREROOMS COOLED BY BRINE.

to be regarded as an absolute necessity. It is not as yet realised generally that cold storage can be carried out on quite a small scale perfectly satisfactorily and efficiently, and for this reason most country houses make shift with a box, or chamber, cooled by ice. While this works all right in cases where articles of food have only to be kept for a few days, it has the disadvantage of being messy and costly by reason of the amount of ice used, whereas in a small larder cooled by using a machine food is kept dry and at any temperature desired, and therefore in good condition as long as necessary. It is probable that in a few years' time a refrigerating machine will come to be considered just as necessary in a country house as the electric-light plant is to-day. The machine, moreover, has been designed and perfected, and the price is moderate for the results obtained. It is, then, only necessary for these points to be realised for the adoption of these machines to become general.

To proceed to details. The smallest size of machine found satisfactory will make a small quantity of ice and cool a chamber measuring six feet square by seven feet high. It will be obvious that this size would not be sufficient for the needs of a very large country house, nor one where game storage is contemplated on a considerable scale. The plan on this page illustrates a smallish plant arranged for the storage of game. From this it will be noticed that there are two rooms, the one being used as a larder for keeping game for short periods for daily use, the other being maintained at a temperature below freezing point, so that the birds can be kept in a frozen condition for any desired period. The machine used is one working on the CO^3 principle, which is by far the most suitable type of machine, owing to its absolute safety combined with the highest efficiency. Though the type of plant is in many ways similar to those described in the last chapter, it is thought well to describe it in detail, even though it involves a certain amount of repetition. The action of the machine is as follows: The gas is compressed in a compressor driven by an electric motor or oil engine, and while under high pressure it is passed through piping which is immersed in cold water, and is known as the condenser. The result of cooling the gas while under high pressure is that it becomes a liquid, and while in this state it passes through a valve known as the regulator, this valve being kept almost shut so that the pressure is high on one side of it and low on the other. The gas passes from the regulator through further piping, and the great drop in pressure causes the liquid to suddenly evaporate into a gas again and become intensely cold. This piping, known as the evaporator, is immersed in brine which cannot freeze, although it is reduced many degrees below freezing point. From the evaporator piping the gas is drawn back to the compressor, and it repeats the same cycle as before, no gas being used except that lost by leakage. The brine cooled by the evaporator piping is circulated by a small pump to any point where the cold is required. In the illustration shown the cooling appliances in the chambers consist of what are known as "brine drums"; these are merely large pipes through which the cold brine is passed. The

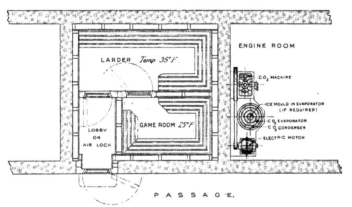

object of having them so big is to keep a large body of cold brine actually in the chamber, which reduces the temperature even when the machine has stopped running. The quantity of brine circulated through the brine drums in each course is controlled from the engine-room, so that the temperature can be maintained at any desired point by varying the amount of brine circulated.

128.—GAMEROOM AND LARDER COOLED BY THE CO^2 METHOD.

In the room used for storing birds for a short period (where the temperature is kept above freezing point) it will be noticed that means are provided for carrying away moisture deposited on the drums, this being necessary because all moisture present in the air is deposited on these drums, with the result that the air in the room is kept perfectly dry. Each time the door is opened and fresh goods brought in, a small amount of warm air is admitted, and the moisture present in this is immediately deposited on the drums. But in the chamber kept below freezing point the moisture is not carried away in this manner, as owing to the low temperature it freezes solid immediately it is deposited.

Another method of cooling the larder would be to circulate the brine through a series of pipes bent into grid form and closely nested together. This stack of piping is placed immediately outside the larder, and air forced over it by means of a fan is circulated through the cold room. In this case the air is cooled and the moisture deposited before actually entering the room. The best method is to combine this system with the one already described, so that a good ventilation is ensured and birds can be rapidly cooled by means of the air-cooler. Then, when the plant stops work, the low temperature is maintained by the brine drums. In constructing any cold store, great care must be taken to see that the insulation is thoroughly efficient. The work of the machine is divided into two parts; first of all, the heat has to be removed from the goods brought into the store, and, secondly, the heat has to be removed which passes through the walls. Now, the amount of heat which has to be removed from the goods cannot be controlled; at whatever temperature the birds come into store they must be cooled down, but the second portion of the work can be controlled. If the insulation is bad, a large quantity of heat will pass through the walls, but good insulation will stop the heat passing through and so make less work for the machine. For this reason it is always worth while to spend a little extra on thoroughly good insulation, and so save not only on the first cost of the machinery, but also on the running expenses during the whole period of the existence of the plant. The insulating material should be from six to eight inches in thickness, varying according to its insulating value and the temperature at which the store is to be kept. The best and most efficient method of insulating a cold store is by means of cork, supplied in slabs formed of small pieces compressed into one piece. Each slab is two inches in thickness, and three layers of this should cover the walls, floor and ceiling of the store. The slabs are laid so as to break joint, and are held in place by means of odourless pitch. The whole surface is then covered with a thin layer of white cement, which gives a very nice finish and enables the chamber to be washed out when desired. A somewhat cheaper method of insulation is to place battens six to eight inches in length against walls, floor and ceiling, and to nail match-boarding to these, the space of six or eight inches thus formed between the boarding and the brickwork being filled with a material known as slag wool or silicate cotton. When this is done it is often well to have a layer of waterproof paper on each side of the slag wool, as it readily absorbs moisture, and when this occurs it loses its value as an insulator. Other materials are sometimes used when insulating with this method, the commonest kind being granulated cork, flake charcoal, sawdust and cowhair.

It will be noticed that the plan shows a lobby or air-lock, out of which the cold chambers open. The object of this is to prevent an inrush of warm air when the cold room is entered. Before opening the larder door the lobby door should be closed, and similarly the larder door should be closed before opening the door of the frozen storage-room. The doors are specially made with a taper, so as to fit tight when they are closed, and are insulated with the same thickness as the walls. The approximate cost of the plant described is three hundred pounds.

Illustrated in Fig. 128A is a very convenient apparatus for hanging the birds in the cold store. This provides for a large number of birds in a small space without their being too tightly packed together. The upper rows hang clear of the lower ones, so that there is no fear of blood dripping on to them; the whole apparatus revolves, which facilitates handling. Without an apparatus of this sort it is difficult to make use of the space in the centre of the store, as birds can only be hung on rails attached to the walls and ceiling. DUDLEY G. GORDON.

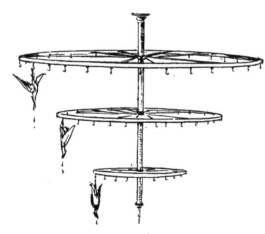

FIG. 128A

THE BATHROOM.

Thackeray on Baths—The Shower—Some Historical Notes—Heating of Bath Water—Treatment
of Walls and Floors—Baths and Lavatory Basins.

BATHS and bathing have become so much a part of one's everyday life that it is a little difficult to
realise that times are not so far distant when they were regarded as luxuries for the over-nice
and as whims of the foolish.   An interesting sidelight is thrown on the subject by Thackeray,
in " Pendennis," when he says : " ' Gentlemen, there can be but little doubt that your ancestors
were the Great Unwashed : and in the Temple especially, it is pretty certain that, only under
the greatest difficulties and restrictions, the virtue which has been pronounced to be next to godliness
could have been practised at all.'   Old Crump, of the Norfolk Circuit, who had lived for more than thirty

years in the chambers under those occupied by
Warrington and Pendennis, and who used to be
awakened by the *roaring of the shower baths* which
those gentlemen had erected in their apartments—
part of the contents of which occasionally trickled
through the roof into Mr. Crump's room—declared
that the practice was an absurd, new-fangled,
dandyfied folly, and daily cursed the laundress
who slopped the staircase by which he had to pass.
Crump, now much more than half a century old,
had indeed never used the luxury in question.   He
had done without water very well, and so had
our fathers before him."   This shower-bath of
Pendennis' must have been of the same type that
Leech drew in his *Punch* pictures—a sort of foot-
bath at the base forming a foundation on which
stand four columns, about as high as a man, and
these in turn support a cistern on top.   There are
curtains between the columns to enshroud the
hardy bather, and a sort of bell-pull arrangement
released the water on to him.   In one of his
pictures, called " Domestic Sanitary Arrangements,"
a stern papa brings four small boys to bathe, all
looking very miserable and protected as to the
head with conical caps.   Meanwhile a page, housemaid and a very fat old cook are filling the upper
reservoir.   One can understand that, in use, such
a shower-bath would roar in quite a terrifying way
for a small boy.

An illustration is given of a modern treatment of this fitting at Ardkinglas, designed by
Sir Robert Lorimer.   Here the walls and floor are
treated with vitreous mosaic, and one imagines

129.—SHOWER BATH AT ARDKINGLAS.

that the only difficulty which would be encountered
with small boys in their use of this shower would
be to persuade them to leave off in time for other people to share its joys.   There are several other
drawings by Leech of baths and bathers, all going to prove that the former were novelties,
and so material for his facile pencil.   One cannot but feel, then, that many of our forbears were
distinctly unsavoury.   Yet it is, perhaps, hardly kindly to probe the past and quote authorities,
though, on the one hand, the subject is of great interest, and it might be found that certain periods of
culture included cleanliness and, on the other hand, times of stress left no leisure for baths.   There are
many references in English literature to the subject, and Shakespeare in " Coriolanus " talks of being
" Conducted to a gentle Bath and balms applied to you."   The scene of the play being Rome recalls the

fact of how large a part bathing played in the life of the Roman, and Sir Alma Tadema's pictures give one a vivid idea of what their bathing establishments were like. Wherever they went, too, they carried their good habits with them, and the Roman bath in the Strand and at Bath are instances. The habit of bathing, though, was, perhaps, less of a virtue in the sunny climate of the Mediterranean than in our own bleaker one—the famous baths of Maria de Padilla at Seville, which form part of the Alcazar, were originally open to the sky, surrounded by orange and lemon trees, and here Pedro's favourite disported herself. It was a mark of gallantry for the knights of the Court to drink the waters after Maria had performed her ablutions, and Mr. Calvert in his book on Seville tells a tale of how the King noticed that one of his knights refrained from so doing, and on being questioned replied, " I dare not drink of the water, lest, having tasted the sauce, I should covet the partridge." In this note of the baths at Seville mention may be made of the Moorish occupation, which terminated in 1248 after over five hundred years, during which time all Mussulmans bathed in accordance with the teachings of the Koran.

It should not be forgotten that the bath has its own order of chivalry, instituted with us at the Coronation of Henry IV. in 1399, and again revived in 1725. It received its name from the candidates for the honour being put into a bath the preceding evening to denote a purification or absolution from evil deeds A bath

130.—STANDING OUT INTO THE ROOM.

opened in 1679 in Bagnio Court off Newgate Street is said to have been the first used for hot bathing in England, while Turkish baths did not appear till 1860. The first public bath was opened in the neighbourhood of the London Docks in 1844. Having thus delicately touched. on the subject of how our forbears did not bathe, it will, perhaps, be fitting to consider how best one can do so to-day, and the first and most vital need is an adequate supply of really hot water. One's bath may be of porphyry, and the bathroom lined with onyx—if the water is lukewarm the result is unsatisfactory. Taking the ordinary small house as an example, the usual method is to have a boiler attached to the kitchen range. If this is to be effective, the fire must be lowered, the boiler damper withdrawn and the oven ones pushed in, so that all the heat of the fire is directed through the arched flue under the boiler. These simple details are generally known and yet just as generally neglected.

Should there be more than one bath in a house, it is essential that an independent boiler with separate furnace be used. At first sight this may appear to be an unnecessary and extravagant arrangement, whereby two fires are needed. This is not the case, though, as the same boiler will be used for all sinks and lavatory basins, and the range then need only be alight when cooking is in progress. Being assured of a sufficient quantity of hot water, the question of the cold supply presents little difficulty, and generally consists of connecting to the water main and storing water in a cistern at a level above the highest fitting. In the country the same system of storage in cisterns obtains, the tanks being filled

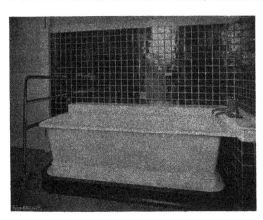

131.—BATH ON BASE: TILED WALLS.

either by gravitation or by water being pumped into the same by electric, gas, oil, or other engine, or by hand power. The next consideration, then, is the actual bathroom ; its size will have to be in proportion to the house, but it should not be too cramped, so that physical drill may be possible to those who start the day in strenuous fashion. Where space can be afforded, the bath looks well standing

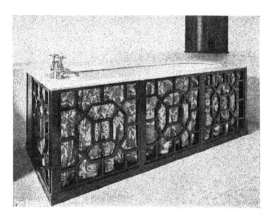

into the room, as shown in Fig. 130. It thus fittingly forms the central feature, and all the other fittings can be grouped round the walls. Water-closets should never be placed in the bathroom. Floors should be tiled if possible, and nothing looks better than a warm red tile wax-polished. The walls in this case will be tiled as well, and the angles where the walls join the floor should be finished with rounded tiles, so that there cannot be any dirty corners ; the same method should be applied to the angles of the walls. The wall tiles can be treated as a dado about 4ft. 6in. high, or, of course, taken all the way up ; if this cannot be afforded, then the walls should be plastered in Keene's cement and finished with a flatted oil paint, and this applies to the plaster ceiling as well. Marble is available for wall lining and floors, but it is a material that wants using with great restraint— if varied colours be introduced, the result is apt to be reminiscent of the cheap

132.—AN ORIGINAL TREATMENT.

restaurant. In all cases, be it bathroom for peasant or millionaire, the effect must be obtained in simple fashion and by the use of suitable materials. There should be little, if any, applied ornamentation ; a man in his pyjamas, or just out of them, is apt to look incongruous in the midst of much elaboration, and though none may witness his discomfiture, yet it is well to avoid it.

The bathroom should be heated and ventilated—in the smaller bathroom a towel-airer will serve to heat, and in larger ones a radiator may be added, as well as an open fireplace. For sheer unadulterated luxury nothing can be compared to the enjoyment of jumping out from a cold bath and dressing in front of a good fire, and the fire is useful if the room be used for children. As to the relation of the bathroom to the bedrooms : If there is only one bathroom, it should never be placed *en suite* with the principal bedroom and dressing-room, as what generally happens is that the master of the house approaches through his dressing-room, locking the other door, and neglects to unlock the same after his bath, with

133.—MARBLE-LINED WALLS.

the result that some unfortunate visitor is left disconsolate on the landing wondering when his turn will come.   We have much to learn from the Americans as to the number of bathrooms to be provided.

Having dealt with the planning and arrangement of the bathroom itself, and its relation to the bedrooms, it is proposed to deal briefly with the various types of fittings.   The bath, naturally, is the important fixture.   In selecting a bath, one of the most important details to be borne in mind is the finish of the surface of the inside.   A few years ago, and in the case of the cheaper ones to-day, baths were " stove enamelled," and though the term has a well-meaning sound, such enamel is really little better than paint, soon wearing off.   As soon as this happens the bath must be repainted, and if used before the same be absolutely hard the paint may again come off, and in any case is a constant source of expense.   The bath itself is made of cast iron, and the best ones now are vitreous enamelled with a thin coating of porcelain, which should not crack unless subjected to very rough usage and is practically indestructible.   Acids must not be used for cleansing purposes—a little paraffin easily removes all grease and soapiness and, in addition, cleanses the trap connection and waste pipes.   The parallel shape is the one generally used, and looks better in the room than the tapered bath, and if placed against a wall does not leave more space at one end than the other between the wall and bath.   It should also be remembered that baths are made of varying lengths, and where the bathroom is of fair size it is best to have a good long bath, so that tall people may bathe with comfort.   The edge should be finished with a wide roll, and the bath looks well standing on a base as in Fig. 131, thus obviating any chance of dirt collecting underneath.   A separate shower bath is shown in Fig. 133, though economy can be effected by having the same fitted to the bath itself ; it also enables one to have a cold shower after a hot bath in the same fitting.   But where it is desirable to have a shower bath only, say, after a game of tennis in the summer, then it is more convenient as a separate fixture.

An original treatment for a bath is shown in Fig. 132, designed by Mr. Lutyens.   The fitting has a marble top, and the sides are framed up with a trellis, made of ebony with chintz hangings behind same. The idea, though, cannot be commended for general use, and it seems better to use only materials like tiles or porcelain, not easily damaged by water.   Sitz and foot baths are sometimes fixed in large bathrooms, and have their uses ;   though in small houses the one bath and shower fitting is really quite sufficient. Canopy baths are those having the waste end enclosed and the shower fitting in the same ;   they can be fitted up as well with a variety of other sprays, the one objection to them being that, so far, the design of the canopy is, as a rule, somewhat cumbersome.   The canopy is sometimes cased with wood panelling, but it is not a practice to be commended.   It is far better in a bathroom to have all surfaces enamelled and easily accessible, and wood, unless very well seasoned, is apt to warp.

Lavatory basins are of many types—of white glazed ware, or with marble top and back ; or, again, they are sometimes fixed on a pedestal.   The main consideration, though, is that they should have a large water area ;   nothing is more annoying than to attempt to wash with only a thimbleful of water.   The soap trays should be so arranged that any water lodging in them is speedily drained off ; if this is neglected the soap soon becomes a sort of " soft soap " not nice to use.   A very delightful and luxurious fitting to a basin is the combined hot and cold shampooing valve.   Everyone has often expressed a desire to have at home apparatus which would enable them (ladies, especially) to enjoy the comfort of a shampoo, a desire which this fitting now will permit them to realise.   By reversing the valve it can be used for spraying the face ; and refreshing indeed is the effect of this operation on the faces of those tried by the heat of a summer's day.

The towel-airer has been mentioned for heating purposes, and should always be provided in the smallest house.   Its heat is just sufficient to make the bathroom pleasantly warm on a very cold morning, and, in addition, gives the luxury of dry towels.   The fittings may be so arranged that they can be shut off by a stop cock if it is found that they make the bathroom too hot in summer.   In small houses where there is not a housemaid's closet, hot and cold draw-off taps should be arranged in the bathroom, so that cans can be filled without the danger of the bath enamel being cracked by their knocking against the sides.

In conclusion, let the keynote of the whole be a bright cleanliness.   If the bathroom faces east, then one's morning tub with the sun streaming in becomes the best of starts for the day's work, and the simpler the place is the better.   One is unsophisticated in the morning, and the complication of things belongs to the night that is passed.   This simplicity should be observed in colour as well ;   the bath and the lavatory will be white glazed.   Let the walls be white too, so that by contrast our bodies may appear ruddy with health ;   and, looking well, we shall feel well.   Our bathroom then will have fulfilled its purpose.   C. H. B. QUENNELL.

REVIEW OF LIGHTING SYSTEMS.

Electricity, Air-gas or Acetylene?—Factors in a Fair Comparison—Questions of First Cost and Upkeep—Typical Examples—Degrees of Skilled Attention Required for Different Systems.

WHEN the lighting of a country house which is not within reach of any public service of gas or electricity comes to be considered, an important question arises for immediate decision: Will electricity, acetylene or air-gas best serve the individual purpose? Anyone who intends to instal a private plant is faced by conflicting advice from the makers and advocates of these varying systems. Some attempt at a fair and impartial comparison is likely therefore to be useful. It is impossible to apply any definite rule or set of rules when making the choice, but it is desirable that the following conditions should be fulfilled:

(1) Low first cost of installation.
(2) Low working cost.
(3) Simplicity of machinery.
(4) Reliability.
(5) Safety and cleanliness.
(6) Adaptability to the decorative scheme.

The size of the installation is the chief factor determining which of the three systems best fulfils the foregoing conditions in any particular case, and this, together with the manner of life of the householder and the style of the house, should form the basis on which the final decision is made. No attempt has been made to write down the above conditions in the order of their importance, as this varies with the personal element in each case. For instance, low first cost will not appeal to the wealthy individual who desires to light up a large country house containing a great drawing-room, a ballroom, and numerous guest chambers, to the same extent as it will to the country clergyman with a small stipend, a small rectory, and a large family. The rich man with a very large establishment will almost certainly declare in favour of electricity, which in his case will probably give the lowest working costs, while his less wealthy neighbour will most likely instal air-gas or acetylene.

The actual first cost is determined by the size of the installation required; but in making a comparison, the annual cost of working must also be taken into consideration, and it is this which makes a fair comparison extremely difficult, as so many things affect it which are not, properly speaking, commercial considerations at all, but rather affairs of domestic concern. In a very large establishment which is run on business lines by the estate agent, it is desirable that the value of the plant should be written down year by year on some properly determined scale of depreciation, that provision for maintenance should be included, and that a certain proportion of the estate engineer's wages should be added to the cost of fuel in order to ascertain rightly the cost of the light.

When, however, we come to consider the case of a small country house built by the occupier, who may be a retired man of business wishing to spend the end of a busy life in surroundings of his own choosing, the case appears entirely different. Should such a man be content to use oil lamps or candles, we should not be likely to find the ironmonger from whom he makes his purchases presenting him with statistical data as to the depreciation and maintenance of his candlesticks, interest on his capital expenditure and the annual cost of labour in lamp trimming. The fittings in this case are regarded as ordinary pieces of household furniture, to be replaced or repaired as may be required, in the same way as the chairs and carpets, and the yearly sum expended on oil and candles does not differ in kind from similar sums spent on bread or coal; they are both part of the ordinary household expenses. The situation is not materially altered by the installation of a small acetylene or air-gas plant; the cost of running it forms part of the ordinary household expenditure, and the repairs that may be necessary to keep the plant in order are not properly assessable on the capital cost of the plant. A concrete example may serve to make the meaning clear; take the case of a very small acetylene installation for five lights costing £15 all told. The calcium carbide to run such a plant for one year cost only £3 in at least one well-authenticated instance. The light was, of course, used sparingly. If we follow the statistician's advice and allow 10 per cent., or £1 5s., for yearly depreciation, 5 per cent., or 12s. 6d., for interest on capital expenditure, and a further 10 per cent., or £1 5s., for labour in connection with the plant, we saddle the lighting bill with a sum of £3 2s. 6d. in addition to the cost of carbide. Now, if the plant is of thoroughly good make, there is no reason to suppose that it will be absolutely valueless at the end of ten years, as the proposed scale of depreciation would lead us to expect; and if we allow 5 per cent. interest on capital for the acetylene plant, it should also be allowed on the lamps and candlesticks. Furthermore, the servants' time in attending to the generator should be considerably less than that required for lamp trimming.

The foregoing view has been set out at some length, as it seems that in the case of small private plants the cost of running is made to appear unduly high by the addition of fixed percentages on capital outlay to running costs. Let us consider the first cost of the plant for supplying 50, 100 and 150 lights. A manufacturer who supplies all three systems, and may therefore be trusted not to enlarge unduly on the merits of any particular one of them, gives the following as the cost of such installations complete from the generator to the lights :

No. of lights.		Electricity.		Air-gas.		Acetylene.
50	..	£130	..	£105	..	£83
100	..	205	..	200	..	150
150	..	275	..	250	..	217

These figures are only approximate, and would vary according to the circumstances in which the installation was to be carried out ; furthermore, in studying the comparisons of this table it should be remembered that the costs given in each class are for one type of plant only. There are more costly forms on the market which have certain advantages. This is more particularly the case with the acetylene system.

Our next consideration is the cost of the fuel necessary to keep these plants at work, and in this we may take as a convenient standard the cost of the fuel required to run a 60 candle-power light for 1,000 hours. In the case of electricity we assume the use of ordinary paraffin oil at 6d. per gallon. The manufacture of air-gas requires the use of petrol, and it should be remembered that the Government duty can be reclaimed on petrol that is not used for driving motor-cars, so we may take the price as 1s. per gallon. Calcium carbide for the manufacture of acetylene costs £12 10s. per ton. Now, an oil engine for driving a dynamo of about the size we are considering would require about one pint of paraffin per horse-power per hour, but we can only reckon on three-quarters of a horse-power being available at the lamps, as we must allow for losses in the dynamo and accumulators. A 60 candle-power metallic filament lamp taking 1·1 watts per candle-power would require 66 Board of Trade units to keep it running for 1,000 hours. As a horse-power for one hour is equivalent to 0·746 Board of Trade units, this is equivalent to 88·5 horse-power hours. Now, we have seen that we can get three-quarters of a horse-power at the lamps for one hour at the cost of one pint of paraffin, so it follows that we should use 88·5 ÷ ¾ = 117½ pints to keep a 60 candle-power lamp going for 1,000 hours ; this works out to 7s. 4d. with paraffin at 6d. per gallon.

In the case of air-gas careful experiments have shown that a 60 candle-power light can be kept going for fifteen hours at the cost of 1d., assuming the cost of petrol at 1s. per gallon. This means that the same light for 1,000 ÷ 15 = 66·6 pence, or about 5s. 6½d. A 60 candle-power open flame acetylene burner consumes about 1½ cubic feet of the gas per hour, and good calcium carbide at £12 10s. per ton will produce 5 cubic feet of acetylene to the pound weight. We therefore require 1,500 cubic feet to keep the burner going for 1,000 hours, that is, 1,500 ÷ 5 = 300lb. of carbide ; the cost of this at, say, 1¼d. per pound works out to £1 11s. 3d. This latter would appear to be a very high figure when compared with the other two, but as will be seen from what follows, there are many circumstances which tend to modify the position when the question becomes the practical one of lighting a house and not a purely academic comparison of fuel against candle-power per hour. Now, it will be observed that the air-gas in this comparison is the cheapest, and in cases where a house is required to be lit throughout by 60 candle-power lights it undoubtedly is so ; but whereas electricity and acetylene can be used in lights of smaller candle-power, thus allowing economies to be made in passages, lobbies, etc., the smallest burner that can be successfully used with air-gas gives 40 to 60 candle-power. Acetylene has the additional advantage that it can be turned down when not required. This, of course, cannot be done with any form of gas lighting that makes use of an incandescent mantle, and the dimming of the electric light is rather a wasteful proceeding, save in cases where the alternate current system is used. In all but very exceptional instances country house plants are designed to give continuous currents, when the use of dimmers is distinctly uneconomical.

In the above comparison table of first costs the lights are not of equal candle-power ; for the electric system they are assumed to be a proportion of 12, 16 and 20 candle-power, for the air-gas they would all be 60 candle-power and for the acetylene they would all be 22 candle-power. This seems to be the fairest way of making the comparison, as it is not a question of obtaining the greatest candle-power at the least cost, but of efficiently lighting a house, and a system which can give a small light where only such is required should be able to claim this advantage. The amount of attention required to operate an air-gas or acetylene plant is very small, and it is not unusual to make it part of the housemaid's duty. In the case of electric light the writer has never heard of this having been done ; male attention of some sort appears to be required, even if it is only such as the bootboy can give. Gardeners can usually undertake the work quite successfully. The writer knows of at least one case where a suction-gas electric plant was put into the gardener's charge. This was before the days of the modern oil and petrol engines, which have so greatly simplified this work. Still, it is undoubtedly a fact that more attendance is required for an electric plant and more expenditure on lubricating oil, stores and maintenance of battery than with either of the other two systems. Electricity, however, has the great advantage of giving a light which neither vitiates the air nor fouls the decorations, and which can be disposed of in such a manner as not to jar with the various historical styles of decoration found in so many country houses. This latter advantage is shared by acetylene, which, in the case of a small, old-fashioned country house, is an ideal method of lighting, for the candle and lantern fittings that can be obtained for use with this gas give a perfect illusive effect, and do not jar in the least with an antique decorative scheme. Of the three systems acetylene has, generally speaking, the simplest machinery ; a fact of some importance when considering the lighting of a small establishment. Air-gas necessitates the use of the incandescent mantle, but where this is not inconsistent with the scheme of decoration it will probably be found to be the cheapest in fuel consumption, though slightly dearer than acetylene in first cost. It should be noted that neither of these gases fouls the decorations and vitiates the air to anything like the same extent as ordinary coal-gas.

If mechanical power is required for pumping water, chaff-cutting, etc., electricity is the only system of the three which can provide it cheaply and conveniently. In the case of some large establishments where a coal-gas plant was in use before the advent of electricity it has been found necessary, even after the installation of the electric plant, to run the gas plant for the sake of the cookers in the kitchen and a few heating stoves about the house. This is an enormously costly proceeding, and now the coal-gas plant is being very generally replaced by an electrically driven air-gas plant, which, being absolutely automatic in its action, reduces the cost of attendance to practically nothing, and is very much cheaper to run in all respects.   MAURICE HIRD.

ELECTRIC LIGHT IN COUNTRY HOUSES

Revolution Effected by Metal Filament Lamps—Electric Heating—Subsidiary Uses of Current—
Costs of Typical Small Plant—Running and Maintenance.

THIS subject has become a matter of general interest to architects and householders since the introduction of the metal filament lamp, which has been shown to reduce the initial outlay to one-half and the working expenses to a fraction of what was formerly necessary. Electric light was admittedly the most luxurious, most convenient and most healthy light ; but it was regarded as beyond the reach of the average man, and architects who have been scheming to provide the required accommodation with eight to twelve bedrooms at cut figures have been compelled to fall back on acetylene or petrol gas for their lighting, scarcely giving electric light a second thought. Electric light was, in fact, in a similar state to gas before the advent of the gas mantle, and what the mantle did for gas the metal filament lamp is rapidly effecting for electricity. Where the current is taken from supply mains at a reasonable price the tables have, in fact, already been turned, and scores of letters are being received from users saying that the actual bills for lighting are considerably less than they formerly paid for gas, apart from the indirect saving in decorations and flowers, which last so much longer when the air currents and sooty products of gas are removed. Where a supply is available, inasmuch as the cost of wiring is not materially greater than tubing and the fittings cost the same, there will doubtless be no hesitation on anyone's part in arranging for electricity.

Until recently there have been two classes of metallic filament lamps, one with a tungsten filament, the other with a tantalum one. While it has been found possible, in spite of its extremely hard and refractory nature, to draw tantalum into a wire, it has not been possible to do the same with tungsten. The tungsten filament had to be made in another way and was far from being as strong as one made by drawing the metal into a fine wire. Users of the first tungsten filament lamps, though they were gratified by the economy effected in consumption of current, have been made sadly aware of the frequency with which the filament broke, adding considerably to the cost by renewals. Since those early days much experience has been gained by lamp manufacturers, which is now having its full effect in the great improvement in the life of the tungsten lamp. But " this 'ere progress keeps on ; you'd 'ardly think as 'ow it *could* keep on," to quote Mr. Tom Smallways ; so, according to the latest reports, tungsten can now be drawn into wire filaments, and the full advantage of the current economy of tungsten combined with the mechanical strength of a wire can be obtained. A further improvement has also been made in the light distribution of the metallic filament lamp. This consists of arranging the filament in such a way that it throws more light downwards and illuminates the space immediately under the lamp more efficiently.

: The problem of lighting the smaller country house is being made less costly by this rapid succession of improvements. Those who at one time were compelled to regard electricity as too expensive an illuminant can now consider the incidental advantages accruing from its use and in many cases decide in favour of its adoption. The great economic advantage that electricity possesses over other forms of illuminant is doubtless that of cleanliness. There is no fouling of the decorations due to its use, and in rooms simply ornamented it is no exaggeration to say that walls and ceilings will last for eight years without requiring to be redecorated. This term, however, may be reduced considerably if an open fire is in constant use.

This brings us to the question of electric radiators, and we must acknowledge at once that it is more costly to warm a room electrically than by means of a fire. But it is not the true function of an electric radiator to warm a room ; it should be used for warming the person. The warming of a bedroom or dressing-room as a whole is not necessary, provided the person occupying it can be kept comfortable. In the case of the bedroom a fire is not a satisfactory method of heating. It goes out in the night and is not available for taking the chill off the air on rising, as a radiator would be. Furthermore, many people do not like sleeping in a warm bedroom. The electric radiator is hot the moment the current is switched on, and by means of a wall plug and connections of flexible wire can be placed anywhere in the room. Dressing operations can be conducted in close proximity to it, and the current switched off the instant it ceases to be required. Used in this way, the radiator is not the expensive luxury that it appears at first sight to be. As the great efficiency of the metallic filament lamp, not to speak of the improvements in other parts of the plant, has brought the cost of light down to less than half what it was in the days of carbon filaments, the users of electricity can well afford themselves the luxury of a radiator or two. Those who have hitherto considered it impossible to instal an electric-light plant on account of the cost will be well advised to think it over again, as the difference in cost that the last few years have made can only be described as colossal. For intermittent requirements, such as the heating of curling-tongs, cigar-lighters and flat-irons, the drying of a lady's hair after shampooing, or the boiling of small quantities of water, the current provides an ever-ready and safe solution of the problems.

To motor-car-owners, present or prospective, the electric installation affords a ready means of charging the ignition cells, for which fancy prices are frequently charged. With low voltage this can be easily done without any loss worth considering, by merely inserting a few lamps in circuit, these being connected on a panel with an ammeter to show the rate at which the current is passing. For photographic work electric light has no rival ; not only is the dark room kept cool and free from carbonic acid gas, which results from the combustion of any form of gas, but the ordinary lamp or red lamp can be extinguished or lit at will. For bromide or other printing processes which require a regular exposure, the constancy of the electric lamp enables exact work to be reproduced if care is taken to keep the distance from the print the same, and for enlargements the electric lamp is equally convenient. Most of 'the farm machinery, as well as the cream separator, the churn and the lathe, can be economically driven by the plant, as also a fan for extracting the smell of cooking, which has a way of pervading some houses.

Let us now consider the cost of an electric-light installation such as would be required for a country house of the size shown in the plans, which may fairly be taken as a type of residence costing from twelve to fifteen hundred pounds. The wiring of the house to thirty-one points, including the wire casing or tube, with thirty-one switches to control twenty-nine ten-candle-power and sixteen-candle-power metallic filament lamps, together with any distribution fuse-boards that may be necessary, would cost forty-seven pounds eighteen shillings. This would not include the cost of the fittings or the lamps, nor the fixing of them ;

134.—GROUND FLOOR PLAN.

but if the fittings chosen were of a simple character, the price for this work, including metallic filament lamps, would be about twenty-seven pounds five shillings. The cost of the generating plant, including oil engine, dynamos, switchboard and set of accumulators, would be ninety pounds, and a further charge of twenty-five pounds ten shillings would be made for erecting the plant and setting it to work ; this is inclusive of a small sum for builders' work in connection with foundations for the engine. We may say the total cost of plant and installation comes roughly to one hundred and ninety pounds. It should be here stated that the wires would be run in wooden casing over the face of the walls and under the floors. If it were required to sink the casing in the walls, the cost of making good the plaster and redecorating would have to be added.

The generating plant would consist of a horizontal engine giving $1\frac{1}{2}$ h.p., using ordinary paraffin oil, directly coupled to a dynamo giving four hundred watts. The accumulators would be capable of supplying current for thirty ten-candle-power metallic filament lamps for nine hours. The engine would use about one pint of paraffin per horse-power per hour, so that for a $1\frac{1}{2}$ h.p. engine a pint and a-half of oil at about sixpence a gallon would be required ; this works out at one and one-eighth pence per hour when the dynamo is giving its full output. When the lights are being supplied by the accumulators it is necessary to make some allowance for the fact that the accumulators will not give out as much electrical energy as is put into them, so that about twenty per cent. should be added to the figure of cost of oil, which will bring it to about three halfpence. It will be safest to take this latter figure as the basis of our calculations, as the occasions when the engine is required to supply all the lights at once will be few. The output of the dynamo when the engine gives $1\frac{1}{2}$ h.p. is four hundred watts, as already mentioned, and, making allowance for the efficiency of the accumulators, we can obtain this for three halfpence per hour. Metallic filament lamps can now be obtained to give one candle-power per watt, so that four hundred watts is sufficient for forty ten-candle-power lamps, and these can be used for an hour at the cost of three halfpence for fuel. In the house we have under consideration the maximum output with all the lamps in use would be about five hundred and fifty watts; but the switching on and off of electric light is such a simple matter that servants and others are less likely to keep the lamps burning uselessly than they would be with other forms of illuminant; we may, therefore, safely assume that the total number of lights will never be on at once. If we assume an average lighting time of four hours per day throughout the year, and allow that something less than half the number of lamps are burning for this time, we can fairly take our fuel cost at three farthings per hour. Of course, this implies care and economy in the use of the light; but there should be no difficulty in obtaining this average if the necessity of switching off, whenever possible, is duly impressed on the servants. This for four hours on each of three hundred and sixty-five days brings the total cost of our fuel for the year to one thousand and ninety-five pence, or four pounds eleven shillings and threepence. There are, of course, other things to be considered besides cost of fuel, such as attendance, lubricating oil and maintenance of the generating plant and accumulators; but the two latter items should not exceed the cost of the fuel, and, as far as attendance goes, the gardener, if an intelligent man, could easily be trained to attend to the plant.

Where there is a chauffeur, minor repairs in connection with the plant and installation naturally become part of his work. The experience gained in dealing with the various forms of electric ignition apparatus used on the modern motor-car implies a rudimentary knowledge of the electric circuit. This will save calling in an electrical contractor in many cases where it would be otherwise necessary. We see, therefore, that if we allow five per cent. interest on the capital outlay, the total cost of lighting such a house as that shown in the plans would not exceed seventeen pounds per annum when all allowances had been made; surely not a very high price when the cleanliness and hygienic properties of electric light are duly considered.   MAURICE HIRD.

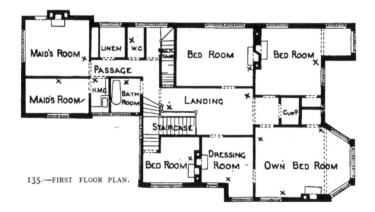

135.—FIRST FLOOR PLAN.

ELECTRICAL WORKING COSTS.

Data Obtained from a Typical Large Country House—Description of the Electrical Plant—And of the Subsidiary Machinery—Meeting the Farm Requirements—Details of Costs for Two Years.

ALTHOUGH one still occasionally hears the remark that electricity is in its infancy, it cannot be denied that it is a singularly well-developed child. Hence it is but natural that a general interest should be evinced in the experience of those who are employing the most modern apparatus obtainable. The particular branch with which we are at present concerned is the utilisation of electricity for country house requirements. It has therefore been thought best to proceed by giving an example of what has actually been done in one instance, rather than to set down the figures of electrical consumption in various classes of machine as given by the manufacturers. It is seldom that accounts and data have been compiled with sufficient care and accuracy to enable an exact comparison to be made, and it is therefore satisfactory to be able, through the courtesy of Mr. Philip Foster, M.P., of Canwell Hall, Sutton Coldfield, to set out the tabulated figures which have been compiled by his staff.

Canwell may be described as a typical country estate, the house containing thirty-seven bedrooms, six reception-rooms, with stabling, garage and farms adjoining. Until 1905 the light and power were obtained from private gasworks, the gas being used everywhere except in the drawing-room. Power was derived from gas engines for both pumping and farm machinery, the gas consumed being charged to the tenants at the ascertained cost of production. In 1905 an electric plant was installed, consisting of two engines, each of 30 h.p., with suction-gas producers and two dynamos, also an accumulator capable of maintaining for nine hours all the lights that are likely to be in simultaneous use, besides supplying current for pumping, sawing and other purposes, at times when the engines are not running. The dynamos are constructed so that the whole or either half of the battery connected to the three-wire system can be charged from either machine.

The engine-house is erected on the site of the old gasworks, the old buildings being used for producer-room, coal store and accumulator-room, and the water supply for the engines is obtained from rain and surface water collected in the old gas-holder, which is used as a storage tank, the water being pumped electrically. One of the illustrations shows the interior of the engine-house, and the main switchboard at which the different circuits are controlled and the consumption recorded. There is also a room for the producers or suction-gas plant, this apparatus, like the engine, being duplicated, and

136.—GAS PRODUCER PLANT.

137.—IN THE POWER-HOUSE.

arrangements are made by which either producer can supply either engine if required. There is an electrically-driven blower for starting the gas generators, which enables the work of starting the large engines to be effected by one man, which would otherwise require two.

The accumulator-room adjoins the engine-house. Power is supplied for an orchestrion in the house by an electric motor, the current being automatically controlled according to the demand. At the ice-well pump-house, a distance of four hundred and fifty yards from the generating station, is located a three-throw pump, which provides the water supply to the house. At the home farm and estate workshops a 15 h.p. motor takes the place of the gas engine formerly employed to drive the farm machinery and a thirty-six-inch saw bench with the lathes and wood-working machinery. The same applies to the Canwell Gate Farm, where another 15 h.p. motor is at work. Meters record the amount of current, which is charged to one of the tenants according to the amount used. In the stables there is a 1½ h.p. motor driving a chaff-cutter, and at the laundry the machinery is also electrically driven.

One of the applications to estate requirements shown is that of circular-sawing, for which electricity is found to be extremely convenient, as the saws can be started at any time without the necessity for getting an engine under way. Under the older methods it is usually necessary to accumulate the wood until there is sufficient to justify the running of the engine; but at Canwell, when other work cannot be carried out owing to rain or other causes, the men can immediately be turned on to sawing, chaff-cutting, grinding or any other indoor work without delay.

The total number of lights installed in the house amounts to six hundred, and in the farms, dairy and outbuildings one hundred and twenty lights. A small church, which is now being built in the park, will be supplied with current from the central station, both for organ-blowing and lighting. The power transmitted amounts to 56 h.p., the furthest motor being located seven hundred and fifty yards from the station. In order to reach this distance

138.—CIRCULAR SAW.

139.—IN THE STABLES.

140.—IN THE LAUNDRY.

with economy it was necessary to employ the standard voltage adopted for most town lighting, viz., four hundred volts for the motors and two hundred volts for the lighting.

    The next question is the comparative cost of gas and electricity. The following are the records of the three previous years when the house was supplied from its own gasworks:

			1902.			1903.			1904.		
Coal	..	..	..	£154	18	3	£126	7	2	£129	6	6
Labour	..	..	65	19	2	65	13	2	66	4	·0
Sundries	..	..	15	7	11	8	16	5		6	9
			236	5	4	200	16	9	195	17	3
Less gas and coke sold			*45	13	0	11	10	0	17	5	9
			£190	12	4	£189	6	9	£178	11	6

* Includes stock from previous year.

After allowing for gas and coke sold, the cost of working the gas amounted to an average of £186 3s. 6d., or about 5s. per thousand cubic feet, a fair average for private gasworks. The following data show the cost of working the electric plant for two years:

			1908.			1909.		
Labour	..	..	..	£98	6	8	£101	16	10
Coal	..	..	..	53	6	3	55	5	10
Waste	..	..	..		10	0	1	10	0
Sundries ..	..	..	6	16	0	6	14	11
Engine repairs ..	..	4	10	1	9	15	2
			£163	9	0	£175	2	9

or an average of £169 5s. 10½d., from which must be deducted £8 charged to one of the tenants, or a total of £161. A sum of about £20 per annum, however, must be credited to the gas account for work previously done by gas, which has not been connected to the electric service, so the cost of electricity is slightly greater. In the house, however, there is more than double the former amount of light. There is no doubt that at the home farm and estate workshops the power has been used to a greater extent owing to the convenience of being able to start any machine at a moment's notice.

    The above comparison will be improved as time goes on, for metal lamps are being perfected to suit the high voltage used. The apparatus, owing to its simplicity, is handled by one attendant. Mr. Foster has noted that in addition to the improved state of the atmosphere and other recognised advantages, he is freed from the damage which was caused to his books by gas. The house decoration, instead of rapidly deteriorating as it did, is as fresh as when done some five years ago. With a well-designed installation, electricity now compares very favourably with gas in the working cost. If, moreover, allowance be made for the increased life of decorations, the advantages to health, the increased light and the usefulness of electricity in the house for. driving labour-saving devices, it would seem to be actually cheaper.   BERNARD MERVYN DRAKE.

WATER-POWER INSTALLATIONS

Nature in Man's Service—Water-power Plants Usually a Blot on the Landscape—Model Treatment by Sir Robert Lorimer—A Beautiful River Happily Unspoilt—The Power-house and Its Equipment.

THE work of an engineer has been defined as "the conversion of the forces of Nature to the use and service of man," and though this is truly the purpose of all the complex mechanisms elaborated by latter-day engineers, the definition is most obviously accurate when he proceeds to dam a stream and make use of the power contained in the falling water which has hitherto run to waste. The definition of an engineer's functions as given above covers a very wide field, and when he has given the time and attention that is necessary to qualify him in one branch of his profession, he usually has little opportunity, or even inclination, for the study of æsthetics. It often happens, therefore, that when he is called upon to perform the particular conversion of Nature's forces just indicated, his dam is a smooth-faced concrete structure with an iron handrail along the top, his power-house is of precisely the same design as he would put up in the meanest of manufacturing towns, and his pipe line joining the two is of tarred cast iron, uncovered and unashamed, the whole forming an ugly blot on what may be an enchanting view. Perhaps one of the worst instances in this country of this lack of care for the beauty of the site of a water-power scheme is to be found at Lynmouth, where the supply of electricity for lighting the towns of Lynton and Lynmouth is obtained by water-power from the river Lyn. Here the water is taken from the upper stream along a straight canal cut, and thence through an iron pipe, or penstock, to the power-house. This is a frankly factory-like structure, and an ugly thing to confront on a spot where one might expect to see the shade of John Ridd meeting that of Lorna Doone.

In order to show how perfectly possible it is to combine use and beauty in these cases, a description of a small plant, where the natural features of the scenery have been conscientiously considered, is here given at some length. At Ardkinglas the crimes complained of have not been committed, and, indeed, with this example before him, the engineer of the future will be the veriest vandal should he ever again perpetrate some of the utilitarian misdemeanours that were due to ignorance rather than vice in the past. The thanks of the whole profession are due to Sir Robert Lorimer of Edinburgh, the architect who designed the structures which are now described and illustrated. When the scheme was first proposed, all the small streams that come down from the mountain and the glen were examined, but it was found that none could be depended upon for a sufficiently constant supply of water, so that in the end the river Kinglas itself had to be pressed into service, and even in this case experience has shown that in long periods of dry weather the water supply is only

141.— THE POWER-HOUSE AT ARDKINGLAS.

just sufficient.   There was no definite cataract in the river to supply a head or fall of water, so it was necessary to adopt what is known as the low-pressure system, *i.e.*, the turbine installed had to be of a design that would work with a low head and a comparatively large quantity of water.   In cases of this sort the turbine is made something like the screw propeller of a ship, boxed in a special casing, through which the water flows evenly.   In cases where there is a high fall and the high-pressure system is adopted, only a small quantity is required, and the turbine takes a form more or less like the old mill-wheel, with jets of water impinging upon its blades.

The fall available at Ardkinglas is twenty-two feet, and this was obtained by damming the stream at a convenient spot and building the power-house five hundred feet further down the stream, the water from above the dam being conveyed to the turbine in a twenty-four-inch riveted steel pipe.   This pipe is laid in the bank of the river, and is entirely covered and out of sight ; even the discharge pipe which conveys the water back to the river-bed after it has given up its power to the turbine is covered with boulders and water-worn stones.   The illustration shows the dam, and it will be seen at once how

142.—THE DAM AND SALMON LADDER.

different it is in appearance from the usual structure that passes by that name.   A long, sloping back has been given to the dam wall, which has been filled in with boulders in such a way as to make it appear part of the river-bed.   The salmon ladder on the left consists of five or six basins in concrete and boulder, which make a series of cascades perfectly natural in appearance and eminently suited to the purpose for which they are designed.   The photograph was taken when there was comparatively little water in the river, and in such conditions salmon could without much difficulty get up the waterfall itself.   The value of the ladder arises when the river is in flood.   The most ardent follower of the cult of the beautiful can find nothing to complain of in the way a practical need has been met.

We pass to the power-house shown in the first illustration.   Sir Robert Lorimer has designed and placed it as though it were a mediæval fort or watch-tower guarding the entrance to the upper glen.   It is built in cement of smooth boulders from the river, is of two storeys, and its reinforced concrete roof is flat and out of sight.

The third illustration shows the interior of the power-house.   The white glazed brick walls and wide marble flags which form the flooring make the turbine and dynamo appear very compact in their position across the end of the room.   The turbine is capable of giving 35 h.p. when running at three hundred revolutions per minute, and the dynamo, which is directly coupled to the turbine shaft, gives its current at a pressure of two hundred volts.   There is a battery of accumulators on the floor above to provide a reserve of electricity should the water supply fail for a short time.   To charge this battery a motor-booster consisting of two four-pole dynamos coupled together has been installed.   This is seen on the left in the illustration.

There is also a motor-driven turbine pump of 20 h.p. that is capable of supplying with water four fire hydrants, each having a nozzle three-quarters of an inch in diameter.   The pressure in the hydrants is sufficient to throw the water over the roof of the house.   At ordinary times water from the dam is allowed to run through the stationary pump, the twenty-two feet of head that it possesses being found sufficient to keep the garden fountain in play and also for watering the garden.

A switch-board for controlling the various lighting and power circuits is placed just in front of the right-hand wall of the power-house.   It is made up of six panels of white marble.   The three upper panels contain the measuring instruments and regulating switches for the dynamo, booster and battery, and also a clock, while the three lower panels are fitted with switches and fuses for the distributing circuits. The plant serves three hundred lights in the house and an electric luggage lift.

The water-power plant at Ardkinglas is an object-lesson to all who desire to make use of water-power amid scenes of natural beauty, and a direct disclaimer to all the objections raised by those ultra-æsthetes who can never hear of some natural source of water-power being put to use without exclaiming against an age so sordid and Philistine.

The world is still waiting for the genius who can supply a design at once efficient and artistic for large hydro-electric power-stations.   It will be a thousand pities if the site of the Victoria Falls on the Zambesi ever becomes cumbered with a collection of buildings which for all the eye can tell are Lancashire cotton-mills without chimney-stacks, as has been done on both banks of the St. Lawrence at Niagara.   The engineering capacities of mankind are great, and are growing from year to year, but we are still unable to construct a Niagara, though by carelessness and parsimony we may readily destroy the sublimity and grandeur which is Nature's gift to us.   Vast quantities of water falling from an immense height are not such common phenomena that we can afford to desecrate the two or three unblemished examples that still remain to us.   The Governments of the countries containing these mighty cataracts will be showing little regard for their national treasures if they leave them to the small mercies of unchecked industrial capital.   MAURICE HIRD.

143.—IN THE DYNAMO ROOM.

THE ILLUMINATION OF ROOMS.

The Conflict Between the Æsthetic and Practical in Illumination—Principles that Make for Efficiency—Avoidance of Light-obscuring Devices—Practical Hints.

THE fact that electric lighting lends itself more readily to æsthetic treatment than any other form has, in the past, tended to its misuse as an illuminant. This may appear paradoxical, but it is a fact that this virtue has been abused. While every fresh artistic possibility is at first overdone, the ultimate reaction is bound to establish it on a utility basis. So it is with the electric illumination of rooms, which, to be effective, involves three main principles, namely, the character of the illuminant, its location, and the distribution of the light, which is accomplished by diffusion and by reflection. The latter is perhaps the most important, as domestic illumination is generally required not so much for the purpose of finding one's way about, as to aid the performance of some definite function, such as dressing, reading or eating. For these purposes it is necessary to have the light more or less concentrated on the particular task, and if this is not done adequately, the results are unsatisfactory to the eyes. Diffusion of light is of importance chiefly in places where a general illumination is required, such as halls, staircases, passages and perhaps drawing-rooms. It is usually necessary to combine diffusion with reflection to some extent, as otherwise all those parts of the room where the light is not concentrated would be in semi-darkness, which is not desirable. Location of the lighting points is also of great importance, because it is of no use attempting to reflect or to diffuse light efficiently if the source of light is not placed in the correct position for the purpose, or if there are not sufficient sources of light to illuminate a given space adequately.

Now the great enemy of economical illumination is absorption, both of direct and reflected light. That is to say, the light may either be absorbed at its source by obscuring devices, or it may be absorbed at its goal by bad colour-schemes and not reflected. In the arrangement of internal home decoration, including electric lighting, there are two factors that enter into every scheme, namely, beauty and utility ; and it is, unfortunately, the case that until quite recently utility has been sacrificed to art. It is not meant to suggest that the furniture or decorations should be ignored in selecting the fittings ; but it should be remembered that the primary object of electric light is to illuminate, and that there are certain styles of decoration which are unsuitable for fittings if good lighting effects are desired. In such cases it were often better to have recourse to concealed lamps, if the simpler kind of fittings are considered unsatisfactory, and this point is dealt with later.

While it is impossible to lay down rigid rules for economical illumination, because every room must be considered on its merits, it is possible to give a few general hints which may enable existing installations to be improved and inefficiency to be avoided in new ones. It should be accepted as an axiom that all light-obscuring devices, such as opaque or coloured glass shades, silk flounces, bead fringes, etc., must be avoided if economy is desired. It is possible to combine art with economy if the art takes the direction of simplicity. Again, rooms decorated in dark colours require more light than those with light colours, so the latter should be used in preference. As to distribution of light, the light given by an electric lamp over a given area depends on its candle-power, on its shade or reflector, on the colour of the room and the height at which it is fixed. If it cannot be placed below the level of the eye with a concentrating shade, it should be well above the line of vision. Distribution is not necessarily obtained by glaring lights ; indeed, the rays from a naked lamp, besides being painful to the eye, produce violent contrasts of light and shadows. Paradoxical though it may appear, the way to obtain the best dispersion or diffusion of light is slightly to obscure its source, but by a device which will absorb as little light as possible and break up the direct rays. The simplest way of doing this is to employ frosted lamps. Another way is to surround the lamp with a cut-glass or moulded glass globe or shade, but care must be taken that the facets of the lenses are properly designed and that good glass is used, as otherwise much light will be reabsorbed. Reflection is a simpler thing to attain, and depends largely on the material used and its shape. It is often complained that electric lamps throw a poor light downwards, but this is due to the bad reflecting devices employed, such as silk, or to their absence. To obtain good reflection, efficient reflectors of proper design must be employed in order to cast the light in the downward or useful plane.

For general dispersed lighting, a bowl or hemisphere of holophane glass, mounted on the ceiling with the lamp inside, gives a soft and pleasing light emanating from above the line of vision, which is suitable for halls, drawing-rooms, etc. For concentrating purposes a small shade or reflector of six inches diameter, placed on a ceiling ten feet high, will, with a sixteen-candle-power lamp, throw downwards about fifty candle-power ; another design can be had to throw most of the light at an angle of, say, thirty degrees ; another to give a combined reflecting and diffusing effect. Such shades or globes can be hung on existing electroliers or brackets, and will often enable one to consume much less current. Where concentration is more important than diffusion, the reflecting shades can still be surrounded by silk hangings, so long as these are fairly translucent. For those, however, who wish to obtain effective illumination by other means there are two methods open. The first is to employ fittings to suit the furniture and decorations, using plenty of them, and avoiding naked lights by obscuring ; the second is to illuminate by means of concealed lamps, *i.e.*, by indirect lighting only. Both these systems tend to use more current than any where the lighting is direct and reflected ; but they may be made effective as well as æsthetic where expense is not the first consideration. Assume that a Louis XVI. room is to be lighted by means of brackets or electroliers of the same style. It is a *sine quâ non* that the candle lamps must be shaded, as otherwise the result will be painful to the eyes, because electric candles give much more light than wax candles. Simple, small conical shades should be used, or small screens. There must be plenty of lamps, and these should not be too high. The result should be a mellow, diffused light with no obtrusive shadows or dark places. Where antique fittings are already available, these may easily be converted for electric lighting by the addition of electric candles. An oak room affords another example. The fittings for such a situation should be of wrought iron or armour bright metal. One form of fitting is the lantern, which may be either attached to brackets on the walls or suspended by chains from the ceiling. Naturally, the colour or finish of the glass panes is an important factor in the determination of the number of lanterns required ; but if the bottom of the fitting be left open and a suitable invisible reflector be fitted in the top behind the lamp, the number need not be unduly increased. Georgian rooms are difficult to light satisfactorily with due regard to their style. The lustre fitting may be a charming thing if designed in the proper way for electric lamps, *i.e.*, concealed within the lustres. A particularly happy effect may also be obtained by concealing the lamps within a hemispherical bowl, constructed of lustre beads wired together. Also, there are handsome Georgian brackets and electroliers for electric candles in steel bronze. In this case it may be better not to place shades on the lamps, but to employ frosted lamps, and to place the fittings fairly high. Rooms with recesses sometimes present a difficult problem if the recesses do not receive adequate light from the main rooms. Where such recesses cannot have fittings of similar style to those in the main room, it is best to place one or more small frosted lamps right against the ceiling in the centre of the panels, and to cover them, perhaps, with a bag of yellow silk. This method gives an adequate illumination without clashing with the decorations.

Lighting by concealed lamps, known as illumination by reflected light, is suitable for most styles of decoration where the structural arrangements permit of concealing the lamps, and is the ideal method where cost is not the first consideration ; but the shape and size of the room itself affect the result considerably, and such an installation should not be attempted by an amateur, or the result will probably be a failure. There are two main ways of doing this—by throwing the light on the ceiling from fittings with inverted shades, and by illuminating the ceiling by lamps hidden by a heavy cornice. The latter is very effective, and can even be employed where there is an oak ceiling, if there is a big whitened cove above the cornice. A large number of lamps has to be used, and they are generally of tubular form, lying in trough-shaped reflectors. In some cases where this method can be used successfully it need not be much more expensive than direct illumination, and when absence of eyestrain is considered it may be cheaper, as it enables those using the room to accomplish more work with less effort. Another method is to transmit light through a translucent ceiling, as in the House of Commons. This is also effective and pleasant, but necessitates a false ceiling fitted with obscured glass panels, and can therefore only be employed in rooms with high ceilings.

In conclusion, effective illumination is a greater factor of good health and contentment of mind than many people appreciate. Poor lighting or dazzling rays are bad for people who have to use their eyes much, and they produce headaches and eyestrain ; while to those who have no occupation they are a source of annoyance and discomfort. V. ZINGLER.

AIR-GAS IN THE COUNTRY HOUSE.

The Demand for More Light—Broad Principles of Air-gas Plants—Motor Drive versus Weight Drive—Rich versus Weak Mixtures of Petrol and Air—Costs of a Typical Small Plant.

THE newest "Darwinism" asserts that environment has a greater effect than inherited faculties on the development of the race. The almost "cat-like" sight whereby our great-grandmothers could thread a needle by the light of a wax candle at the far end of the room has certainly not descended to us, and every improvement in the quality of artificial light has resulted in an immediate demand for a greater quantity, till we are led to wonder what amount of light our grandchildren will consider essential for their comfort. The problem of lighting the smaller country house entered upon another phase with the advent of what we may call single-house lighting installations. The householder who requires only some twenty-five or thirty lights in his house may be rather alarmed at the idea of installing a miniature gasworks or electric-light station of his own ; but it is often to his advantage to do so, even in places where there is a public supply.

The apparatus used for the manufacture of air-gas is very simple and requires no skilled attendance ; the plant described below is worked with complete success by the housemaid. Air-gas is merely a mixture of petrol vapour and air. The difference between the mixture used in the cylinder of the motor-car engine and that used in the burner of an air-gas system is simply that a much larger quantity of air is added in the latter case, whereby it is rendered non-explosive. The broad principles on which most air-gas generators work may be described as follows : A small motor drives an air-pump or blower which sucks or forces air, either directly or through a small air-container, into a carburettor, where it mixes with the petrol vapour and then passes directly to the gas pipes and burners, or into a small gas-container connected with the supply pipes. The function of the container is to keep the pressure constant, so that those systems which use an air-container do not require a gas-container, and *vice versâ*. The motor takes various forms to suit particular cases. Where there is a disused well available, or the clear side of a house wall, the gradual falling of a weight, as in a grandfather's clock, can be made to drive the pump. If there is a cheap water supply, a water motor can be installed for this purpose ; but the form of motor applicable to the case where these conditions do not exist is a small hot-air engine driven by means of the gas it generates. A few turns have to be given by hand to the motor at starting. This is sufficient to generate a little gas, which passes to the burner under the motor cylinder. When this has been burning several minutes a few more turns will set the motor running, and the rest of the control is entirely automatic. If it is desired that a supply of gas shall always be available at times when the engine is not running, a small gas-holder of limited capacity can be installed without adding greatly to the capital cost ; but this is rarely necessary, as in most houses gas is only required during certain hours. An electric switch can be fixed in the householder's bedroom, or any part of the house, by means of which the engine can be stopped. This is found to be an exceedingly useful contrivance by those who have tried it, saving as it does a visit to the engine-house the last thing at night, such a visit being particularly tiresome on a dark winter night when the engine-house is situated some distance away from the residence, as has happened in some instances we have known. In the case of the weight-driven machines, when no gas is being used, an automatic inlet valve cuts off the supply of air from the pump. The partial vacuum so created is sufficient to hold up the weight, which ceases falling until the gas is turned on again, and the air inlet is automatically opened in consequence. It should be noted, however, that with some plants the pressure of the gas drops when the weight is wound up, and any burners in use at the time would probably go out. Care should therefore be taken not to wind up the weight when gas is being used.

The machines driven by water motors are usually provided with an automatic regulator, which turns off the water supply and the gas when no light is on, and turns it on again as soon as the first burner is lit. Some systems are arranged to use a gas much richer in petrol vapour than others. These naturally require a less volume of gas to give the same light for a given time, so that the strength of mixture adopted does not materially affect the cost of illumination. The advocates of a weak mixture claim that, as all the air required for perfect combustion is supplied in the gas, no vitiation of the atmosphere takes place. Those who favour the use of a richer air-gas and employ a Bunsen burner claim that the additional air drawn in by the gas during combustion has a cooling effect on the burner and results in a longer life for the mantles and fittings. Arrangements are made in most forms of generator for automatically controlling the mixture of petrol and air and for keeping the proportions constant at the strength found most suitable for the system in question. Discrimination is very necessary at the present time, when so many different forms of generators are on the market, and the advice of a consulting engineer is even more important in the case of an air-gas installation than in electric light or acetylene. The cheap plant should be avoided, or the first cost will be supplemented by a considerable account for renewals and repairs. The supply piping is the same as used for ordinary coal-gas. In houses piped for the latter, it is not usually needful to make any alterations, though when a weak mixture is used it may be necessary to increase the size of one or two main pipes in order to keep an even distribution of pressure throughout the house. It is desirable to have the generating plant fixed in as central a position as possible, because this tends to avoid great differences of pressure at the burners. The burners used with air-gas vary according to the system. Each maker of the apparatus supplies the burner which he considers best suited to the strength of gas that his generator turns out. The differences consist mainly in using a Bunsen burner admitting a greater or less amount of air to the flame, according to whether the gas is rich or poor in quality, or in cutting off external air supply altogether and only using the air already mixed in the gas for purposes of combustion, as is done in the case of very weak mixtures.

The cost of installation of an air-gas plant is, of course, the first consideration to anyone who may be thinking of adopting this form of lighting. The plans here reproduced are those of a country doctor's house in which air-gas has been installed. The building itself, as will be seen from the plans, is a very fair type of house costing from one thousand two hundred pounds to one thousand five hundred pounds. The total cost of the generating plant, which is listed as for forty to fifty lights, including pipes for three gas rings, two radiators, and thirty-one points as shown on the plans, also the cost of supplying thirty-two burners, three gas rings and flexible tubing, was seventy-six pounds ten shillings and sixpence. This price included all erection work connected with the plant and

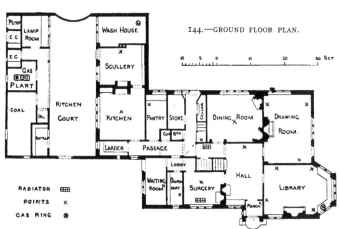

144.—GROUND FLOOR PLAN.

supply pipes, and also the erection of the brackets, pendants, etc. The cost of the latter, all very simple in design, was eleven pounds ten shillings. An electric switch for stopping the engine and a pneumatic switch for operating the gas-tap at a distance were fixed in the doctor's bedroom at an extra cost of two guineas. Two heating radiators were provided, one in the study and one in the drawing-room, at a cost of eight pounds eight shillings. The grand total may be taken, therefore, at one hundred pounds; but the fact that the small sum of eleven pounds only was allowed for fittings must not be lost sight of.

In a larger house, say, with three more bedrooms, making nine in all, correspondingly larger reception-rooms and proportionately increased offices, it would be necessary to instal a fifty to sixty light plant, and the number of points would be increased to about forty. This would leave a fair margin of capacity on the generating plant for radiators or future extensions. Such a plant, including the extra pipework and fittings, fixed complete, would cost about twenty-two pounds more, providing that the fittings were of the same simple character as in the house described. Three or four radiators of the size mentioned could be put in if desired, and it may be noted in this connection that the smaller size radiators appear to be much more efficient than the larger ones. Other accessories, such as gas fires, cooking stoves, laundry irons, etc., are made for use with air-gas and do not differ much in design from those used with coal-gas.

The last word has not yet been said in the matter of design of air-gas plant, and it is fairly obvious that, with the number of plants being turned out and the keen competition between the makers, progress is likely to be rapid and continuous in the near future. At present there appear to be few designs of fitting which can be guaranteed to give a perfectly noiseless light under all natural working conditions.   It is necessary, for the sake of safety, to store the petrol outside the room containing the generating plant. This need cause no inconvenience, as the petrol tank can be connected to the plant by means of a small tube, through which the petrol flows automatically as required.   The light obtainable for one penny from air-gas ranges from forty to sixty candle-power for fifteen hours with petrol at one shilling per gallon. If we base our calculations on the lower figure, and compare the cost with a forty candle-power burner taking gas from a town supply at four shillings per thousand cubic feet, we find that it consumes two and two-thirds cubic feet per hour, and in fifteen hours, therefore, forty cubic feet will have been used, costing 48d. $\div$ 1,000 $\times$ 40 = 1·92d., or very nearly twice as much as the air-gas.   With petrol at more than a shilling a gallon the comparison is less favourable.   The amount of coal-gas used per annum for a house such as shown in the plans would probably not be less than one hundred and fifty thousand cubic feet. With gas at four shillings per thousand cubic feet this would amount to thirty pounds ; whereas, using air-gas, the cost would be fifteen pounds thirteen shillings for the equivalent amount of light.   Assuming about five per cent. per annum on the capital cost of the installation to be put by for renewals and repairs —a liberal allowance—we still have a net saving of over ten pounds in favour of air-gas.   It is claimed that the absence of colour in the light produced by means of air-gas makes it the nearest approach to day-light that we possess in any commercial system of artificial lighting.   Its products of combustion do not contain either sulphur or ammonia, and are therefore far less injurious than those of ordinary coal-gas ; furthermore, it is non-explosive.   It has, unquestionably, a great future for country-house lighting.

MAURICE HIRD.

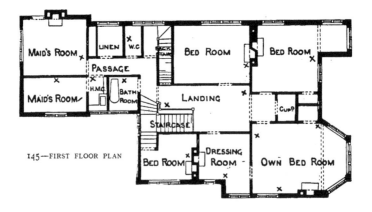

145—FIRST FLOOR PLAN

ACETYLENE IN THE COUNTRY HOUSE

Concerning Carbide—The Two Main Types of Acetylene Generators—No Necessity for Incandescent Burners—Adaptability to Old Types of Fittings—Simplicity of Apparatus—Costs of Installation and Upkeep.

THE pioneers of acetylene lighting can claim the credit of being the first to relieve the small country householder from the comparative gloom and discomfort of oil lamps and candles.   So recently as 1892 there were no means available for artificially lighting the isolated country house, except by installing a private coal-gas or electric-light plant at a cost which in those days was prohibitive to all but the wealthy, or by putting up with the old-fashioned illuminants referred to above. Although the commercial development of acetylene lighting is so recent, the discovery of the gas itself dates back to 1836, and it was suggested even at that early date that the gas could be used as an artificial illuminant.   There was no possibility of doing so, however, until a commercial method of manufacturing carbide had been discovered.   The commercial process for the manufacture of calcium carbide, which was at last developed in 1892, is so simple that it is curious that it should not have been thought of before. It consists of fusing lime and carbon together in an electric furnace.   The resultant material, calcium carbide, has only to be brought into contact with water, when decomposition takes place and acetylene is given off, so that the manufacture of the gas from the carbide is also a very simple process.   In spite, or perhaps because, of this very simplicity, the number of forms of acetylene generator that have been invented for the purpose of bringing the water and the calcium carbide together runs to some hundreds ; but the few that have survived the test of time can be conveniently divided into two classes.   In the first, and doubtless the most usual class, the water is allowed to flow into the generator, which has previously been charged with calcium carbide.   The gas evolved is taken through a pipe into a gas-holder or small gasometer. As the gas-holder rises, due to the inflow of gas, it pushes against a movable stop, which cuts off the water supply, and consequently checks the manufacture of the gas, until the emptying of the gas-holder into the house supply main causes it to sink ; in doing so it again operates the stop, this time admitting water to the generator, and starts the process of acetylene generation once more.   In the second class the generator is charged with water, and a series of buckets are filled with carbide, which are emptied into the generator automatically, one by one, as required ; but this latter system is rarely

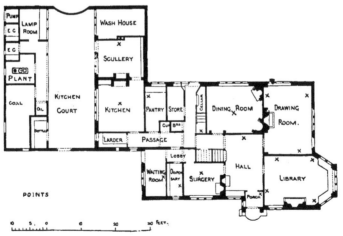

146.—GROUND FLOOR PLAN.

employed in this country. It is usual to pass the gas through a purifier before letting it into the supply main, in order to abstract any foreign gases which it may contain, due to impurities in the carbide. The resulting acetylene gives a pure white light without any noxious fumes, and the abstraction of oxygen from the air is, light for light, far

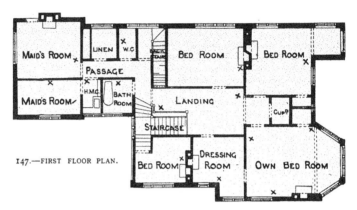

147.—FIRST FLOOR PLAN.

less than with ordinary coal gas. A theoretical saving in the quantity of gas used may be made by adopting the incandescent mantle; but the great point of acetylene lighting to the householder who is so fortunate as to possess a really old-fashioned country house, and wishes to have a style of lighting in keeping with an antique decorative scheme, is that it can be used in candle and lantern fittings with an open and suitably-shaped flame, giving a perfect illusive effect and at the same time a brilliant light. There is no way of attaining this very desirable end if the incandescent mantle is used. It sounds a modern note which, however well disguised, is bound to jar in such a decorative scheme as we have in mind. The accompanying illustrations of two charming fittings done in armour bright steel, to the designs of Sir Robert Lorimer, are a good example of what can be done in this respect. Though made for electric light instead of gas, they can be readily adapted for the latter, and a tube run through the chain of the pendant. When all these points are given due weight, and maintenance of mantles taken into consideration, and also the fact that any form of gas used in a mantle cannot be turned down, it will be seen that the economy of the mantle disappears in practice. The turning down of acetylene when not required has been solved, by at least one large firm of acetylene plant manufacturers, who have devised a bye-pass arrangement that can be fitted near the door. This controls all the lights in the room, so that they cna be turned down when not wanted and turned on immediately they are required. A new type of burner, designed not to carbonise when turned down, has been on the market for some time. A further source of économy, due to the absence of mantles, can be made use of in the ease with which it is possible to fix a burner to give exactly the amount of light required in any given situation. The lighting of small lavatories, landings, etc., can often be quite efficiently done with five candle-power, whereas the smallest mantle generally used gives twenty-five candle-power, and uses a corresponding amount of gas. The simplicity of the apparatus used for generating acetylene is such that it can be worked with safety by the most unskilled of attendants. This is, of course, a great advantage in the smaller country house where one or two servants only are kept, and where it is impossible, therefore, that any great amount of time can be spent in attending to the lighting plant. Half-an-hour is ample to allow for recharging a generator of modern design, and it should be clearly understood that this is not a matter of daily occurrence. One charge a week will often be found sufficient during the summer months, if a generator of ample capacity has been chosen. The plans illustrated are those already used as exemplars in the previous chapters on electric and air-gas lighting. The following is an estimate of what it

148.—A CHANDELIER IN STEEL.

would cost to light such a house with acetylene. The cost of a generating plant for, say, forty lights capacity for six hours would be about £23 15s. ; that is, if a cheap but quite efficient form of generator were used. It is, of course, possible to obtain more elaborate forms, which would be a little more convenient to operate and of stronger construction, in which case the price may run as high as £45. The cost of erecting this plant and laying a galvanised steel main to the house from the generator, with a controlling stop-cock in the kitchen or scullery, together with all the necessary mains, branches and connections to the thirty-one points shown on the plan, the whole in screwed wrought-iron pipe, tested to high pressure, would be about £30. This would not include any cutting away of walls or making good and redecorating, as we are assuming that the pipes will be laid while the house is being built. If quite simple fittings are used, we can average the price at 10s. 6d. each. This price would include plain wrought-iron or brass fittings with burners and shades, and would amount in all to £16 5s. 6d. The cost of fixing the fittings would not be likely to exceed £3. We now have a total price for the complete installation, excluding builders' and decorators' work, of £73 if the inexpensive form of generator is used, or £94 5s. 6d. if the most elaborate generator on the market is installed.

A pound of calcium carbide costs about 1½d., and will generate five cubic feet of gas, so that if all the lights were of the usual nominal twenty-five candle-power each, taking one-half of a cubic foot per hour, it would cost 7½d. to keep fifteen burning for four hours. This might be taken as a fair average of the number of lights and hours of burning of each of the three hundred and sixty-five days in the year, in which case the cost for carbide for the year would amount to £11 7s. ; such a result would only be obtained if care were taken not to waste the gas. In certain cases, where great care has been exercised in putting in the right size of burner to suit the situation and making use of a bye-pass arrangement for turning down the light when it is not required, the yearly cost of carbide for such a plant has been reduced to as low as £6. The sum of £4 per annum should easily cover the cost of attendance and maintenance, making the total lighting bill for a forty-light plant about £15. This estimate applies to a house of moderate size, but in the case of a little cottage requiring, say, ten lights, the advantage of acetylene as against other systems is great. Some makers claim to have completed an installation of this size for the sum of £15, and that the yearly cost of running the same amounts to £3 only.

Lastly, readers who think of installing acetylene lighting would be well advised to go to a recognised firm who make a speciality of this class of work ; it is by no means the sort of thing that the local plumber can satisfactorily carry out.   MAURICE HIRD.

149.—WALL FITTING FOR TWO CANDLES.

HOUSE TELEPHONE INSTALLATIONS.

A Necessity for the Large Country House—Intercommunicating Systems—The Central Switchboard
Type—Costs of Systems for Large and Small Houses.

THE transmission of the human voice to a distance is a problem which, like so many others, has been finally solved by the use of electricity. It is true that prior to the invention of the electric telephone voice transmission over short distances had been practised by means of the speaking-tube. It is, however, hardly necessary in these ultra-hygienic days to point out what a very insanitary piece of apparatus the speaking-tube must be. Our forefathers, who were not so versed in germ theories as we are, might possibly use it without feeling that they were catching something all the time. However that may be, the sight of a speaking-tube suggests to the modern mind the story of the Imperial Yeoman who would have been successful in administering a pill to his horse through a tube had not the horse " blown first." The oracles of the ancients were probably worked by some means of voice transmission through a tube. We can picture the awe and reverence of the ancient Greek as the muffled voice of the oracle spoke in admonition or prophecy. The picture has nothing in common with that of the modern gentleman, frenzied with irritation because he cannot hear his friend quite distinctly over three hundred or four hundred miles of telephone wire. The two cases are, however, alike in this, that the working of the oracle was not a greater mystery to the ancient than the working of the telephone to the average man of to-day. The miracle is, indeed, greater in the latter case ; though, as the object of the priests of science is not to mystify but to serve, its miraculous nature passes unnoticed. The telephone was invented and patented independently by Professor Graham Bell and Professor Grey in 1876. It was not the perfect instrument that we have now, but the root from which the later improvements have sprung. Indeed, the telephone receiver has not been altered at all in principle, but the transmitter, *i.e.*, the part into which one speaks, has undergone two great improvements in the addition of the microphone and the induction coil. It is not necessary for the purpose of this article to go deeply into the principles involved in the modern telephone. Suffice it to say that the sound vibrations issuing from the speaker's mouth are enabled, by the mechanism of the telephone transmitter, to control an electric current from a battery in such a manner that the current flows down the telephone wires in a series of impulses, which bear a direct relation to the sound vibrations producing them. These electric impulses are reconverted into sound vibrations when passing through the telephone receiver.

The telephone is now one of the usual modern conveniences found in the country house. Its use, however, is frequently restricted to giving orders to servants, whereas, although this in itself is a great convenience, there is no reason why the system should not be laid out in such a manner as to make the communication of guests with each other a possibility. The convenience of being able to do this is not always realised. In a large establishment it is impossible to know exactly where everybody is at any given time ; but with an "intercommunication" system of telephones in the house, room after room can be quickly and easily "rung up," and the required individual found at once. Moreover, when this happens, conversation can immediately take place. This saves a double journey to the servants, who can receive their orders at once instead of answering a bell to receive them. It puts each guest in direct communication with the whole staff and also enables the members of the household to make arrangements with each other with the minimum of trouble. If asked to prophesy as to its future, we should say that in a few years no good country house will be built without an installation of "intercommunication" telephones. The "intercommunication" system, as its name implies, is one by which every telephone can be used for speaking to every other telephone on the system. This is done without the intervention of a telephone operator. Each instrument is supplied with a switch having a number of contacts corresponding to the number of telephones on the system. The operation of calling up any particular instrument is merely to move the switch to the corresponding contact, which is, of course, appropriately numbered or labelled, and press the bell push. When receiving a call from another instrument the switch has to be moved to the contact labelled "reply" before conversation can ensue.

There is now an improvement on the multiple contact switch, which consists of a little board attached to each instrument on which are arranged a number of push buttons. These buttons are numbered or labelled in the same way as were the contacts of the multiple way switch, and there is one button provided for every telephone on the system. In this arrangement it is only necessary to press the correct button. This connects the speaker up to the instrument he requires and rings up at the same time. The act of replacing the receiver on its hook when the conversation is over releases the press button, and the line is clear for receiving the next call.

The " central switchboard " system differs from the ' intercommunication " system by the fact that an operator is needed to connect the instruments through which conversation is required, and to disconnect them when the conversation is over, leaving them free to be used for other connections. It is obvious that the efficient working of such a system depends upon an operator being constantly in attendance ; but the switchboard is so simple that there is no reason why every servant in the house should not be taught to manipulate it. It is necessary, however, to make such rules that the switchboard shall never be left unattended, and probably the best results are obtained when one servant is stationed permanently at the switchboard. This would only be possible, of course, in a very large establishment.

There are certain classes of communications that can very conveniently be left to the servant operating the switchboard to transmit to their final destination. " Ring up the garage, and tell the chauffeur to bring the car round in ten minutes." " Tell the gardener I wish to see him in the orchid-house in half-an-hour," and so on. In this sense the presence of an operator saves time ; but the efficiency of the system as a whole will largely depend on the operator at the switchboard, and in making comparisons between the initial costs of the ' intercommunication " and " switchboard " systems the wages of the operator required in the latter case should not be forgotten. In the case of the " intercommunication " system it is necessary to run a wire from every instrument to.every other instrument on the system. This is done in practice by making up a cable with the same number of wires as there are instruments plus one extra pair, which is used by all the instruments for ringing up, and also as a return path for the telephone current. It will be seen, therefore, that if this cable has to be run from the house to some outlying building the cost may be greatly increased. The cable must then either be carried overhead on insulators or, what is more costly, be armoured and protected to make it suitable for burying in the ground. Consider a typical instance of a country house compactly built and fitted up with an " intercommunication " system for seventeen instruments. The cost of the installation would be about sixty pounds complete. Now, supposing that one of these instruments was required at the lodge three hundred yards away, another at the stables one hundred yards away, and a third at the game-keeper's cottage four hundred yards away, leaving fourteen instruments in the house itself. The cable necessary for connecting these instruments into the system would be eight hundred yards in length and contain nineteen wires. Even if this were run overhead it would probably not cost less than one hundred and twenty pounds. It would obviously be better in a case like this to connect the outlying instruments to one special instrument in the house, situated in some central position, like the entrance hall, and to restrict the ' intercommunication " system to the house itself.

A single pair of wires eight hundred yards long run on insulators overhead could be put up for about ten pounds, provided that the insulators could be fixed to trees or house walls and no poles were needed. So that, by using one special instrument in the house and connecting the outlying instruments to it, great saving in initial cost would be effected. In the case of a " central switchboard " system these outlying instruments would be connected to the switchboard in just the same way as the others, and no special arrangements would be needed. If the same compactly-built house were fitted up with the same number of telephones arranged on the " central switchboard " system, the cost, including the switchboard, would be about forty-five pounds. If the outbuildings were situated some distance off, as in the previous example, the sum of ten pounds already mentioned would have to be included for overhead wires. In a smaller establishment than the foregoing an " intercommunication " system for six instruments only has been fitted at a cost of. thirty-seven pounds.

In the smaller country house where extensive telephonic communication is not required, it may be found convenient to instal a small system of telephones directly connected with each other. Supposing, for instance, that it is required to communicate between the dining-room and kitchen. A telephone in each of these rooms, with a pair of wires connecting them together, and the necessary electric batteries for ringing and speaking, are all that is required If in addition to this it were desired to speak from the bedroom of the mistress of the house to the kitchen, a telephone with a pair of wires connected to the kitchen ·telephone could be fixed. It would then be possible to speak to the kitchen from either the dining-room or bedroom, but it would not be possible to speak from the bedroom to the dining-room. This system is very inexpensive. There are, indeed, instruments on the market costing only seven shillings and sixpence each which can be used, and if there are electric bells in the house the same battery and wires will also serve for the telephones. It should be noted, however, that if the bells and telephones are in frequent use there is danger of the electric battery running down after a short time, in which case both bells and telephone will cease to work. Good results can be, and have been, obtained from these telephones, probably in those cases where someone in the house with an interest in electrical matters has looked to the battery from time to time, or possibly in cases where the bells and telephones are not in constant use. Nevertheless, it is usual for telephone contractors to recommend a more expensive instrument and a separate system of electric batteries and wires.

The cost of an installation of three instruments as described, making use of existing bell batteries and wires, would only amount to the cost of the instruments and the electrician's fee for fixing them. This latter could not amount to more than a few shillings, so we may safely say that about thirty-three shillings would complete the installation.   If better-class instruments were used and a separate system of wiring and batteries installed, the cost would be increased to something like five pounds, but there is no question that it would be very much more reliable.

In giving the approximate cost of various systems it has been assumed that the instruments will be of the type suitable for fixing to the wall of the room.   Table sets would be somewhat more expensive. Finally, when considering the installation of a telephone system, it is worth while to spend a little time in making the requirements of the case quite clear to the prospective contractor.   It is not always the simple matter that it appears on first sight, and a clear understanding before the work is started will often save considerable confusion and disappointment.   MAURICE HIRD.

LIGHTNING CONDUCTORS.

Causes of Lightning—Popular Scepticism About Conductors—Views of Sir Oliver Lodge—The " Cage " System—Copper versus Galvanised Iron—Safety in a Storm.

THUNDER and lightning have been the most universally awe-inspiring of Nature's phenomena in all ages of the world, and lightning was, undoubtedly, the first manifestation of electricity to be vouchsafed to man. This being so, it seems strange that in these days of advanced electrical research there should be so little positive knowledge available concerning it. Lightning was not identified with electricity until the eighteenth century, and in the twentieth we cannot better protect our buildings from the ravages of the lightning stroke than by following the precepts of Franklin as elaborated by Maxwell. Maxwell in this, as in other matters, has proved himself the greatest of electrical prophets, his proposed modifications of Franklin's isolated lightning rods into a network of conductors running along the angles of a building being very much on the lines of the latest recommendations of the Lightning Research Committee.

There does not yet appear to be any general consensus of opinion among those who have studied the question as to how the clouds acquire a charge of electricity sufficiently great to cause repeated lightning flashes sometimes as much as two miles long. Recent research into the electrical conditions at high altitudes shows that the air there is electrically charged. In that case, the theory that it is the coalition of minute particles of vapour, ultimately forming raindrops, which causes the high charge of electricity in a thunder-cloud, would seem to be a feasible one. The minute vapour particles have a much larger superficial area in the aggregate than the raindrop which contains many of them, and as the electrical charge resides entirely on the surface, there is less room for any given quantity of electricity after the coalescence has taken place than there was before, and consequently the potential of the charge is greatly increased. It also seems to be proved that the light and heat of the sun to some extent electrically charge the bodies on which they fall directly, and that the interposition of a cloud annuls this effect. It is, therefore, possible to assume this to be one of the contributory causes of a thunder-cloud. Cyclonic winds with horizontal axes, which are assumed to act in the manner of a frictional electrical machine, and other natural phenomena, have at one time and another been pressed into the service of furnishing explanations of the electrical charge. Whichever of the above theories may be the true one, and it is quite possible that all are true to some extent, it is to the avoidance of damage to life and property that the designers of lightning conductors must address themselves ; and the problem is a difficult one on account of the cataclysmic nature of the lightning stroke. During the short period that it lasts many thousands of horse-power have to be dissipated, and this must be done harmlessly.

The fact that a building protected by lightning conductors is occasionally struck has given rise to a certain amount of popular scepticism as to their utility. This is unfortunate if it leads anyone to neglect this means of protection, which, if properly carried out, is undoubtedly a very great safeguard, though never an absolute specific against the ravages of the storm. Perhaps the following analogy may help the non-technical reader to an understanding of the matter : Supposing that all the culverts which run through a railway embankment for the purpose of conveying away the surface drainage water were suddenly called upon to deal with a flood caused by a bursting reservoir. They would obviously be incapable of doing it as designed at present, and though they would ultimately carry away all the water, some slight damage might be caused. Suppose, further, that the bursting of the reservoir was a more or less frequent occurrence, and culverts were designed to meet the case. They would have to be of enormous size to be capable of dealing with such a cataclysmic contingency. It may be asked, " Is it, then, merely a question of making the lightning conductor big enough ? " No ! for if we pursue our analogy still further, and assume that there is a row of cottages facing our railway embankment on the lower side, we find that while these would suffer little if the culverts through the embankment were of normal size, they might be altogether swept away if large culverts capable of dealing with the flood had been put in. So it is with the lightning conductor ; a large conductor is rather a source of danger than otherwise. A flash of lightning develops enormous energy, and this must be got rid of. It cannot be conjured out of existence by conducting it too easily to earth ; in that case it will run up again, surging backwards and forwards many times, before it finally dies away, and may do much damage in the process.

Sir Oliver Lodge, who has perhaps been more active in lightning research than any other scientist in this country, divides lightning strokes into two classes—Class A, when a cloud becomes highly charged and discharges steadily on to the earth beneath, occasional flashes between cloud and earth may pass; but these can be readily dealt with by an efficient system of lightning conductors. In any case, the points of the conductors are a means of silently discharging that part of the cloud which lies immediately above them, so that the stroke is less likely to take place in their immediate vicinity. A stroke of the B class is much more complicated, and occurs when a flash passes between cloud and cloud, leaving an unbalanced charge of electricity on the lower side of the lower cloud, which immediately flashes to earth with terrible violence and travels in a most erratic path. Cases have been known where the flash has travelled halfway down an isolated lightning conductor and then left it, piercing brick walls and running to earth through gas pipes, water pipes and even bell wires.

The only way to protect a building absolutely from such flashes would be to build a gigantic wire cage over it; and as this is impracticable, the next best arrangement is to fix lightning conductors in a manner representing the framework of such a cage. This can be done by erecting a number of small rods on the various prominent features of the building (one is wholly insufficient, save in very exceptional cases) and connecting them all together by means of conductors running along the roof ridges and supported a few inches above them. Horizontal conductors should also be run to the rain-water pipes, iron finials, etc.; in short, to all the *external* metal-work on the building. The vertical conductors which join the rods to earth should run straight down the side of the building, and to enable this to be done easily they should be held a few inches away from the wall by special bolts so that they will clear any projecting masonry without leaving the direct line. The bottom end of the conductor should be connected to a metallic plate surrounded by a quantity of broken coke and buried in permanently damp ground. If this last condition cannot be fulfilled without excavating to a great depth, a "tubular earth" can be used; in this case the conductor is led into a pointed iron tube which is driven well into the ground and filled with broken carbon, a little water from the nearest rain-water pipe is diverted into this tube, and leaks through the bottom of it, keeping the ground moist all round.

The manufacturers of lightning conductors still make them, for the most part, of copper, though the best scientific authorities have declared iron to be quite as good from an electrical point of view, the disadvantage being that it corrodes more easily. In the case of a country house well away from the smoky atmosphere of towns, galvanised iron conductors ought to be quite satisfactory, and, of course, very much cheaper. The very fact that they are more liable to corrosion than copper is an additional element of safety, because it makes a periodical inspection necessary. It is most unwise to assume that lightning conductors in copper or any other material, having once been erected, require no further supervision. In the course of time many things may happen to them at the hands of workmen engaged in repairs to the building, and a thorough inspection by a qualified person, say, once in three years, would appear to be a very necessary precaution.

There is no reason why a system of lightning conductors should be at all unsightly; but British manufacturers do not seem to have grasped the fact that the terminal of a lightning rod is necessarily part of the decorative scheme of the building, and one sometimes sees some grotesque examples of scientific Philistinism which architects and electricians on the Continent would have avoided. A finial containing numerous small points is better electrically than one containing few large ones, and can in most cases be adapted more easily to the architectural scheme. It is sometimes asked, "Which is the safest place during a storm?" A banker's steel strong-room would protect anyone inside it absolutely, but few would allow their fear of lightning to carry them so far as to make use of that. The next safest place is a house with an efficient system of lightning conductors. It is perhaps needless to say that lightning conductors should not be handled or even approached too nearly during a storm, and the same caution applies to any metal-work connected to them. For the same reason it is inadvisable to walk in close proximity to a long stretch of iron railing when caught out in a storm, and the old caution against sheltering under a tree holds as good to-day as ever. The danger here is twofold, for if the tree is struck by a powerful flash it may burst into hundreds of pieces, which will be projected outwards over a large area, killing or maiming anyone in their path, or if the flash is not powerful enough to burst the tree, it still may find a passage to earth for part of its charge through a human body standing near.

MAURICE HIRD.

DRY ROT.

Warning Signs of Dry Rot—Its Causes—Precautionary Measures—Treatment and Cure.

LET no one be so presumptuous as to say that " dry rot " has no terrors for him. He may, for twenty years past, have lived in his house in comfort, assuring himself, in the words of his boast, that it was as " dry as a bone," and that an attack of dry rot was an impossibility. And yet, all the time, the evil day was approaching. Unwittingly, the gardener had, year by year, earthed up the flower-beds next the walls, each year's top-dressing raising them a little higher than the year before, until at last they reached above the damp-course and choked up the air bricks which ventilated the under-floor space. The ends of the floor-joists had become damp, the air beneath the floor stagnant, and the dry rot spore, after so long and so patiently biding its opportunity, had not been slow to seize it, now that it had come. An unpleasant, musty or cellar smell pervades the room. The skirtings, and even the door linings, are observed to be cracked and blistered, and, on removing the sideboard, a growth as of mildew is found covering both it and the adjacent wall. On removing the floorboards a truly wonderful sight is revealed, for the joists appear to be cased in cotton-wool of snowy whiteness, or in grey and brown leather jackets cold and clammy to the touch.

Now this dry rot is a fungus (Merulius lacrymans) allied to the mushroom tribe, and it feeds on the substance of coniferous wood, on deal and pitch pine. It requires moisture and a certain amount of warmth, and flourishes best in a dark, warm, stagnant atmosphere. A drying wind is fatal to it ; but, on the other hand, if the conditions are favourable to its growth, it will spread with amazing rapidity. If one would escape its ravages, one must assume the existence of living spores about the house, on the alert, as it were, to commence their devastating course, and act accordingly. These spores may have been brought on a carpenter's saw or on his clothes, or they may have been blown hither by the wind. But they are there, waiting ! A leaky down-pipe may supply the moisture. The modern hot-water apparatus is a prolific cause, for its joints often leak and its pipes provide the necessary warmth to the cellars and under-floor spaces. For if these spaces have not been covered with concrete, and properly, even abundantly, ventilated at the time that the house was built, the risk of dry rot is very considerable. Let anyone, therefore, who contemplates the introduction of a heating apparatus into an old house be wise in time and take precautions against damp and stagnant air, for many old buildings have no damp-course. Even if a damp-course is present and the soil has been concreted and the under-floor space ventilated, it must be remembered that there is still a part of the wall below the damp-course in contact with the damp earth, unless an external air channel, itself ventilated, has been wisely provided. Moreover, care should have been taken that the ground floor-joists are not built into the wall, but rest on an oversailing course, covered by the damp-course. Perhaps, however, the most frequent cause is the foolish hurry to inhabit a new house. It is not that the shell of the house has been built too rapidly, for it is an advantage to get the roof on and protect the building from the weather ; but the windows are glazed and the floors laid too soon. Skirtings and dadoes are fixed against the damp walls to wood plugs driven into the brick-joints, and all too soon they are painted or varnished, and the damp which they have absorbed is imprisoned. In the same way, kamptulicon or thick carpets, but especially the former, imprison the moisture of the half-dried floors. The tongueing also of ground flooring, otherwise desirable, prevents the passage of air between the open joints which would otherwise help to dry them. And then, the crowning folly ! the house is heated up to dry the walls. By all means have a gentle heat from open fires, and keep all the windows open except at dewfall. Often, however, the windows are kept closed, and the moisture which is drawn from the walls during the day is condensed on them and re-absorbed by the walls at night. There is a yet greater depth of stupidity, and that is to attempt to dry the house by lighting the gas. Water is largely produced in the combustion of gas, as one may ascertain by observing that a cold glass vessel held above the flame becomes dimmed with moisture. This water of combustion is condensed on the cold walls, and may be seen streaming down them if the drying operation has been carried far enough. The Terk system of drying new buildings, recently introduced, rests on sound principles, and may be employed with advantage.

Floor-boarding is sometimes laid direct on concrete, nailed to wood strips embedded in its substance. This is a reprehensible practice. Coke breeze fixing-blocks should be set in the concrete, and, after the latter is set and dry, it should be covered with bitumen preparatory to nailing down the floor-boards. But even with these precautions, neither will such a floor nor one composed of wood blocks be immune from dry rot if it is continually being washed in a careless manner and the water allowed to soak into its joints. Let it, however, be supposed that a spore has eluded our precautions, or, rather, has availed itself of some fatal omission in them.   On germinating, it sends out minute tubular thread-like growths, which penetrate the cells of which timber is composed, feeding upon them, and in the process reducing them almost to powder.   If the air is damp and stagnant, as in cellars and under-floor spaces, the growth develops rapidly on the outside as well as in the inside of the timber attacked, and the fungus will spread from its point of origin in the most surprising way, until it may, if not checked, envelop a whole house.   The reason why it can do this is that, if, after it has once made a start, it is in contact with a source of moisture at any part of its growth, and with timber, not necessarily damp, at any other part, it can pass on the fluid from the one and the nutrient substances from the other to extend its growth in any direction.   In this way it will spread across materials like brickwork or glass, which afford it neither moisture nor nourishment, until it again reaches woodwork.   It will thus be seen that a whole house may be attacked by this insidious fungus, even if the carpentry is dry, so long as at one point of its growth it is supplied with sufficient moisture.   Under such circumstances it will no longer manifest itself on the outside, but will permeate the interior of beams, or joists, or the inner face of skirtings, so that these may still present the appearance of being sound, while, in fact, they are rotten at the core.   At length, even the exterior appears cracked, warped and blistered, and the wood is by this time reduced practically to tinder.

Sometimes, in chinks or corners of the building, or behind furniture, leathery corrugated patches may be found covered with dust of a golden brown colour, from which an occasional drop of clear water, like a tear, exudes, a circumstance which has given the fungus its specific name, "lacrymans."   This is the fructification, or spore-bearing surface, corresponding to the gills of a mushroom.   This brown dust is seen, under the microscope, to consist of countless thousands of spores, each about one-three-thousandth of an inch in diameter, so minute, in fact, as to be readily dispersed by the wind, yet each one capable of producing a new fungus sufficient to wreck a building.   When these brown patches are discovered, they should be handled with extreme care so as not to disturb the "dust," and should be burnt instantly.   If they are first soaked with paraffin, so much the better, as the spores will then be prevented from dispersing and they will burn the more readily.   All the timber that is infected should be taken out and burnt on the spot without delay.   It is a false economy to leave infected timber in the building on the ground that it is not badly attacked, unless it be in such a position that it must always in the future remain isolated from damp or any fungus that could convey damp to it, or unless it has been most efficiently treated with some antiseptic.   For this purpose corrosive sublimate dissolved in methylated spirit may be used, although it should be remembered that this substance is an extremely deadly poison ; or carbolic acid, or a hot wash of sulphate of copper (blue vitriol) may be substituted.   Several substances like carbolineum or solignum are also on the market.   But the work must be efficiently done, and the wash must not be restricted to timber, but brick walls, concrete, or the earth beneath the floors, which may, and probably will, be permeated by the living fungus, must also be soaked.   W. H. BIDLAKE.

THE CARE OF THE HOUSE.

The Need for Regular and Systematic Examination—Exterior and Interior Features Needing Attention—Concerning Gutters—Pavings—Smoky Chimneys, Their Cause and Treatment— Noting the Costs of Maintenance.

THERE is no little responsibility in maintaining the fabric of a building in sound repair. Great care is needed to ensure that no decay of any sort shall be allowed to mature, and systematic and regular examination is required to prevent it. In the treatment of the diseases of materials used in building, the nature and cause of the trouble must be ascertained before right remedies can be applied. Much money is uselessly spent and much labour lost by the common habit of applying a " remedy " hastily before the disease has been diagnosed, a course which generally results in work having to be re-done. This chapter is intended to help those who have the care of a house and to guide them in examining its fabric, so that repairs may be effective and lasting. Two things are essential—*regular* examination and *systematic* examination. The first can be easily arranged. Buildings should have a thorough examination at least twice in the year, of which once should be after the fall of the leaf. For the purposes of proper inspection, it is desirable to deal with the parts of the structure separately, and the obviously convenient division is into exterior and interior. Starting at the top of the building, the exterior is naturally divided into (a) chimneys and structures above roof, (b) roof coverings, (c) exterior of walls, fittings and attachments, (d) external pavings and adjoining structures, (e) external tanks, pipes, wires and other work, and the interior into (a) roof construction and structures, such as chimney passings through roofs, (b) ceilings, (c) walls and fittings attached, (d) floors, (e) internal tanks, pipes, wires, etc. Roof coverings should be kept in thorough repair, and care is needed during their examination, thick felt shoes being worn. A careless man on the roofs can do more damage in half-an-hour than the weather will do in twelve months. Before examining the roofs outside, it will save time to search for any sign of dampness in the interior ; the cause of the trouble can then be generally found quickly outside. Every piece of ridge on a pitched roof should be seen to ascertain that the pointing is sound and all broken or loose tiles marked for immediate attention. All leadwork and flashings, especially those round chimneys, should be closely dressed to the adjoining work. Lead gutters and flats mostly give trouble at the drips and rolls, caused often by dust and leaves. Solder should never be used with any metal in repairing joints in roof coverings or flashings. Lead has a great tendency to " creep," forming ridges on the surface and retarding the flow of water, and all parts of the roof should give water the easiest possible way of escape. If ridges so caused retard the flow, the lead should be taken up and relaid in shorter lengths, with more drips inserted in the gutter. Secret gutters, *i.e.*, gutters hidden by the overlapping of other roof coverings, are a source of trouble owing to their being out of sight, and, being generally of small section, quickly get clogged. Chimney stacks and pots should be examined, the pointing of brickwork kept sound and the pots well bedded and weathered, both to keep damp away from the smoke flues and to prevent chimney-pots blowing off. All parapet walls and copings should be examined, and cracked or loose joints and defective cement rendering or plaster carefully noted for repair. Eaves gutters should be examined for cracks or loose joints, and the brackets and screws securing them need special attention. Gutters of every description should be often and thoroughly cleaned out, especially after the fall of the leaf in the autumn, care being taken that all lead or wire balloons, domes and protections over the rain-water pipes and heads and other outlets are properly cleaned and replaced. Nothing is more likely to cause overflow and leaks, with consequent damage inside the house, and nothing is more objectionable than decayed vegetable matter. Roof lights, owing to their exposed position, need careful examination and repair.

External walls require as much care as the roofs. Practically all materials used in walls are porous— it is only a question of degree. No matter what the material, it is essential that the pointing of the joints should be kept in thoroughly good condition, both to preserve the materials of which the wall is composed and to prevent moisture penetrating. If the walling has " settled " or cracked, the rain is not only driven into the structure, but capillary attraction sets up, and causes the very heart of the work to decay, a defect which cannot be found out until considerable damage has been done. The expansion and contraction of practically all materials used in buildings vary, and wherever two different materials join small cracks and openings may develop. The pointing to all window and door frames should therefore be kept thoroughly tight. Nearly all materials when first exposed to the atmosphere undergo a kind of oxidising process, which forms a thin protecting skin on the face. Once this is damaged by frost following rain, or by the bruising of the wall by misuse of ladders, the material will seldom coat over again. The outside surface of the walling should be treated as gently as internal plastering. The examination of the external walls should be started at the top. Dampness from leaking gutters, etc., should be looked for. With the constant closing of windows the mortar often gets cracked and loose, not only round the frame, but also under the sills, which is a favourable place for trouble. The under-side of most projecting sills have a groove of sufficient size to prevent water meeting the surface of the wall ; this often gets filled up, and should be raked clean. The condition of all horizontal and vertical damp-proof courses should be ascertained as far as possible. Arches and lintels quickly record any settlement in the structure. When cracks appear, the *cause* of the trouble should be first ascertained. Merely to cut out the cracked part and make it good is but temporarily to hide the warning that something is wrong. When cracks occur it is necessary to examine them all systematically. It may be found that the roof and floors transmit undue strain to the wall, and before the foundations are blamed all other causes should be eliminated. If there is foundation trouble, it may be due to innumerable reasons, such as the gradual destroying of the bearing surface by leakage from waste or other pipes, by underground drains or water-pipes which may be allowing percolation of liquids. Excavations should not be made anywhere near the building to a greater depth than the foundations. The effect of weather on different subsoils varies considerably ; clay may become dry and cracked at a depth of six feet below the ground, and during a long spell of dry weather will probably be affected at a much greater depth.

Decaying stone and brickwork should be thoroughly cleaned down, and may be treated with one of the many preservatives on the market. All decaying woodwork should be immediately cut out and replaced with new. Cutting out, however, should be the last resort in almost all other materials. If the smaller, but important items, such as the flashings, pointings, fillets and water-grooves, are kept in good condition, little replacing will be required. Pavings around buildings should, if necessary, be relaid so that the water is discharged away from the walls, and if immediately next to the building, should be kept with good waterproof joints. Where there are pavings, the ground beneath is apt to retain water to a considerable extent owing to lack of evaporation. In dry weather, pavings round buildings are an advantage, as the ground beneath is kept moist, and, provided the joints are good, they are no disadvantage in winter. All gulleys, traps and other water conveyors should be kept water-tight. External ironwork should be kept absolutely clear of rust. At the point where ironwork is built into walls moisture is certain to be found. To overcome consequent decay a small cement band should be formed round the iron next the wall.

All putty to glazing should be kept in good condition, otherwise wood sashes will suffer. The leads in leaded lights occasionally require to be run over and dressed close to the glass. All external pumps, tanks, pipes, wires and other conductors should be examined for leakages and defects, and the tanks emptied and cleaned periodically. All taps should have a clear flow and be free from leakages. All external painted work should be thoroughly cleaned and painted not less often than every three years. The basis of the paint used should be either of pure English genuine white lead or zinc.

Turning now to the inside of the house, the roof should be the first point of examination. In timber-work there is a constant movement taking place. It is therefore necessary to examine periodically bolts and straps and joints of all woodwork. If bolts are not kept tightened up, the timbers are apt to spread and cause considerable movement, both in the roof-coverings and in the walls. Rafters and purlins, etc., should be examined, including the beams and joists carrying the ceiling below. Chimney-stacks passing through the roof require inspection, as many fires have arisen from the mortar becoming defective. Where stacks pass through the thickness of the roof they should be coated with cement plaster.

In examining the rooms, it is convenient to start with the top floor and work down. Ceilings, walls, doors and windows, with their fittings, should be looked at in turn, and any defects or loose parts noted. All ventilators should be clean and in working condition. Ventilating gratings in walls and floors are the cause of trouble unless properly protected. The wind drives rain through them, which saturates adjoining materials, and is often the cause of rot and other forms of decay and damage. Ventilators should be so arranged that air can freely pass and that all rain and snow is excluded. Signs of dampness behind panelling or skirtings should be sought, also openings where dust can accumulate. This may be particularly noticeable at the point where the skirtings join the floor. If a small quarter-round oak fillet be added, it will not only form a cover, but will protect the painted skirting from being damaged by constant cleaning of the floor. All fireplaces, fines and mantel-pieces should be very carefully gone over. Smoky chimneys can often be remedied if the cause is ascertained. They are, however, among the most difficult defects to deal with, and often require long examination and trials by an expert before their real cause is found. The following notes on the causes of down-draught may be useful : (*a*) An adjoining flue may be of a much lower temperature and thus cool the rising gases and smoke too quickly ; (*b*) the chimney may not be high enough to cause an adequate upward draught ; (*c*) an adjoining flue, or even a part of the building, such as a staircase or open gallery, may act as an upward shaft which controls the circulation of the air of the flue and actually makes the flue an intake instead of an out-take The last may be remedied either by increasing the height of the chimney or by the erection of screens to prevent the air being drawn from the fireplace into such air-shafts. This trouble often occurs where the supply of air to the fireplace is insufficient, and may sometimes be remedied by making additional openings in the larger air-shaft by windows or other means at the lower part of the building. Flues are subjected to very considerable wear and tear, and, consequently, the bricks and materials with which they are made and lined are easily displaced. It is difficult and costly to examine and repair flues continually, and where they give constant trouble it may be cheaper and more satisfactory to line the flues with fire-resisting linings, and thus allow them to be kept in a cleaner condition. Generally speaking, if the smoke and fumes successfully pass up the first ten feet of the flue, little trouble is found. This portion of the flue should be the first point of inspection. Additional air supplied to the fireplace is sometimes more or less successful, but will never be entirely successful so long as there is a greater air-shaft or a higher air-shaft in close proximity which has not in itself a sufficient air supply. All fireplaces should be built with solid backs, otherwise soot will accumulate. Cracked hearths should have immediate attention, as they are the cause of many avoidable outbreaks of fire. Floors should be free of coverings before inspection. Open joints are caused by the wood shrinking owing to the wood before use not being properly seasoned or being laid too soon after exposure to wet or damp weather, or may be caused, perhaps, by being exposed to excessive heat from adjoining heating-pipes, radiators, fireplaces or flues. Open joints in the boarding should be filled in with fillets to prevent damage to ceilings underneath from water percolating during the process of cleaning. Floors out of level may be caused through the joists and floor generally being too weak to carry the weight put on them by continual excessive vibration, by deterioration of the timber, or by settlement of the walls or other supports, or by the end of the supporting timbers having rotted. Interior pavings of wood blocks, tiles, marble and other materials should be inspected for cracks and loose parts. When any part is relaid care should be taken that all edges of the old work are thoroughly clean and that new work is laid with a solid bed. All internal pipes, wires and other conductors should be tested throughout the various systems, all tanks noted where requiring cleaning out, all valves should be labelled to allow of further easy inspection, and all safety valves, expansion pipes and exhausts tried.

The last items for inspection, but by no means the least important, are the interior sanitary fittings and the connecting pipes and fittings. All traps, inspection caps and chambers should be clear and clean, and the whole of the pipes above ground should be tested with smoke. The whole of the underground work should also be tested with smoke or water, care being taken that all fresh air intakes and ventilating pipes are clear at the completion of the test and that all inspection caps and covers are properly replaced with sufficient bedding.

To complete the survey, carefully note any matters which might affect the structure, such as undue watering of the garden immediately next the house. Care should be taken that the ground adjoining the building is at a proper level, *i.e.*, well below the damp-courses, and that all dry drains around the premises are in a proper state of cleanliness and repair.

In conclusion, the careful man will keep detailed accounts of the expenditure on maintenance, so that he may see year by year what part of the property is costing an excessive amount to keep in repair. This will indicate where radical restoration, or even partial rebuilding, is required, and thus reduce the annual drain for excessive maintenance. A. ALBAN H. SCOTT.

ON GARDEN DESIGN GENERALLY.

Beginnings of Gardening in England—Italian Influences—Fountains—Grottoes—Stairways—Terraces—
Parterres—Clipped Hedges—Statues and Vases in Stone and Lead—Need for Restraint in
Garden Ornaments.

150.—RAPE OF THE SABINES AT PAIN'S HILL.

AMONG all the older of the important gardens that are so numerous throughout the British Islands, there is but little that remains to us in the way of garden ornament that is of an earlier date than the first three decades of the sixteenth century. It may well be supposed that there were ornamental gardens attached to the villas built in Britain by her Roman conquerors, for the great gardens of Rome and its environment, profusely ornamented with sculpture and architectural detail, with many beautiful ways of using water, and ordered alleys of clipped evergreens, were still maintained in their original splendour. But this we can only conjecture, for there remains no existing proof or written record. We hear of a pleasure garden made in the thirteenth century by King Henry III. at Woodstock, but it is an isolated fact in the history of horticulture. Manuscripts of the fifteenth century show small walled gardens with arbours, fountains and turfed seats, with trellises and covered alleys, where suitable shrubs and trees were trained over a wooden framework. It must be remembered that before the time of King Henry VIII. the great houses were still places of defence, closely encompassed by moat or wall, and that the spaces within were small, and, therefore, necessarily given to herbs and plants for use in the kitchen and pharmacy. Gardens for pleasure and beauty were thus almost unknown. But when the country became more settled, and a private house was no longer a fortress, and the windows of the main rooms, that formerly might only look into an enclosed court, could now be large and wide and could look abroad without fear into the open country—with this wholesome and comfortable expansion of the house came also the widening of the hitherto cramped garden spaces.

Gardens for pleasure might now be made, and every house had its roomy bowling green. Then, with increasing enjoyment of garden delights came the desire for garden ornaments. Sundials had long been in use, but now they were to be for ornament as well as utility, placed as centres and at other salient points of garden schemes. No fewer than sixteen dials were made for the King's new garden

151.—A PIPING BOY IN LEAD MODELLED BY MR. BUHRER.

at Hampton Court. But garden expansion and the worthiest forms of ornament did not come at once, for we read of much that was meretricious, such as an abundance of painted woodwork, painted wooden figures of heraldic animals, and, still worse, gilt bird-cages and objects of coloured glass. Still, it is a matter for regret that no one example of this manner of gardening should remain to us, such as this garden of Hampton Court as laid out by King Henry VIII. after the fall of Cardinal Wolsey, or the King's next enterprise of the same nature—the creation of the palace and garden of Nonesuch. One of the ornamental features of these Tudor gardens was the "knotted" garden, a compact space laid out in a symmetrical design, whose character was not unlike that of the elaborate braided and corded work on the full-dress clothing of the day. That curious and perplexing toy, the maze, was also usual, both this and the

152.—AT HARTHAM PARK.

153.—PAN AT ROUSHAM.

"knotted" garden being outlined with edgings of tufted herbs or plants of sub-shrubby growth, such as thyme, dwarf box, hyssop, lavender, rosemary and lavender-cotton, though frequently the maze was of clipped trees six to seven feet high, in which case its walls were usually of yew or hornbeam. But in what remains to us in existence or record of these Tudor gardens there is still a slight feeling of cramped space—there is not yet perfect freedom. That was to follow later, as the outcome of influences from Southern Europe. Hitherto no distinct style of architecture had been known in England other than the Gothic, some of whose structural ornamental developments were carried further in our country than in any other of Northern Europe.

But that extraordinary revival of learning and new life in the fine arts that we know as the Italian Renaissance, whose dawning was in the end of the thirteenth century, and whose noontide was towards the close of the fifteenth-century, was destined to extend its influences to the gardens of England. Meanwhile, one of its conspicuous effects in Italy was the building of stately villas, the term "villa" comprehending both house

and garden.   The garden was equally the work of the architect ;. indeed, in many, if not most, cases the garden was more lavishly treated with architectural enrichment than the house itself.   Many of these gardens have perished, some, indeed, quite recently, but enough remain to impress us with a just idea of the sense of dignity and harmony with which the minds of their designers were saturated.   No doubt they had the advantage of a simplicity of apprehension and aim which to modern designers is a thing of the past.   For they had the ancient classical models and tradition alone, while we of modern days have our minds encumbered and distracted, and our sense of fitness perplexed, by a vast number of influences bearing upon questions of ornament.   For to us the word ornament means decoration, not of one, but of many styles ; not classical only, but of Gothic, Egyptian, Assyrian, Indian, Arab and Moorish, and numberless base hybrids of these well-defined styles.   We have to allow that the marvellous discoveries and inventions of the nineteenth century and the diffusion of education have had some evil effects among their many good ones.   Easy production by casting and stamping of metal by machinery, facility of communication combined with superficial smatterings of many branches of knowledge, trade competition (that greatest of all enemies to artistic production), that during the last century have flooded the world with masses of cheap rubbish, falsely called ornamental because covered with some kind of

·155.—A COPY OF THE WARWICK VASE.

pattern—all these influences tend to debase and confuse public taste.   The honest student of pure decoration, faced at every step with some one or other ignoble, if not actually vile, design in building, in furniture, in every kind of public erection and domestic appointment, has, with infinite labour and difficulty, to free his mind from all this mass of clogging impediment and to begin quite afresh ; moreover, he must acquire a considerable measure of critical discernment before he can find his way through the maze of so-called ornament, false, intrusive and meretricious, that surrounds him on every side.   It is sad to think of this and to know that it is an apparently unavoidable side-issue of our progress—all this ill-directed effort, all this toilsome production of bad and debasing inutility.

The artists of the Renaissance had no such stumbling-blocks.   They had, it is true, some knowledge of Gothic architecture ; but it was never rooted in Italy as was the Classical ; and when the great upheaval came, when the men of wealth and influence searched for and endowed and upheld those who were already possessed of learning, industry and genius, it was to the classical literature of Greece and Rome, to their architecture, sculpture and decoration, that the energy of these giants of the Middle Ages was directed. Then were created those wonderful gardens whose general designs have remained to us as superb models, the precious quality of whose decorative detail as garden ornament has never been surpassed or even approached.   Their influence was to reach our English gardens in late Tudor days, though in the earlier

156.—A KNEELING SLAVE AT MELBOURNE, DERBYSHIRE.

Tudor gardens there were already some features that recalled some of those of the pleasure grounds of antiquity.   For the maze was the direct descendant of the older labyrinth, and flower gardens were very small and closely surrounded by clipped hedges of evergreens.   The " covert alleys," too, had their ancient counterpart and the aviaries of singing birds.
    English architects travelled and studied in Italy and returned with minds widened and stored with methods of taking advantage of the new freedom.   Then it was that some of the greatest houses of the English Renaissance arose—Hardwick, Wollaton, Longleat—and with them the wide garden spaces and an adaptation of the methods of the gardens of Italy.   But there can be little doubt that the true Italian garden cannot be rightly transplanted into our climate.   It always remains exotic, and yet it so happens that in the only portions of our islands where some illusion of Italian conditions might be gained, namely, in the Isle of Wight and the southern coasts of Devon and Cornwall, it has scarcely been attempted. Those who are acquainted with the gardens of Italy at first hand cannot help feeling this comparative unsuitability.   We have not the sky, or we have it only on but few days in the year ;. we have not the temperature ; above all, we have not the endless abundance of rushing water.
    The villas of antiquity and of the Italian Renaissance were almost invariably on hilly ground, needing steep terracing in some place where there was an ample water supply.   There are cases where

157.—SUNDIAL AT CRICHEL.

there are whole rivers of water rushing down long flights of steps, plunging at intervals into pools or basins and then flowing on in endless variety. of invention for garden beneficence or garden delight. Cisterns on high ground were so arranged as to give ample pressure for fountain jets.   The wealth of invention, in fountains alone, if described from known examples, would fill a book. Fountains in the open formed centres of garden schemes in relation to the parterre, and were commonly known by the name of the deity whose sculptured figure formed the central ornament.   On rising ground a frequent form was the wall-fountain, sometimes expanded into the still more important " theatre."   Here, in a space more or less semi-circular, would be a colossal group of Tritons, or a Neptune with attendants of human shape, or water monsters, and boldly-rusticated architectural forms cunningly intergrouped with masses of the living rock.   Over or through the rock, only partly tamed by the guiding of the design, the water would come thundering into the great pool or basin, the sound reverberating from the wing-walls and gaining both in volume and mystery.   Then in another part of the garden where steps descended from the higher ground, little runnels were often built in order that the wayfarer might be accompanied on either side. by the sweet tinkling and musical gurgle of the running rills.   Near a seat there was always, as in the more ancient days, a fountain for the enjoyment of the pleasant, refreshing sound of falling water.   In comparing the ornamental possibilities of our English gardens with those of Italy, this lack of water is a conspicuous deficiency, and it is the more to be regretted in these days when the reposeful and soothing qualities of pleasure grounds are more than ever important. For to a tired brain there is nothing more healing or refreshing than the sound of falling or moving water. It is difficult to describe the mental effect ; but all who have noticed it and felt its salutary kindness will probably agree with the present writer that, even with closed eyes, it occupies the mind without strain in a way that no visible beauty can do. Other obvious delights of a garden are comparatively enlivening and awakening, but in days of summer heat the sound of water is lulling, tending to internal dreaming and refreshing brain-sleep. It may be that the contemplation of flower-border and parterre leads the mind to the thought of their production and maintenance and mutability, but the sound of water is final and eternal. Be this how it may, that garden is a happy one where running water may be freely used. But even when we have water we are apt to misuse it—we are strangely careless. Nothing is more frequent than to see some garden pool or fountain basin with a little water in the bottom only, and nothing looks worse or more neglectful. The proper water-level should be maintained and never relaxed ; moreover, it should be near the level of the inner edge of the kerb or parapet—the nearer the better. If there is not a sufficient supply to feed the basin, the thing is a sham and a fraud, and ought

158.—LEAD VASE AT PAINS' HILL.

not to be there. Gardens can quite well be designed without fountains or pools, but a water-space which is half empty shames and debases the garden. Often in the gardens of Italy the whole basin is raised and the water-level is raised with it. A fine example of such treatment is the Fountain of Neptune in the gardens of the Palazzo Doria at Genoa. The whole design is large and bold. The raised basin has an outline of eight segments of circles, four large and four smaller, with projecting bracketed plinths bearing figures of eagles. There is an inner basin whose lines are reversed. Each panel is a great hollow shell, and each pier, bearing sculptures suggesting the forms of swan and dolphin, is surmounted by an infant Triton. In the centre is the huge figure of Neptune in his car, drawn by sea-horses. This is an example of the greater fountains ; more frequently they were of one basin with a central figure or group, the kerb of some well-designed plan often treated with dwarf plinths and statues.

Balustraded basins of considerable size were of fine effect, especially in connection with the thick groves of ilex and cypress that so usually encompassed the pleasure ground. Of these there are good examples in the gardens at Frascati. But when such a basin is transplanted into an English garden with an open environment it only shows how bald and dull such treatment may be in itself. An example of this is at that fine place, Montacute in Somerset. There is an important fountain at Hewell Grange, a

159.—LEAD FIGURES AT POWIS CASTLE.

copy of the one in the market-place of Perugia. It has a good deal of panelled decoration, and is set in a basin of fair size. But the surroundings are quite inadequate, especially the very plain and wearisomely monotonous rounded kerb. Such examples show the dangers that beset the imitation and importation of isolated objects. It is bad enough in England, but far worse in the Northern States of America, where the pleasure grounds seem still less fitted for the reception of Italian garden ornaments. If in England they often look out of place, in the States they have the appearance of unhappy exiles. It is true that there is a certain measure of success in the case of some of the Italian gardens in England, but this success may be nearly always traced to the strong individuality of some highly-cultured owner whose mind had become saturated with the spirit of the older work, and who was, therefore, able to reproduce it. Some notable examples (among others) that come to mind are the gardens made in recent years by Mr. John Morant at Brockenhurst in the New Forest, the parterre and other portions at Castle Ashby in Northamptonshire, and those of Balcarres and Balcaskie, both in Fifeshire. But even in these one misses the delightful *abandon* of the design, the way the Renaissance artist let himself go, bursting with the wealth of his fancy and the over-mastering force of his conviction. ·

The Italian garden designers of the fifteenth century, imbued with the spirit of the ancient work and with their own traditions of nearly two centuries, showed an astonishing boldness of conception and

160.—THE CÆSARS AT CASSIOBURY PARK.

fertility of invention. The whole thing was done with a kind of passion of spontaneous exuberance. It came straight out of the artist's mind and is instinct with his vitality of imagination ; his sense of beauty and fitness insisting on adequate and unrestrained expression. We, on the contrary, import a Venetian *pozzo* and put it as a centre ornament *on gravel* in the middle of a hybrid parterre in an open garden, where the poor exile cries aloud for its old environment of wall-encompassed courtyard and flagged pavement ; or, if we are more ambitious, we bring over a pair of highly-decorated marble vases and erect them on plain plinths with a very slight and thin moulding at the base, as an ornament to the top of a short flight of unmoulded garden steps !

Such are the usual results of our attempts to introduce the Italian character into our gardens, although there is now and then a glimpse of the true Italian feeling, as in the well-designed box-planted parterre at Balcarres, and the view up the south walk at Chatsworth. In the latter case, and one or two others, the pleasant southern effect is gained by the straight outline of the masses of trees, recalling the *bosco*, the woodland frame that commonly surrounds the picture in the gardens of Italy.

Another of the many uses of water in the Italian gardens was in the grotto, to which the hillside building readily lent itself. Sometimes these grottoes were actual caverns in the mountain, sometimes hollow places under terraces—entirely artificial. In some cases they were not accessible, the floor spaces being pools, with hidden mysteries of falling water, faintly visible—distinctly to be heard. Or they were cavernous cool retreats for hottest summer, with sprays of water rising from the floors and spouting from the sides, and strange hydrostatic toys—water-organs. The pool and tunnel grotto at Albury in Surrey, part of the garden design of John Evelyn, were adapted from his recollection of the grottoes of Italian gardens. He probably set the fashion for grottoes in English pleasure grounds, for many still remain. They had their predecessors in ancient days, when in places near the sea they were sometimes lined with sea-shells worked in patterns, or mosaics, or designs of curious stones. In the grottoes of the Renaissance gardens we see audacious mixtures of natural and artificial rock, and roofs adorned with bold masses of stalactite, so cleverly combined with architectural form and so completely harmonised by the water mosses and other growths that there is no sense of incongruity; only one of admiration for the boldness of the artist's invention and the skill with which he has brought order out of chaos.

Stairways are always beautiful in garden design ; nothing gives a more distinct impression of nobility than a perspective of a succession of always ascending flights of steps rising into higher ground. Especially is this so where the individual steps are long and shallow, with a moulded edge that gives a shadow below, and when they are bounded by a balustrade of refined design. Then the balustrade runs out to right and left, crowning the retaining wall of the terrace, and leaving the best of places below for well-arranged groupings of plants in the flower border, itself one of the best of garden ornaments. There is something peculiarly satisfying in stairways descending to water. There is a fine example at Stoneleigh Abbey in Warwickshire, where there are important water-stairs and a stone embankment with balustraded parapet. Such stairs were also worthily designed in the Italian villas that adjoined water, as in those of the Italian lakes.

Flagged terraces with porches were beautifully treated in the time of the English Renaissance ; of these there are good examples at Bramshill in Hampshire and Fountains Hall in Yorkshire. Careful planting will always enhance the value of beautiful architecture, but it must, indeed, be careful, and in some cases studiously restrained. Nothing is more frequent than to see good architectural detail smothered and obscured by masses of climbing plants. Here and there a cluster-rose may be allowed to fling its long branches over the sculptured balustrade, or a clematis, jasmine or honeysuckle may lightly drape it ; but to keep them within due bounds they need the most careful watching, guiding and regulating. It is the work of the artist-gardener.

Only too often handsome gate-piers may be seen choked with ivy, and walls of ornamental brick-work, with important copings, completely obliterated. But there is many a garden on sloping ground where delicate architectural forms would be out of place, but where the steps are needed and also the retaining wall. Here is the opportunity for making the stonework grow its own ornament by laying the walling dry, that is to say, without mortar, but with earth joints, to be planted with all the good things that are suitable.

The parterre of the Italian garden took a firm hold in England, and showed a distinct development on diverging lines. It grew into a design of bright flower masses rather than one of firmly-drawn outline. In the Italian parterre the pattern was in strong lines of box-bordering, from two to three feet high and wide. Frequently the whole design was planted in box. The garden at Balcarres shows one of the best examples in our islands of a box-planted parterre ; there are others in English gardens, but perhaps none that is so good in design or so entirely Italian in feeling. In the gardens of antiquity we learn that the parterre was also solidly edged. Here it was always small. For one thing, they had but few kinds of flowers—rose, iris, jasmine, poppy, violet, narcissus and not many others. The gardens of Italy were nearly always encompassed by masses of trees—ilex and cypress for the most part. It is interesting to observe that with us also those gardens are the most beautiful and restfully satisfying that have bounding encirclements of large tree form ; the trees distant enough to allow plenty of air and sunlight, and for the flowers to be safe from the most far-travelling roots, but so closely associated with the garden scheme that they frame it distinctly, and do not allow the eye to travel into distant landscape.

Parterre and wide, far-away view are too much material for one picture. The mind is distracted between the two. But the tree-girt parterre is one complete picture ; and before or after it the distant landscape, also suitably framed by trees, acquires its own value and becomes far more enjoyable. One of the weaker points of the development of the parterre when the beds were set in gravel, was that the gravel spaces became much too large ; quite out of proportion with the design. This is a frequent fault in our gardens. It is not only unsightly in itself, but a waste of one of the best features of our pleasure grounds, namely, their delightful expanse of that fine turf that comes to greater perfection here than in any other country.

Except in the case of bounding or sheltering walls of greenery, chiefly of box and ilex, which were kept closely trimmed, there was very little of topiary work in the gardens of the Italian Renaissance. In ancient time much more was done, and the topiarius was a chief among the slaves. But the clipping of evergreens, either into neat walls or some symmetrical or ornamental pattern, has always been a

161.—GARDEN STAIRS AT STONELEIGH ABBEY

distinct feature in English gardens, perhaps because our native yew is of all evergreens the most docile to such treatment.   There are great hedges of clipped yew in old English gardens that are not only delightful objects in themselves, but most beneficent for shelter.   They are also the best of backgrounds to masses of flowers, and delightful companions to great stretches of velvet-like turf.   At Cleeve Prior in Worcestershire there is a remarkable double hedge of continuous arches of clipped yews.   It ranges along on each side of the flagged entrance path, each opening giving pleasant garden views.   At

162.—FOUNTAIN AT HEWELL GRANGE.

Elvaston are some extraordinary specimens of topiary work in yew.   One example, called the Moor's Arch, has a symmetrical figure carried on two green-clothed stems.   From the shoulders of the green roofing-mass rises a well-designed crown, and between the arches of the crown are rounded lugs, reminding one of those on the monolithic roof of the Mausoleum of Theodoric at Ravenna.   This garden is rich in cut yews ;   many are shaped into crowned cones, others into peacocks and architectural forms.   Some of the most curiously-shaped yews are at Levens in Westmorland, a garden full of charm, where the best of hardy flowers are seen most happily against a background of yew, clipped into strange and fantastic shapes.   The form of the garden and its topiary work cannot have been that of the designer.   It is a charming *scherzo* that has run riot through the centuries in its own sweet way.   This curious place must be regarded as an exception, for there is no real excuse for topiary work except in the case of definite design, when living vegetation is treated as walling and when trees are cut into points of distinctly architectural effect.   But where such design is absent, and where trees stand isolated, serving no purpose of wall, arch, arbour or perspective, they should not be trimmed into bosses or fantastic forms.   All that should be done is to so regulate their growth as to keep it in harmony with what is near.

Of sculptured ornament set up in gardens, the shaft of the sundial belongs most typically to the pleasure grounds of the British Isles, and it is among those of pillar or baluster form that we find the most satisfactory examples as garden ornaments.   The eighteenth century gave us some admirable ornaments in lead, a material better suited for our garden sculpture than stone or marble.   There is a well-known figure—for it occurs in several gardens—of a kneeling black slave supporting a table bearing a sundial. These figures belong to a phase of ornament of a certain date, originally Italian, and for the most part Venetian, for in Venice the blackamoor as a subject for decoration was overdone.   The gardens of Melbourne in Derbyshire are rich in lead sculpture of a fine type ; Powis Castle, too, has some good examples of the French classical-pastoral type.   There are also remarkably fine leaden vases.   A large one is at Melbourne ; others at Hampton Court and elsewhere.   Sculptures in stone and marble are in many of our larger gardens—much of it brought from Italy.   In the Renaissance gardens, the architectural niches in which many of the figures stood were often in England replaced by niches cut in yew hedges. This has an excellent effect, but has the drawback that the niche, from inaccurate clipping, often gets out of shape and proportion.

The orangeries for the winter housing of tender plants in tubs were usually of good design and took their place among the ornamental features of the eighteenth century gardens.   The tubs themselves, of round or square pattern, were probably painted of the pleasant, rather light green that has become traditional in France.   They are often disfigured in our gardens by being painted a crude raw green colour and the hoops coloured black, a quite needless ugliness.   A quiet green of rather neutral tone all over is the best in England, care being taken to keep the green lower in tone than any foliage that is likely to come near it.   A matter of proportion that is very often overlooked is the relation in size between the tub or. vase and the plant that is to grow in it.   The plant is hardly ever large enough.   No doubt it is difficult to get them rightly adjusted, but it is a matter about which it is well to take pains.

Stone seats of good design are not often seen in English gardens, but there are good examples at Danby and Hackwood.   The garden temple or pavilion is only suitable in large places of classical design.   A fine one occurs in the Palladian Bridge at Prior Park, near Bath.   There is grave risk in the over-doing of decorative accessories.   Many a garden of formal design is spoilt by a multiplicity and variety of ornament, for there is danger in the employment of treatment that embraces the use of geometrical form and yet lacks unity and cohesion.   And there are other gardens of this class in our country whose effect is chilling and unsympathetic.   The design may be good, the details correct, and yet the thing that is most important is wanting.   You have the body without the soul.

GERTRUDE JEKYLL.

163.—A GARDEN SEAT BY MR. LUTYENS.

GARDEN-HOUSES.

Dutch Origin of Gazebos and Garden-houses—Mottoes for Their Doors—Their Popularity in England—Two-storeyed Examples—The Most Suitable Materials for Their Building.

OF all the accessories of a garden, from Tudor days until modern times, the garden-house has been the most important. In the fifteenth, and until the middle of the eighteenth, century every care was taken that, besides being ornamental features, they should also be able thoroughly to withstand the vagaries of our climate ; but with the dilettantism of the latter half of the eighteenth century the substantial summer-house gave place to the Greek temple and Chinese pagoda, which in their turn have been succeeded by the spidery rustic wooden arbour of to-day, all freshly varnished and thatched with heather, that in no way takes the place of the comfortable stone or brick built garden-house of the eighteenth century.

164.—A GAZEBO AT WESTBURY COURT.

Banqueting-houses, gazebos and garden-houses all mean pretty much the same thing in an old English garden. The origin . of the word gazebo is undoubtedly Dutch, and signifies particularly that type of summer-house built at the corner of a terrace, or angle of a moated garden, where from its position it could command a widespread view. Such summer - houses are important features in every Dutch garden, and great variety is shown in their design. They are usually built of brick or stone, panelled in wood, often containing fireplaces, and in every way are intended as living-rooms and comfortable places for retreat. They are generally disposed at convenient points about the garden ; but whenever the house should chance to be situated near the high road, we are certain to find at least one of them in a position to command the passing traffic. I remember a delightful " zomerhuis " on the high road not far from Haarlem, overlooking a moat, and nestling amid a grove of limes, its casement thrown wide open, allowing a peep of the cosy panelled interior. Here in the long summer evenings the men were wont to bring their pipes and the ladies their needlework, and gossip of the passers-by was freely indulged in. In bygone days the citizens would often erect such gazebos in the neighbourhood of large towns upon some little patch of ground outside the town, to which they could retire with their families after the business of the day. These little buildings in Holland were formerly quite characteristic features of the highway, and we still come across a few that have escaped destruction, decorated with quaint names or mottoes painted above the door. Thus may be read such inscriptions as " Lust en rust " (Pleasure and ease), " Wel tevreeden " (Well content), " Nood gedacht " (Never expected), " Vriendschap en gezelschap " (Friendship and sociability), " Het vermaak is in t'hovenieren " (There is pleasure in gardening), and many a similar quaint phrase indicating a feeling of content and comfort on the part of the owner.

165.—AN ANGLE PAVILION AT MONTACUTE.

166.—GAZEBO AT BECKINGTON : OF BRICK WITH STONE-TILED ROOF.

Most of the eighteenth century gardens have now disappeared, for the Dutch have long ceased to cultivate their gardens in the old manner.   Unhappily, in the early years of the nineteenth century one or two English gardeners, following in the footsteps of Capability Brown, crôssed over to The Hague and in an incredibly short space of time succeeded in completely demolishing nearly all the delightful old gardens of the wealthier merchants that had been laid out in the style of Le Notre around the suburbs of The Hague, Haarlem, Amsterdam and other important centres.   If we would know something of their appearance, and something of the design of their quaint gazebos, we must examine the old Dutch garden pictures that fortunately have been engraved by the hundred, or else seek out some old Delft panel or plate, on which they are often painted with all their quaintly fantastic roof forms, with walls of intermingled brick and stone.   In the Ryks Museum at Amsterdam there is a typical eighteenth century summer-house, an oblong building, with mullioned windows and a long sun-shelter upheld by two large wooden swans.   If I have dwelt somewhat at length on the Dutch gazebo it is because of the influence this type of summer-house had on the English examples illustrated in this chapter.   That, for example, at Westbury Court, a peaceful old manor house overlooking the river Severn on the main road from Monmouth to Gloucester, is an excellent example of the gazebo (Fig. 164) ; on one side its windows overlook an old-world walled garden with lavender walks, and long, straight canals bordered with prim hedges of yew, while on the opposite side the windows look on to the dusty high road separated from the gardens by a moss-grown wall broken here and there by a *clairvoyée* of delicately-wrought ironwork.   The example from Beckington, (Fig. 166), a small square brick building with stone quoins and a handsome pedimented doorway, is in a similar position to the Westbury example, with one window overlooking the roadway and others the bowling green and garden.

167.—GARDEN-HOUSE BY STEW-POND : KING'S WESTON.

A very favourite position for a garden-house was at the end of a long walk, enclosing a vista or overlooking a bowling green, and many such examples might be noted.   John Worlidge, writing in 1677, advises that they should be placed at an angle of the garden with windows and doors commanding " every coast, the windows to be glazed with the clearest glass and to have screens of printed and painted sarcenet for day use, and shutters of thin wainscot for night use."   It is evident from this remark that the garden-house was occasionally used by the master of the house for a day or two's retreat when he wanted quiet.   At Wilton House, terminating a long walk leading through the Italian garden is a stone summer-house of two storeys, believed to have been designed by no less an artist than Hans Holbein.   It is indeed a beautiful piece of work.   At Haddon Hall are the remains of a stone garden-house which overlooked the bowling green.   This had an outside staircase, by which spectators ascended to the flat roof to watch the progress of the game or admire the scenery.   Such buildings were generally fitted up

168.—AT LYDDINGTON BEDE.

with panelled woodwork round the walls, window seats, and often with a fireplace.   At Heslington, not far from York, is a two-storeyed building with an external flight of stone stairs leading to the first floor, while below is an open arbour overlooking the bowling green.   At Nun Moncton, on the opposite side of York, there is a very good example of a square brick summer-house with ogee leaded roof surmounted by an elaborately wrought vane.   In some cases garden-houses were used as retreats and consisted of two or more apartments.   There is a delightful example of such a retreat at Severn End, near Worcester, erected in 1661 by Judge Letchmere ; here he was wont to retire, perhaps for several days together, for

169.—AT CHARLTON HOUSE, KENT.

quiet contemplation among his books.   From his study a little kind of leper's squint enabled him from time to time to cast a glance into his orchard, whose deeply-laden branches were doubtless not unknown to the idle youth of the village. The well-known garden-house, built by William III., overlooking the river at Hampton Court, is also an interesting example of such a garden retreat.

Another favourite position for garden-houses was at the two angles of a court, like the superb examples at Montacute in Somersetshire (Fig. 165), the finest of their kind to be found in England.   They are two storeys in height and are square in plan with small circular-shaped bay windows on either side ; the lower room appears to have been always intended for the storage of fruit and tools, and the upper room

170.—AT IFORD MANOR.

171.—AT NETHERSWELL MANOR.   DESIGNED BY MR. E. GUY DAWBER.

for a garden-room comfortably arranged as a retreat from all weathers. The garden-houses overlook what was originally an entrance forecourt, and our illustration shows a part of the well-proportioned wall enclosing the courtyard. It is broken at intervals by small pavilions of clustered Doric columns, around which the roses grow in luxuriant profusion. At King's Weston in Gloucestershire (Fig. 167) the garden-house overlooks a small enclosure and stew-pond surrounded by a high wall and a wealth of lovely flowers. It was probably intended to be used as a fishing lodge, like the delightful little lodge designed by Inigo Jones for Becket Park, near Shrivenham. The garden-house at Apethorpe belongs to a more open type. It overlooks the rose garden and a circular lily pool. Apethorpe still retains some of its old-world characteristics, including a very fine yew hedge and wonderful lawns.

An immense variety of garden-houses are to be found in the engravings of Kip, Badeslade, Adkyns, Dugdale, Switzer and other engravers of the eighteenth century. In these realistic bird's-eye views of country seats, with their avenues, courtyards and trim parterres, we may find an immense variety of garden-houses; but perhaps the quaintest of all are those in Loggan's views of the colleges of Oxford and Cambridge. A word as to the materials for building a summer-house. Best of all is hand-made brick, especially the small bricks of a warm tone, which seem to harmonise better than any other material with the verdure of grass and trees. In stone districts a warm yellow stone is very suitable. White stone should be avoided—it looks hard and uninteresting. The covering should, if possible, be of stone slates, each course diminishing as it gets near the apex of the roof. Concrete is a material that might be used for garden-houses if designed by a skilled hand; the surface may be finished with fine rough-cast, and the walls should be coloured, as cement takes many years to tone down. Where rough-cast is used the surface should be coloured a warm yellow or, as an alternative, white, mixed with a good proportion of carmine, imparting a rosy tone that is particularly effective in a garden. In a chalk district this material mixed with flint might be used, especially in a round garden-house. That chalk is durable and weather-proof is proved by many old buildings, such as the church at Stoke Poges, where chalk walls have withstood the weather for at least three centuries. The one objection to chalk is its glaring whiteness, but this might be overcome by very broad overhanging eaves. Treillage is a material which we find largely used in French gardens; the graceful Temple d'Amour at Chantilly or the little pavilions at Bagatelle or Versailles show how well the material may be used; but in England a garden-house is generally needed to withstand the weather, and is therefore required to be of a more solid material. The cheapest forms of garden-houses are those of wood, and if well designed and harmoniously coloured in browns and greens without too much white, such a form of garden-house has much to commend it.

Unpainted elm boarding is also a suitable material; left to itself it turns a delightful colour. The modern craze for painting all garden woodwork and furniture white tends to give far too great a contrast and to break the harmony of colouring that should always exist between the works of Nature and those of man.   H. INIGO TRIGGS.

172.—AT AVON TYRRELL. DESIGNED BY PROFESSOR LETHABY.

OUTDOOR   DINING-ROOMS.

Modern Habits in Favour of Dining Out-of-Doors—Examples Stately and Simple—Treatment of Tea-room Windows at Grey Walls—A Scheme for an Ideal Outdoor Room.

FASHIONS change. Our grandfathers were apt to close up their bedroom windows prudently, being convinced of the poisonous character of the night air.   Some of us, on the contrary, are getting into the way, anyhow in the dog-days, of dragging our beds out under the stars, and with most people there is more of the open-air life than there used to be.   The garden is becoming a place not for a hurried walk, but for the enjoyment of many a long hour.   It needs modification to suit it to its new and enlarged uses, so that shelters, loggias, arbours and garden-houses take a large place in modern garden design. There is no better moment to enjoy the fresh air and garden outlook than at mealtimes, and arrangements that make this possible and pleasant should receive due consideration.   The occasional picnic may be all very well, but as a regular habit meals should be served easily, comfortably and securely, whether they take place in a closed room or in an open space. In our changeable climate it is impossible to feel security if that space is not roofed and sheltered from driving winds.   I remember suffering frequent humiliation when the terrace where I used to breakfast lacked such a contrivance. I would over-rule my servant's strong objection to laying the breakfast there when the sky threatened, and often enough, by the time I sat myself down, a shower or a drizzle would set in. Even if, to save my dignity, I was prepared to face the elements, the salt was not, and the effect was disastrous also on the cutlery So I had to ring the bell, confess my error of judgment and beg that everything might be removed hurriedly indoors.

173.—AT IFORD.

A roofed space, then, is a *sine quâ non*, but it is only the first of the requirements. The situation and the disposition of the building also need careful consideration. It should be easily get-at-able by those who serve as well as by those who partake of the meal. If all the food and the numerous adjuncts and implements that play their part in its presentment and consumption are to be brought circuitously and from afar, outdoor meals will be highly unpopular with the household and there will be persistent attempts to confine them to the dining-room.

In building a loggia or shed for the purpose its position should make it as accessible from the kitchen and pantry as the dining-room itself. The next point to settle is the extent to which it is to be open-sided. That, and the detail of whether there should be means of partially closing the sides at will, depends very much upon the site. If the house stands high and exposed to winds, and if the loggia or shed is placed projectingly, it will be necessary to prevent the wind blowing through, as, besides creating much draught, it would certainly bring the rain with it. In such a case it is better to have an open arcade to the south, or wherever the warmest and stillest quarter may be, and fill in the sides ; but if windows or shutters that hook back can be arranged in them, so much the better.

174.—AT MUNSTEAD.

On the other hand, if the domicile is in a sheltered nook, or if its own wings and projections protect the loggia, two at least of the sides of the latter may be open. It is, of course, not very difficult to fulfil all such requirements when a place is being laid out anew and the open-air room is an integral part of the original design. But where it has to be added to a house built at a time when such a feature was undreamt of, it is more difficult to make the thing really practical, and some compromise or makeshift will be often necessary. The consideration of how to incorporate such a feature in a new design will be dealt with ; but examples may first be given of how the problem has been solved in the case of existing houses. Of such attempts, several are here illustrated, and they have been chosen as showing much divergence both of style and position. The one at Iford is an adjunct to a stately Palladian house, and is treated as an elaborate and sympathetic architectural feature (Fig. 173). It occupies part of the space where a useless and derelict annexe had stood, and the fine ashlar of the walling, architraves and cornices of the annexe provided most of the material. Certain ornamental portions, such as the inserted roundels and the ironwork of the balcony above, were among the owner's collection of Italian antiques. The wrought stonework of the triple arcade and the columns that support it were the only important portions that had to be new made. The house is on a rapid slope, and some of the principal sitting-rooms are on the first floor. although the rapidly rising ground makes the garden accessible from them at the back. A considerable part of the ground floor is occupied by the hall, one screened-off section of which is frequently used as a dining-room, and from it the loggia is immediately reached. Convenience of access is therefore fully attained. The open arcade faces south-east into an extremely sheltered enclosed garden, while to the south-west is a window which may be opened or shut. Nothing

175.—AT MATHERN.

can be more beautiful, more agreeable, or more practical than this clever adaptation of a useless building into one of the most enticing parts of the house.

The open-air dining-room at Munstead, though conceived on much simpler lines, has also architectural character (Fig. 174). It stands at right angles to the house and forms the termination of the terrace. In winter it presents the appearance of an orangery and shelters the baytrees and other shrubs in tubs that need protection from hard weather. But when warmth shows signs of advent the great glazed doors and windows (which are made movable) are taken away, and the loggia thus obtained makes an altogether apt and convenient summer refectory. The photograph was taken just before this time, so that, though many of its winter occupants have come forth on to the terrace, the glazing remains. The area is ample for a considerable party, being twenty-eight feet long by fourteen feet wide. There are, besides, recesses for two great marble-topped service tables. The west side of the room has a door on to a small back-yard, just across which is the kitchen. The arrangement permits of easy, if not quite perfect, service.

The next two pictures show buildings conceived in much humbler spirit. They may be termed sheds rather than loggias, but they serve their intended purpose excellently, and should be noticed by those who wish to have these conveniences without much outlay. That at Mathern (Fig. 175) was a shed opening from a

farm kitchen, and was with a copper and fitted apparatus for washing dairy and other household utensils. When the house was re-arranged some years ago, its position in what had become a sheltered and flowery part of the garden, and its direct connection with a room arranged for dining in, made it fulfil all the requirements for open-air meals. The copper and other utilitarian adjuncts were swept away, the walls were rough plastered, an oak post and braces were set up on its open side, and the appearance presented in the illustration was obtained.

176.—AT LLANWERN.

At Llanwern the shed has the fault of being detached from the house. That was inevitable, for the house was a great square, dignified Georgian building that did not easily admit of architectural additions or modifications even if expense had been no object. As a matter of fact, it was then occupied on lease, and the tenant very naturally wished to gain his end with small expense. The shed was, therefore, placed on the edge of a Dutch garden near to one of the doors of the house from which the kitchen was immediately accessible. The way, from the spot where the meals are cooked to where they are consumed is short and easy, the only inconvenience being that it is across the open and, therefore, damping to the food and its carriers during transit if rain should come on. The shed is open to the south and west towards house and garden, but closed in to the north and east. It is composed of posts supporting a pantile roof and with weather-boards nailed on for the closed portions. It is quite a simple, picturesque garden object, bosomed as it is in rambler roses. It is comfortable and practical as a room, and the outlook from it on to the garden is extremely agreeable.

Although for tea rather than dinner, the outdoor room at Grey Walls, Gullane, designed by Mr. Lutyens, is a very instructive example. It is approached only from the garden, and being in some sort, therefore, cut off from the house and difficult to serve, would not be convenient for more serious meals than tea. Its planning, however, is full of suggestion The window openings facing north and east are glazed,

177.—OUTDOOR ROOM AT GREY WALLS.

but those to the south and west are fitted with shutters, which roll up and leave the whole opening free. While there are views from the room to all quarters of the compass, only the warm winds have access. It will be seen from Fig. 177 that the room is built between a corner of the house and the garden wall, and thus forms an integral part of the architectural scheme, while it is for practical purposes distinct.

All the examples so far given, except the last, which was not intended for dining, are adjuncts to existing houses, and it is difficult in those circumstances to reach the perfection of arrangement—that is to say, to provide a place with every amenity of exposure and outlook at a point where service from the kitchen is easy. There is, therefore, added a set of drawings and a plan by Mr. C. E. Mallows showing the corner of a proposed house carefully designed to provide large spaces, covered and uncovered, for the enjoyment of sedentary outdoor life. The scheme is an example of due consideration being given to the ideal features of an outdoor meal-room. The inner dining-room faces east, and is pushed out with a great bay that enables it to have a south window, and the loggia, or open-air room, is a continuation of this bay, which has three large window-doors opening on to it.

The north wall of this projecting wing masks the back-yard, and there is no aperture in it, partly on that account and partly because protection from the winds of that quarter is desirable. But the east

178.—AN IDEAL OUTDOOR ROOM: LOOKING ACROSS THE LOGGIA.

end has three apertures between massive pillars corresponding to the door-windows of the bay, and there are three others towards the south. Thus a particularly charming garden picture is obtained from the dining-room, whence, across the shaded area of the loggia, the sun is seen playing upon lawn and flower-bed and lighting up the distant landscape. A somewhat greater intimacy with the garden is reached in the loggia itself. An ample stairway descends southward on to the great plat before the house, while to the east three steps lead to a random-flagged terrace sheltered from the north by a high wall. On this terrace, when the summer evenings are particularly warm and settled, dinner may be served. For there is no doubt that the perfection of open-air dining is to have nothing overhead between you and the sky. The fading of the daylight, the lighting up of the western sky, the sudden beaming forth of the evening star, at first occupying alone the pearly grey of the heavens, but shortly joined by myriad companions as night gains the ascendency—all this can only be thoroughly enjoyed and appreciated on such a terrace as Mr. Mallows here gives us.

But ours is not a climate where evenings of settled warmth and calm are frequent or to be depended upon, and dinner will, therefore, be far more often served within the eighteen-foot square of the loggia,

179.—THE OPEN-AIR ROOM OF A DREAM.

180.—THE PROJECTING WING WHICH FORMS THE OPEN-AIR ROOM.

with its ceiling and two sides offering shelter from the haphazard little inclemencies—a dash of rain, a whirl of wind, a rush of chilly air—to which we are ever subject in this country. At other moments and for other meals it is shelter from sun that this building affords. It is excellent for both lunch and tea in hot weather, while at breakfast-time the table may be either put forward towards the eastern apertures to get the early sun in spring and autumn mornings or kept well back towards the dining-room in the dog-days. The offices and service lobby lie to the north side of the dining-room, so that meals may be carried out without walking across the whole length or breadth of the dining-room, and thus creating a sense of discomfort should it be used for reading or writing. Certainly, it is a well-thought-out scheme, and if it at all fits in with the conditions and site where the lover of the open-air can construct a dining-place, it would certainly be adapted for use during a long part of the year, and even, occasionally, at seasons when resort to the fireside is more normal. For there are quite sunny days in November and March when it is really delicious to begin the day by drinking in fresh air at breakfast-time if only a little care and forethought has been exercised to provide the rightly-constituted spot.   . H. AVRAY TIPPING

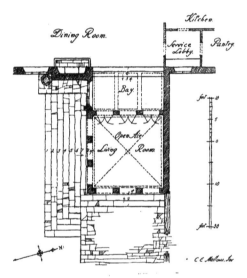

181.—PLAN FOR AN OPEN-AIR LIVING-ROOM.

THE ART OF TREILLAGE.

Treillage and Its Uses—Mr. John Belcher, R.A., on its Value to the Architect—Its History in Classical and Mediæval Times—Methods of Construction—Its Place in Bacon's Ideal Garden—Practical Suggestions for its Use.

AMONG the many modern revivals of decorative features that gave to old gardens so much of their charm, the re-introduction of treillage should surely be encouraged. In laying out a garden, there is very much to be gained by partially concealing and judiciously screening certain parts from immediate view. By this means the imagination is tempted to conjecture the presence of hidden delights beyond, and our interest is aroused in expectation of some further enchantment. A walled-in garden, or one divided by hedges of yew, generally owes its charm to the fact that we are induced to wander from garden to garden, never quite aware of the end. Besides the fact that such divisions of a garden give pleasure to the casual visitor, they have always the additional advantage of affording seclusion, quiet and comfort. Brick walls and hedges of yew, laurel and holly form substantial screens; but in these days of short leases and gardens quickly made, how few there are who will care to incur the expense of solid walls or wait ten years and more before such hedges can be effective! In treillage we have an excellent substitute; against it the hedge can be planted and protected and trained; roses, clematis, jasmine and honeysuckle will climb readily and show their preference for it to cold and uncongenial iron rods and wire.

The word " treillage " is said to have been derived from the Latin *trichila* and also from the *treille* or tendril of a vine. The French word is now generally adopted, and it is, perhaps, better than " trellis."

182.—LA MAISON DE SYLVIE: CHANTILLY.

If there is any distinction between trellis and treillage, it would seem to be that the latter implies a combination of posts and rails forming an architectural design, while the former is appropriate to the mere lattice-work filling. The reason why trellis-work does not suggest the same meaning to the mind as the word treillage is that usually it does not presuppose the existence of design of an architectural character, which is invariably present in good French examples. Porticoes for the decoration of the ends of vistas and niches for statues and busts, pavilions and summer-houses were built of treillage, and sometimes the entrances to the mazes and small groves which were part of all the larger French gardens of the eighteenth century. A *berceau* was either a long gallery of trellis-work, occasionally combined with a garden-house, or else a shaded walk formed of small clipped trees with pleached branches.

In a paper on " Treillage," written many years ago, Mr. John Belcher, R.A., pointed out that it has a poetical and romantic as well as a useful side. " Such a medium," he says, " may be to the Architect what clay is to the Sculptor :

183.—TREILLAGE DESIGNED BY LE PAUTRE.

in it he may venture to give shape to some poetic dream of ethereal architecture which has visited his brain, or at any rate (if this seem too large a flight of fancy) he may realise, if only temporarily, some playful fancy for his own satisfaction in work, which from the very nature of its material cannot be taken seriously, or raise great expectations. It is the ease and facility with which daring experiments can be made which render it valuable. It can be altered and shifted at pleasure until the desired effect is obtained in a way which more solid and valuable materials prohibit. And it thus affords opportunities for judging effects which may subsequently be translated into stone or brick."

That the use of trellis is extremely ancient is proved by the frescoes that have been discovered in Rome, and many of those found at Pompeii have supplemented the not too abundant knowledge of ancient gardens contained in passages among the classical poets and *litterateurs*. These wall paintings have proved quite a mine of information concerning the flowers grown in ancient gardens, and more than three-score ornamental trees, shrubs and flowers thus represented have been already identified. Both at Herculaneum and Pompeii complete schemes of trellis-work made of intertwined reeds and canes are represented : fountains, nymphæa, shrines, aviaries, summer-houses and other varieties of ephemeral struc-tures. In the peristyle of the House of Sallust is an excellent representa-tion of an ancient garden, with small circular trellis niches and bubbling water-jets. China and Japan have each their characteristic treatment worked out with wonderful elaboration and finish. Examine a willow-pattern plate, and see how trellis enters into the garden design,' the palisading, the bridge and the varied patterns suggested in the margin. The familiar lattice-work of Cairo seems to be another variety of the same thing and, no doubt, is a direct descendant of the Egyptian trellis so often represented in ancient paintings. Of late years much of the best Arab woodwork has left the country, and, indeed, a few years ago it was

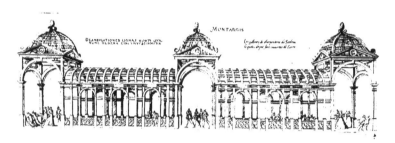

184.—WOODEN GALLERY IN THE GARDEN AT MONTARGIS.

vanishing so fast that its exportation was prohibited. In Italy treillage was in full use as a garden ornament as early as the fourteenth century. In Andrea Orcagna's fresco at the Campo Santo at Pisa, painted about 1350, a festive company of ladies and gallants, apparently just returned from the chase, sit laughing and singing under a group of orange trees, before a background of trellis upon which oranges have been trained. Again, in Pinturicchio's picture of "Susanna and the Elders," the garden is shown surrounded by a low trellis wall and a hedge of roses trained upon a lattice of gilded reeds. The very remarkable and rare book, printed by Aldus of Venice in 1499, known as "Poliphili Hypnerotomachia," abounds in woodcuts of the gardens of the period, with several designs for treillage and wooden arbours. Luini's superb " Madonna of the Rose " in the Brera Gallery, which was painted about 1490, shows a square lattice of reeds upon which the roses forming the background are trained.

In France the use of trellis dates from mediæval days ; an early illustration may be seen in the beautiful illumination of the " Romance of the Rose " in the British Museum, dating from the latter part of the fifteenth century, the finest illustration of a mediæval garden extant ; the garden is divided in two by a low fence with a high gateway in the middle ; both fence and gateway are of trellis, The unique collection of drawings on parchment of French châteaux by Androuet du Cerceau, preserved in the British Museum, are most valuable documents illustrating the great châteaux of Francis I. Many of the gardens

185.—TRELLIS-WORK AT CHANTILLY.

186.—L'ILE D'AMOUR : THE PARK, CHANTILLY.

187.—THE BASSIN D'ANTIN AT VERSAILLES.

188.—DESIGN FROM A DUTCH GARDEN BOOK.

Pierre Betin, Jean Marot, Jacques Boyceau and Mariette. Treillage was especially used in the gardens of town houses, as we see it still so much in Paris to-day. At Chantilly there is the graceful little Temple d'Amour ; this example shows the art of treillage at its very best, and, although of no great antiquity, it deserves to rank with the best work of the eighteenth century. At the entrance to the Ile d'Amour, in which this pavilion stands, are two pyramids of treillage on either side of the bridge connecting the island. We may gather much about French treillage of the eighteenth century from a rare work, " L'Art du Treillageur," published in Paris in 1745. In his introduction the author rightly gives all credit to the French for the perfection to which the art had then been brought. Treillage, he says, like other arts, was simple in its origin and limited to utilitarian purposes, such as the support of the treilles· Until the eighteenth century it was only used to train the young branches of fruit trees or of hedges dividing garden walks and the different parts of the vegetable garden ; when used for these purposes it had no decorative value, and, with few exceptions. such as the great treillis, which was one of the principal ornaments of the gardens of Charles VI. and his successors in the

that are shown have designs for treillage. The great galleries of Montargis had quite a solid architectural appearance. At Blois the privy garden · was entirely surrounded with treillage berceaux and trellis covering the walks in the kitchen gardens. At Beauregard treillage galleries formed the boundaries of the herb gardens, and at Gaillon an elaborate pavilion occupied a large space in the centre of the parterre. These examples of treillage were constructed of very light chestnut laths, fastened together with small wooden pegs, and towards the end of the fifteenth century iron wire was more generally used. As early as the thirteenth century the " treille " was to be found in the citizens' gardens at Paris, and in the time of Saint Louis these berceaux were much appreciated. The idea of an architectural treillage was introduced into France from Italy at the beginning of the sixteenth century.

In the next century there was a more extended use of treillage, and in the eighteenth century every garden must have abounded in elaborate examples. Many of these designs are to be found in the engravings of Le Pautre,

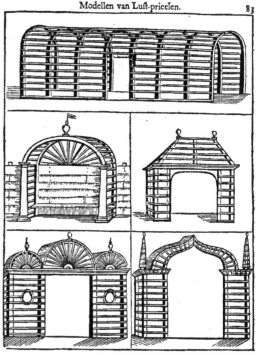

189.—DUTCH DESIGNS FOR TREILLAGE.

Hotel de St. Pol, Paris, was useful rather than ornamental. (The site is still remembered in the Rue Beautreillis.) It was not until the days of Le Nôtre and of Mansart, who laid out the superb gardens of Versailles, Clagny and Marly, that the art of treillage began to be recognised as a most effective decorative adjunct, and its construction was handed over to workmen who made it their sole occupation. The treillageur became a craftsman of importance, and, working either from his own or from architects' designs, found plenty of occupation in the châteaux round Paris. In 1769 the craft was officially recog.- nised and united to the Corps d e Menuisiers.

After describing the orders of architecture and their application to treillage motifs, the author of " L'Art du Treillageur " gives elaborate directions for the setting out of vaulting, the construction of columns, cornices and other details. Iron was largely used in building up the constructional members, in strengthening the vaults and the angles, both in order to give a lightness and delicacy that would have been impossible if only wood were used, and also on account of its being better able to resist climatic effects. Where iron is used it is recommended that it should be painted the same colour as the wood. Diagrams are given showing the most effective means of spacing the laths together, with designs for a variety of ways of filling in the compartments, a n d

190.—THE TEMPLE D'AMOUR, CHANTILLY.

stress is laid on the importance of properly proportioning the solids and the voids, which, as the author says, "distinguishes the work of the real artist of genius from that of the ordinary mechanical labourer who only works by routine " Chestnut, oak and ash were the woods most generally used, but almost any pliant wood served the purpose equally well. Chestnut laths. of lengths varying from

191.—DUTCH TRELLIS-WORK : XVII. CENTURY.

two feet to nine feet by about one inch in breadth, were sold in bundles for this purpose. The most general method of fastening the laths together was by means of one strand of iron wire, and not by nails (which is the method usual nowadays). When tied with wire the treillage lasts longer and any little irregularity in its lines is by no means objectionable.

Besides the construction of berceaux and all kinds of architectural features, the treillageur was expected to be skilful in the modelling of flowers and in composing garlands and bouquets, the leaves of which cut out from thin sheet-iron, were afterwards painted or gilt : " Garlands of jasmine, roses, honeysuckle and other creeping plants arranged in a happy disorder leave us in doubt as to whether we are the more affected by nature or by art. . . . The science of the Treillageur is not confined to their ateliers, it is not an art of routine, but wants experience, taste and a knowledge of geometry, of architecture (as regards decoration), of drawing and of design ; above all of flowers, to fashion them well and to compose garlands and bouquets."

There is no lack of engravings of French treillage. Mariette's ' Architecture à la Mode " gives many examples, and besides these there are the designs of Perelle, Langlois, Sylvestre, Le Pautre, Le Barbier, Née d'Argeuville and Jacques Boyceau. Watteau's well-known picture," Le Joueur de Flûte," and Lancret's " Partie des Plaisirs " have delightful circular treillage temples. Some drawings of Hutin preserved in the Bibliothèque Nationale show the superb treillage pavilions erected by the City of Paris in the Place Louis le Grand on the occasion of the marriage of the Dauphin in 1745. Baudoin's pictures

192 —TRELLISED WALL AND PERGOLA

of ' Le Midi" and " Le Goûter" and Binet's " La Nourrice Elegante " all show treillage designs.
Debucourt's engraving, " La Promenade de Paris," shows the circular pavilions that were erected at the
Palais Royal.

In Holland, trellis, or" latwerk," as it was called, was largely in demand for all classes of garden.
It is generally very solid in construction, and though lacking the grace of the French examples, it has,

193.—AT BRIDGE HOUSE.

nevertheless, a quaint charm of its own. A few examples are illustrated from " Den Nederlandtsen
Hovenier," a curious garden book published in 1670. At Broek, in one of the small gardens, 'there
is an elaborate pyramid of trellis, formed of laths not more than half an inch in width. There
is a curious collection of drawings of Dutch trellis in the Bibliothèque Nationale, Paris. Examples
are also to be found in many of the old books of views of the smaller country seats, such as

Van Nidek's " Het Zegepralend Kennemerland." As a rule, in Dutch treillage, ironwork was not so largely used as in French.

In England, trellis-work remained in fashion with but slight variations from Tudor days until the early part of the nineteenth century. It was first used to surround the flower-beds. In a painting representing Henry VIII. and his family at Hampton Court we see a garden with flower-beds surrounded by low trellis-work with intervening posts, upon which, were fixed heraldic beasts bearing vanes and shields with the King's arms and badges, and, judging from the accounts preserved of work done by Henry VIII. at Hampton Court after Wolsey's death in 1530, he must have made use of treillage very largely. We find described 180 posts and " 960yds. of rayle " painted white and green. In several illuminated MSS. in the British Museum are ·delightful little pictures of mediæval gardens giving examples of trellis ; in one a screen about four feet high and an arched gateway, the laths fixed diagonally with square posts ; in another the laths are spaced much wider apart to allow a hedge of roses to be trained. There is a very suggestive example in Didymus Mountaine's " The Gardener's Labyrinth," published in 1577 ; this shows a square enclosure with an inner parterre protected by a low trellis screen with ornamental pilasters surmounted by baskets of flowers. Bacon in his essay on the ideal garden does not despise trellis. " For the ordering of the ground . . . I leave it to a variety of device. . . . Little low hedges round like welts, with some pretty pyramids I like well ; and in some places fair columns upon frames of carpenters' work." The use of trellis in England was stimulated for a short time by the extraordinary Chinese craze, which followed the publication of Sir

194.—TREILLAGE PORTICO.

William Chambers' " Dissertation on Oriental Gardening " in 1772. The work created a commotion quite out of keeping with its value, and it·is said that, with the exception of·the preface, which is in earnest enough, the book is really a solemn joke, intended to mystify the public. Several of the pavilions he constructed at Kew are still remaining, but it is doubtful if any of his treillage could now be found. Examples of treillage will be recalled in many localities now remote and retired, but fashionable in the eighteenth century—screens, colonnades, verandahs and porches. In Chelsea and other parts of London that were fashionable in the late eighteenth century we may still occasionally come across some stray examples.

With regard to the further use of treillage, there are many purposes to which it is admirably suited. It has been used effectively in an eighteenth century house to enclose the well of a staircase. For a conservatory or winter-garden—parts of a house that are usually tacked on in so unsatisfactory a manner—the material is just sufficiently architectural to add to instead of detracting from the effect of the building, and a sage green treillage design against a plain white background has a pleasing effect. In covering up a blank wall no better means could be found than treillage decoration. In the garden it is suitable for every form of ephemeral structure : for a bandstand, a small garden theatre, a rose arbour or a porch. In many positions where light ironwork is too brittle, treillage might be substituted with advantage ; it is not nearly so costly, can be repaired with ease and any small broken piece restored. For all forms of enclosure it is particularly fitted, being so quickly and easily erected, and its position can be changed if required without much trouble. With treillage screens a garden in a new piece of ground is divided up and made " habitable " in a few weeks where hedges would have taken years to cultivate.

As to its colour, when oak is used, it attains in course of time a delightful silvery grey ; sometimes in the cheaper forms the brown tones of wood-preservatives are not unpleasing. Where it is coloured, the many tones of sage and peacock greens seem to be best, but very pleasing effects may be obtained by the use of two or more tints ; thus the front of the lath might be painted blue and the sides green, with emphasis given to certain small parts by touches of white or red   H. INIGO TRIGGS.

[An interesting example of a design obviously inspired by wood treillage, but translated into ironwork, is to be seen in the garden-house, Melbourne, Derbyshire, and is illustrated in Fig. 195.—ED.]

195 — AT MELBOURNE. DERBYSHIRE.

PERGOLAS.

The Need for Restrained Design in Garden Woodwork—French Influences—Admirable Examples at Easton Lodge—Pergolas and Their Greenery—Tea-house in Japanese Manner—Rustic Work.

IN all gardening of the formal type architectural details play a part of importance. The garden designer must be, indeed, either a trained architect or a man who has a very thorough acquaintance with certain phases of architectural practice, if he is to deal with the formal garden in the right spirit and to bring it into accord with the best traditions. It does not matter whether his design is to be carried out solely in growing vegetation which has to be clipped and shaped into definite and exactly calculated forms, or whether he proposes to associate trees and shrubs with structures in stone or wood which will count as salient facts in his plan and contrast picturesquely with the foliage in which they are set; the architectural spirit must prevail, or the result will be weak and unconvincing.

This is certainly true of pergolas, and, indeed, of all kinds of wood construction in the garden, which, whether plainly designed or fantastically and elaborately treated, must all have their due measure of artistic intention. Their effect must be considered beforehand, and the way in which they will contribute to the pictorial scheme which it should be the aim of every sincere garden-maker to work out must be fully foreseen. Chance should scarcely come within the view of their designer, or, at all events, only to a very limited extent; his accidents must be premeditated and prepared for, carefully led up to by judicious contrivances, and watched always in development lest they should get out of control.

196.—PERGOLA AT EASTON LODGE.

197.—RUSTIC PERGOLA AT APETHORPE.

So, it is necessary that any structure in wood, erected for the adornment of a garden, should agree in character and manner of construction with the character of the garden in which it is placed, and should be arranged in such a way that its specific architectural qualities cannot be destroyed by any over-growth of the creeping plants which this structure may be called upon to support. How admirably the adaptation

198.—AT EASTON LODGE: DESIGNED BY MR. PETO.

of wooden constructions to their surroundings can be managed is proved by the many important examples which can be referred to in the older French gardens, the designers of which appreciated fully the advantage of such additions to enhance the charm of the effects which they sought to produce. In France, indeed, the value of this type of erection, its suitability for its special purposes, its convenience and its many possibilities of picturesqueness have been fully understood and as fully demonstrated ; and the fashion which was established there so many years ago has found many followers in other countries.

Decidedly, our own garden designers have learned from their French predecessors a good deal worth knowing in this matter of constructing varieties of woodwork, and, what is more important, they have learned thoroughly how to adapt them to the requirements of British gardens. An excellent example of this judicious management of accessory details in garden design is afforded in what has been accomplished by Mr. H. A. Peto at Easton Lodge in Essex. The grounds of this house he has adorned with many architectural features ; some of these are in stone, but the rest are in wood, and are carried out with an amount of inventiveness and sincerity that would delight the most earnest of the older garden artists. Mr. Peto has fully appreciated the special advantages of wood construction in garden decoration and the way in which it can be introduced congruously among masses of trees and shrubs, and he has succeeded perfectly in bringing the forms of the erections he has designed into agreement with their surroundings. The most conspicuous feature of his design is the series of finely-proportioned pergolas which stretch along each side of the croquet lawn. These pergolas, with arched roofs carried on slender pillars, and with a central dome to break the great length of roof-line, are admirable illustrations of what can be done by a garden designer who respects the genius of his materials and has that sense of fitness upon which all real artistic achievement is founded. The purpose of the pergola—to be a support for climbing and flowering plants and to be covered eventually with masses of greenery—is by no means forgotten ; but equally the designer has remembered that the structure when completely covered with vegetation, and when its external details are hidden by leaves and flowers, should still be, when seen from within, an architectural fact showing a serious decorative intention and right consideration as a design. In such examples there is proof enough that wood construction, frankly and characteristically used, can be made dignified in effect and yet agreeably unpretentious. Indeed, not a little of the beauty of these particular pergolas comes from their simplicity ; no fantastic devices are employed in them to give an unnecessary quaintness and no purposeless ornament is introduced.

There is a similar reticence in the treatment of another feature which Mr. Peto has placed on the edge of the lake at Easton Lodge. Though it is used as a tea-house, it may well be included with pergolas, as the decorative problems involved are the same. In this case he has looked to the Japanese rather than to the French for inspiration, but he has used his own discretion freely in turning this inspiration to practical account, and the tea-house as he has designed it is much more an expression of his own artistic feeling than a reproduction of anything existing elsewhere. It is an attractive piece of wood construction, solid and substantial, and yet light and graceful in general effect. The true genius of building in wood is observed both in the main lines and in the smaller ornamental additions, and the proportion of the whole thing is very rightly adjusted.

It must not be forgotten that the essentially architectural type of pergola is not the only one which is permissible ; the familiar rustic kind is not unworthy of consideration. Such a one as exists at Apethorpe can be included among the varieties of wood construction. In this type the designer, having a general scheme of arrangement, profits by the accidents of line which come from the use of curiously curved and contorted pieces of wood. If he does not allow his taste for irregularity to get out of reasonable control, he can produce effects undeniably picturesque. But the hand of the artist is as necessary here as in more formal designing. In one case everything is thought out beforehand ; in the other the designer trusts to some extent to the inspiration of the moment and modifies his first intention as circumstances dictate. In both cases, however, the artist does not forget that there lies upon him an obligation to be true to the vital principles of his craft.   A. LYS BALDRY.

199.—A TEA-HOUSE.

ORANGERIES.

*The Orangery a Northern Device—Wren's Work at Kensington—The Value of Thick Sash-bars—
Exuberance of Treatment Permissible—The Orangery of a Dream.*

THE orangery is essentially a Northern type of building.   In Italy and the South of Europe
generally the orange tree is accustomed to winter out of doors; but when it began to be
imported into more Northern latitudes, winter housing was found to be a necessity.   It is
reputed to have been introduced into England by Sir Thomas Gresham, and he is shown in a
contemporary portrait with an orange in his hand.   But it seems more than probable that
his reputation for having done so has grown out of a momentary whim of the painter, who no doubt felt
the need of this colour note in a scheme of general sobriety, for it is certain that oranges were imported
and grown in England long before his time.   As early as Necham refers to their growth in a garden
at Holborn, and in 1480 it is on record that ten oranges could be procured in London for a silver penny.
By the year 1600 they must have been extensively cultivated, as at the end of the seventeenth century
a writer of the time gives a yield of Carew's orangery at Beddington as being upwards of ten
thousand oranges, the trees being one hundred years old at that time.   The building at Beddington
as two hundred feet long and, contrary to the usual custom, the trees were planted in the ground and
not in tubs.

At Versailles is an orangery of magnificent proportions   It lies to the south of the Parterre du
Midi, between two long
flights of marble stairs and
faces the Pièce d'eau des
Suisses.   It is vaulted inside, and the Doric columns
and entablature that form
the front are of truly colossal
dimensions.

In this country there
is probably no finer orangery
than that at Kensington
Palace. Coming, as it does,
from the hands of Wren, one
would naturally expect
much ; but it is wonderful
to see how by dint of simple,
just proportions and relief
he has invested a plain
oblong with so much in-
ferest.   Since it is in the
public part of the gardens,
there is no reason to de-
scribe it further ; but set

200.—AT LONG LEAT.

back, as it is, among the trees, the building might easily escape the notice of the passer-by in the Broad
Walk.   Happily, the ground in front of the Palace, till lately used for garden frames and manure, has
now been laid out again in a formal manner as a fit approach to the orangery.

Orangeries were rising in many directions while William III. and Anne were at work at Kensington,
and it is to this period that the fine, if reserved, example at Apethorpe belongs (Fig. 202).   It was
erected by the sixth Earl of Westmorland and stands on the west terrace, facing full south.   It is
of so simple an architectural character that it depends largely for effect on the thick sash-barring, which
has luckily escaped the nineteenth century plate-glass rage, now, fortunately, subsiding.   In the manner
of this old example, but much more ornate and full of its own individuality, is the new orangery at
Hestercombe designed by Mr. Lutyens (Fig. 203).   He was fortunate in persuading his client to revert
to this valuable form of garden architecture, and he has seized his opportunity with delightful result.
The Longleat orangery (Fig. 200) again shows the importance of adequately framing the great glazed voids.
Here it is carried out with wood mullions of considerable substance, each subsidiary section being

sub - divided with sash-barring. The effect is perfectly satisfying and gay.

At Margam the orangery is a really fine building, and the impression the photograph gives (Fig. 201) hardly does justice to its dimensions. Like so many buildings, it is attributed locally to Inigo Jones, though evidently of the period and probably the handiwork of Sir William Chambers. There is a delightful fragment at one end of it—the front of a porch or garden-house—that might well have been by Inigo Jones ; but this is probably not in its original position, and the two buildings are entirely distinct in any case.

201.—AT MARGAM.

The much smaller example at Heveningham (Fig. 205) has the appearance of emanating from the brain of Sir William Chambers' better-known contemporary, Robert Adam. The cold, restrained effect which he sought to give to his buildings finds expression also in the thinner sash-bars which he introduced. The glass roof, however, with its ornamental cast-iron work, is no part of his design, but a later addition, and the alteration results in a half-bred conservatory, partly because the walls are unnecessarily strong to carry the light glass roof, and also because they are excluding an unnecessary amount of sunshine for the altered purpose of the building. It would be easy to mention other instances up and down England, but, generally speaking, they are not possessed of much architectural quality. The ruling type has been that with tall sash windows between brick or stone piers and a hipped roof behind a parapet. But the architectural possibilities in orangery building are not yet exhausted. With very few exceptions, but little effort has been expended on them, and so long as they are used solely for their original purpose of

202.—AT APETHORPE.

housing the trees, any expense on the interior would be out of place. But now they are felt to be of so much use in the summer for social purposes, there is no reason why they should be left behind any other reception-room in the matter of decoration so long as it is of a permanent nature. There is a fine field on their north walls awaiting the skill of the fresco painter, and in their broad ceiling spaces lie opportunities for the worker in stucco, or for painters on whom the mantle of Tiepolo may have fallen.

If the orangery stands by itself as the focus of the garden, there is nothing on which fine workmanship

203.—THE ORANGERY AT HESTERCOMBE.

may be more fitly lavished.   Whether it be in sculptured caryatides along the front or graceful lead figures over the parapet, a certain exuberance of ornament will not be out of place here, or clash with the sobriety of the house.   It stands for the modern temple of Flora, and that is sufficient excuse.   But it is as an annexe to the house that the future of the orangery probably lies, and in that position its exterior ornateness must be subservient to the rest of the scheme.   Fashion has changed nowadays in several matters that intimately affect country-house building.   In the first place, people pay much shorter visits than they did in the old days, so that less accommodation is required.   The brewhouse, and often the laundry too, is no longer a requirement, as these things are " done out," and, lastly, motors do not need anything like the space that used to be taken up with long ranges of stabling and coach-houses. In short, the dependencies are fewer and the roof area less, and without a certain range of buildings to treat it is difficult—nay, impossible—for the architect to get much effect out of any scheme.   But we still have the orangery, and in this connection it is a godsend.   It must almost of necessity cover a good deal of ground, and it may be marshalled with the main building so as to save the situation.

In the ideal home that I have half promised myself to build for my declining years you will come to the orangery on the left as you step out into the court garden from the corridor beyond the hall.   It will balance the kitchen wing on the right, and the sun will begin to creep in a little before midday.   It

204.—AT CASSIOBURY PARK.

will be paved in stone diamonds and softly carpeted down the centre, and will form the buffer state between my own sancta at the end and the rest of the house, which may be as noisy as it likes with women and children.   You can picture to yourself the double row of well-kept shrubs, down which the servant will come with noiseless tread to announce an intruder on my solitude, and the pleasant odours of flowering things that will take their place in the summer

As the orangery is essentially for winter housing of the trees which, in summer, will stand out in the paved court or border the parterre, it forms a capital place when empty for wet-day games or tor tea during garden-parties, as the practice is at Osterley and elsewhere.   Some years ago it was not unusual for an architect to be told that a conservatory in connection with the new house was to be worked in at any cost. He could see the request coming and it always made him sad.   Happily, it is not so common now, though ants in the house have possibly had more to do with it than a better understanding of architecture.   An

205.—AT HEVENINGHAM.

f certain solidity in construction, while a conservatory must be all voids. From an of view there is very little to be done with the latter. As soon as a support is thickened obliterated there is the gardener to reckon with. But orangeries since first adopted , roofed in, and the piers between the windows have generally been of ample width to the wall surface. Hence they are to the architect as welcome an appendage to a house the reverse. F. INIGO THOMAS.

GLASSHOUSES.

Greenhouse or Conservatory?—Need for Simplicity in Greenhouse Design—Conservatories for a Moving Pageant of Garden Life—An Interesting Glass Corridor.

WE generally class our glasshouses, according as they are in close association with the dwelling or away in the kitchen garden, under the two headings of conservatory and greenhouse. Neither of these two words do we now use with etymological correctness. A glasshouse opening from the dwelling is, or should be, for the temporary display of plants at their best and not for their continued conservation. The term "greenhouse" dates from those Queen Anne days when the fashionable collections of evergreens needed protection, and their collector loved to be described as "a master of curious greens." To-day the greenhouse is the place for the propagation. and growth of plants—it is the workshop and store rather than the showroom. Therefore, the more light and air the better, and it should have as much glass surface and as complete a ventilation system as possible. Such buildings cannot have the least claim to beauty. They are tiresome in form, tone and texture. They should be in a special and well-screened section of the kitchen garden, and designed as simply as possible, with avoidance of decorative ridges, finials and such-like trivialities. This, unfortunately, has not been fully realised by the general run of either the makers or users of this very necessary adjunct to the country house, and it has often been thoughtlessly located in reference to the general lay out of a place. It is true that greenhouses—like the kitchen garden in general—want to be in a thoroughly open situation, and such is apt to be conspicuous. It is, however, almost invariably possible in making a general design to find means to hide them. This may be difficult where a very extensive range of houses, intended for every sort and condition of plant-life, is deemed essential. For the ordinary requirements of a moderate-sized country house, however, a set of fairly low span-roofed houses (with, perhaps the addition of a still lower line of heated frames and melon-houses running in front of them) satisfies all requirements, and is perfectly practical and handy. No form of arrangement, be it for plant or fruit growing, can more effectually meet all cultural requirements at moderate cost. There are few places where a set of houses such as the group of three that is illustrated cannot be so placed as to be invisible from house and grounds either through natural conditions of site or by the interposition of outbuildings and walls or the planting of an evergreen belt or massif. It is therefore much to be hoped that Messrs. Boulton and Paul will instil this truth into their clients' minds, and so be able constantly to repeat variations of this simple design, which only needs the abandonment of the perfectly useless though, in this case, not very objectionable finial to make it satisfactory. Should a complete screen be impossible, it is well to paint all the woodwork of such houses a dull light green or lead colour on

206.—SIMPLE GLASSHOUSES.

the outside. But the inside should still be white, as conducive to that thorough cleanliness and light that are among the first desiderata where plant-growing is the object.

With regard to the conservatory, it is quite a different matter. This is a building for another purpose and in another place, and therefore quite distinct principles should prevail. It is part of the dwelling, and should harmonise and group with it in the matter of both form and material. Nothing can be more distressing than the glass and iron adjuncts that are so often tacked on to houses, and are made all the more painfully obtrusive by attempts at cheap ornamentation. Many a well-designed house, old and new, has been degraded by such association. Leading makers have sought to rival each other in the production of every sort of gimcrack ornament, of every exaggeration of sky-line, of every impossible combination of architectural forms reduced to irritating exiguity in combination with sheets of glass developed to the utmost extent. Now the strange thing is that this class of conservatory is not only unbeautiful in itself, but also is ill-fitted for its purpose. Once a plant has been brought to perfection and is decked with its blooms, it ceases to require excessive light, which only causes the flowers to pass away rapidly and fade. For the purpose of the display of plants the area of transparent glass need certainly not be greater than the area of opaque material. Architecture, therefore, becomes possible, and a design in sympathy with that of the rest of the building may perfectly well be devised. If the conservatory is arranged as a sort of wing touching the house on one side only, and with the other three sides open to the air, the orangery type that arose before the end of the seventeenth century and continued throughout the eighteenth century will answer perfectly. So placed, the conservatory may depend for light and air upon glazed-in arches on its three sides, and there need be no glass in the roof. But a roof all, or partly, of glass will be needed if the site and conditions make it impossible to introduce glass in as many as three sides; in that case the glass in the roof may be screened by a parapet. What has been termed the "orangery type" associates charmingly with houses of its own period—that is, with the various manifestations of classic architecture from the time of Christopher Wren to that of Robert Adam.

207.—A NEW CONSERVATORY ADDED TO AN OLD HOUSE.

It is more difficult to get the right thing when the house is in an earlier manner, as the original designers knew of nothing of the kind. Still, the problem is perfectly capable of solution, and one such attempt shall now be described and illustrated. It was desired to have a place for the display of plants opening out of a room of a house that originated in the fifteenth century and had nothing later about it than the first decade of the seventeenth. Some of the older portions of the house were ruined, and there was a space enclosed on three sides by the remaining walls of a destroyed dining-hall. This was fixed on as the site of the conservatory. It will be seen that the fourth side is composed, above a stone plinth, of a framework of oak, formed into a continuous line of transomed leaded casements, the line being only broken by a double oak door in the centre, and being surmounted by an oak entablature that screens the glazed portion of the roof. This occupies two-thirds of the roof space, the remaining one-third being a ferro-concrete flat, forming a walk reached by a little stone stairway up one of the ancient walls and being used for the service of outside blinds that shade the roof glass. The glazed side faces north-west, and does not admit so much sun as to make blinds necessary. The whole of the upper range of casements is made to open. This, with the doorway, provides ample ventilation; while a through draught can be created on sultry days by also opening a door in the opposite wall. The conservatory is warmed by a large radiator, served by the same furnace that heats the house. Every week there is a partial change in the plants that tenant it. Such a conservatory should never be crowded—should never be congested with

208.—CONSERVATORY AT EYDON HALL

209.—THE CONSERVATORY AT RANELAGH.

a little of everything at all stages of growth, but adorned with a few kinds of plants in considerable batches, freely disposed and left there only as long as they are at their best. Towards the close of the year the chrysanthemum, with its many manifestations, will reign supreme. It should not, however, monopolise the whole space. A very satisfactory and easily-treated plant of quite contrasting aspect is Saxifraga Fortunei. Except in favoured spots it is not quite hardy, but it may be grown on out of doors through spring and summer, and will produce an abundance of its feathery white panicles rising from fleshy leaves for a November display under cover.

With the beginning of the year come the forced bulbs—freesias, hyacinths, polyantha daffodils and the like. Height, greenery and form may be given to the grouping by palms for those who like them, or by a good batch of Nandina domestica where palms are unsympathetic. A dozen or two of great pots full of clivias may be used with effect throughout February and March, and there will be such annuals as schizanthus, primula and Cineraria stellata. Easily-forced hardy shrubs will now begin to be introduced.

210.—AT THE PLEASANCE, GULLANE.

The earliest may well be the forsythias, and the single kerria should be used to continue the yellow colouring. Lilacs and cherries, bladder nuts and mock oranges are just a sample of the many shrubs that with very little trouble and very little greenhouse space may be used to make the conservatory a place of continuous and varied beauty and interest throughout the colder months of the year. In summer it is of less importance. Yet it needs decking, and this is easily done by geraniums, begonias, gloxinias and a host of other beautiful florists' flowers, above whose somewhat lowly growth of steeple-like plants of Campanula pyramidalis and groups of the taller lilies may rise in their due season.

Another quite satisfactory scheme is the glass corridor at the Pleasance, Gullane (designed by Mr. Sydney Mitchell to connect a drawing-room and music-room), of which both exterior and interior views are shown. The glazed side is the same in feeling as the example just described, but is made to consort with a rather later style of architecture. The roof is wholly of glass, as a good many permanently-planted subjects, especially climbers, were desired, and this called for abundant light. But the glass roof is unobtrusive, its flatness rendering it almost imperceptible from the outside, while, within, it is much screened by the pergola fashion adopted for the training of the climbers. Even those who aim at a sort of winter garden—that is, a large, light glazed and warmed space where sizable shrubs and plants that give foliage and flower effect in winter may be grown—can easily develop this idea and create a building of the required size that does not jar with the house to which it is attached. Such has been successfully attempted at Ranelagh in full architectural manner, while the simple example at Eydon Hall is in full harmony with the ancient and quiet flavour of that delightful little Derbyshire seat.   H. AVRAY TIPPING.

211.—GLASS CORRIDOR.

IRON GATES AND RAILINGS.

Jean Tijou and His Work—The Novelty of His Technique—The Greatest Designer of Ironwork· in England—An Injustice to His Memory.

THE arrival of the Prince and Princess of Orange in 1689 was a momentous event in the history of English smithcraft, for soon afterwards we hear for the first time of a famous craftsman and designer, M. Jean Tijou. He was a Protestant and apparently a Frenchman, but came over presumably with his great patrons, whence it may be concluded that he was a Huguenot refugee in Holland. He may have worked there, for many engravings of the great Dutch châteaux show lofty and impressive iron screens to forecourts and gardens, but neither there nor in France is his name recorded. He came to settle and to work, and before the close of 1690 had rendered two bills for work executed at Hampton Court, the first for six iron vanes and a rich balcony, " finely wrought in leaves and Scrollwork," and the second for the garden screen with two pairs of great iron gates and two other little gates on each side, eight square pillars of ornaments, twelve panels and ten pilasters between them ' for the circle of the Fountain Garden at Hampton Court." The two bills came to £80 and £755 7s. respectively. The Fountain Garden was the semi-circular garden on the east or principal front, formed at the expense of the Home Park by Charles II., and which Evelyn saw being finished in 1689. The great gates and pillars are the still existing " Lion Gates," which closed the two broad walks which were continued as avenues in the Home Park, and the panels and pilasters are the famous screens, which after three removals have been re-erected on their old foundations in the Privy Garden by the Office of Works, in the belief that this was their original position. The Fountain Garden was originally small, and the high and rich screens were valuable as shutting it out from the public gaze. There has been

212.—PANEL IN GARDEN SCREEN AT HAMPTON COURT BY TIJOU.

much misunderstanding as to the original position of the screen ; but it is quite clear, first, that it was completed in 1690 ; secondly, that it was not in the Privy Garden when the Queen died in 1694, because Sutton Nicholl's remarkably clear engraving of this in 1695 does not show it there ; and Gibson describes the Hampton Court Garden in 1691 as a large plat " environed with an iron palisade round about next the park, laid out with walks," etc. " The Fountain Garden " was the then new garden with five fountains and three broad, radiating walks, two of which led directly to and were continuous with the avennes in the Home Park, and required large gates to close them, while the third led straight to the long-water. The Privy Garden was not taken in hand till some years later ; it over-looks the river and did not need such a screen, and never could have comprised large carriage gates and wickets, which would have opened on to the foreshore, and for which there is no room. Mr. Law in his exhaustive account of Hampton Court states, on the authority of the gardener Switzer, that little work was done at Hampton Court between the death of the Queen in 1694 and the burning of

213.—THE FORECOURT GATES TO DRAYTON HOUSE: PROBABLY BY JEAN TIJOU.

Whitehall Palace in 1698, when the works were resumed with vigour. An outer semi-circle of eight new fountains was added, necessitating an outlay of £987 14s. for lead pipes, and £2,132 16s. for 1,442ft. of iron railing to enclose the garden on both sides. The screen could not maintain its position in the enlarged scheme, but the great gates did, being merely removed further from the house and still closing the avenues. Simultaneously £832 was expended in masonry for the Privy Garden, which was sunk 10ft., the old mount removed and utilised to form a raised walk around with a semi-circular end to receive the screen minus the gates, as shown in Kip's view of 1708. We learn from Ralph Thoresby that it was painted and gilt in parts when he saw it in 1712. The screen was not wanted in its new

214.—GATES AT BURLEY-ON-HILL: PROBABLY BY JEAN TIJOU.

215.—WILLIAM III. GATE AT ALDERMASTON.

216.—GATES OF 1709 AT BEDDINGTON.

position, and, in fact. must have blocked the view which had been obtained at great expense—necessitating the removal of the old garden mount and the newly-built water gallery. It was removed some time prior to 1782, when the Hon. Daines Barrington described it to the Society of Antiquaries as forming part of the " magnificent gates and rails of iron," extending parallel to the Thames for six hundred yards. One of the twelve panels with their pilasters formed a break at intervals of fifty yards, and a set of the larger gates formed a centre, and the plain rails between are perhaps those which stretched the whole width of the east or garden front of the Palace. The panels were removed in 1865 to South Kensington Museum, then scantily filled, and later were distributed over other museums ; they have recently, after somewhat injudicious restoration, been replaced on their old foundations at the end of the Privy Garden by the river. No such sumptuous garden screen has been produced before or since.

The novelty of Tijou's work consisted in his lavish use of sheet iron, embossed into acanthus leaves, rosettes, masks, garlands, crowns and various insignia, in the French manner, not previously seen in England, indeed, as almost to conceal the forgings. It is quite clear from the book of designs published by Tijou in 1693 that he was a practical designer of embossing, and not of

217.—INWOOD: BY A CONTEMPORARY OF TIJOU.

smith's work, which he did not at that time understand. He probably worked personally at least on the masks and difficult pieces, for they are full of expression and of a fine character never attained by anyone else. He met at the outset his greatest patron, Queen Mary, and all his sumptuous designs for Hampton Court were made and arranged to be executed before her death, Estimates for them were apparently not required. His gratitude is fittingly expressed, in the French manner, on the title-page of his book. There the Queen reclines as Juno. attended by Vulcan, Mercury, Saturn, Amorini and a group of the Arts, inspecting specimens of the work. Tijou also appears to have had a free hand at Burleigh, at Chatsworth and a few places elsewhere ; but the Queen's early death was a blow from which he perhaps never quite recovered. When work was resumed at Hampton Court after an interval of four years, Tijou was required to give estimates, and only one piece of his rich work was required, the balustrade for the King's staircase designed while the Queen was living. The King's death in 1702 deprived him of his remaining Royal

218.—ITALIAN GATES AT INWOOD.

219.—GATES AT HARROWDEN HALL.

patron, for Queen Anne does not seem to have given him commissions, and some of the work for Hampton Court appears to be by other hands. Nor does she seem to have been anxious to pay his accounts which were disputed. His work at St. Paul's, magnificent as it is, does not appear to have been given him freely, and the ironwork there was shared with two other smiths. Wren apparently never liked him, and never mentions him, and there were again difficulties with the accounts. Tijou, disappointed and poor, quitted the country about 1710 or 1711, leaving his wife to collect a balance due for work at St. Paul's. A living descendant informs me that he died abroad, broken-hearted, leaving two sons. He came over accompanied probably by assistants, seeing the large amount of work he accomplished in the first year, and that he would not have found craftsmen here at once capable of embossing. Some may have been of his own name, for there are records of the burial of a Mrs. Ann Tijou, died 1708, and of a Mr. Tijou without initials, who died 1709, in St. Martin's Church, where his daughter was married to the celebrated artist Laguerre. He describes himself in his book as " of London," and his works were thus no doubt in St. Martin's parish, where the name still lingers. His death probably took place in Paris, for a smith, Louis Fordrin of that city, became possessed of the engraved copper plates and issued reprints from them in his own name, claiming to be designer and executant. He must have had Tijou's drawings as well, for he made good use of them.

Tijon was the greatest designer and worker in iron who has appeared in England. Whether, as a foreigner, his memory should be perpetuated is a matter for others to decide ; but French authorities class his work as English. In the meantime the greatest possible injustice has been done to his memory. Among the statues on the exterior of the new Victoria and Albert Museum is one to a person named Huntington Shaw, from Nottingham, who is put there to represent ·British smithcraft. Nothing whatever is known of him except that in Hampton Church there is a marble tablet to his memory, which formed part of a large and fantastic monument twelve feet high, erected in the churchyard against the wall of the church by Benjamin Jackson, Queen Anne's Master Mason at Hampton Court, apparently as a labour of love, for he was sole executor. Shaw died in 1710, aged fifty-one, and the inscription ended, " he was an artist in his way," as recorded by Lyson, leaving half the tablet vacant to commemorate his widow. The church was burnt and the monument destroyed, except the tablet, which was scraped, cleaned and fixed inside the church in 1833. The vacant space was tnen filled up by the addition of the following words, " he·designed and executed the ornamental ironwork at Hampton Court Palace." The Board of Education should be perfectly aware that there is not a particle of truth in this assertion, as an official enquiry was made on their behalf [313, 25-7-'83] which failed to find any mention of such a person, and placed beyond all doubt that Tijou was alone responsible for all the important work there. There is no mention anywhere of Huntington Shaw, and ·Nottingham was not, and never has been, a school of artistic smithing. As far as is known he may equally well have been a stone-mason or wood-carver. Anyhow, if Tijou is not to be honoured, and I believe we have his portrait if it should be required, there are many other great English smiths, his contemporaries, who deserve to occupy the position accorded to this entirely mythic smith.   J. STARKIE GARDNER.

220.—THE CLOSED GATES OF TRAQUAIR.

STATUES ON GATEPIERS.

*The Decorative Value of Statues on Gatepiers—Examples at Hertford, Maidenhead and
Temple Dinsley—The Alternative Use of Vases—And the Most Suitable Types.*

IN the last chapter Mr. Starkie Gardner gave an account of the greatest influence that English ironwork has known, Jean Tijou.   In the complete picture presented by a beautiful entrance, however,
the adornment of the gatepiers often plays a very important part, as will now appear.   At Christ's
Hospital, Hertford, the gatepiers and adjoining screen walls were fortunately left unharmed when
the rest of the Hospital was lately rebuilt.   Fig. 221 shows them surmounted by a pair
of Bluecoat Boys in lead.   The following extract from a minute of the Court of Christ's Hospital,
held on March 27th, 1696, enables the work to be dated with reasonable accuracy : " It was thought fit
that the Pieres on each side of the gate be adorned with a Blewcoat Boy on the top thereof for incitement
to Travellers and others to be charitable to the Hospitall."

The faith of the Governors seems to have been justified, for some benefactor provided them in lead.
It cannot have been long after the beginning of the eighteenth century that the boys seen in the picture

221.—AT CHRIST'S HOSPITAL, HERTFORD.

of the gates took their place.   One of them is also illustrated to a larger scale in Fig. 223.   When
taken down about thirty years ago for repairs they were found to be very heavy and full of sand, the
remains of the casting core.   Doubtless, in those days the figures were painted as they are to-day in

their proper colours, and the familiar blue gown and yellow stockings would have attracted the passer-by and incited him to charity more vigorously than if left in the natural grey of the unpainted lead.

About the gatepiers at Hall Place, Maidenhead, the residence of Sir Gilbert A. Clayton East, there is a gayer atmosphere (Fig. 225). The children there bear a rake and hayfork, and suggest the care of the trim lawns within the gates they guard. They are pleasant little people; the maiden with the fork has a string of flowers round her neck, and her hair is twisted into an engaging little knot. The gates are not at the main entrance, but lead to the Swan Garden. They were not made for Hall Place, but came from a house at Hampton Court. As they bear the initials "J.E.," and as there has been no John in the East family since the John East who died in 1679, it seems reasonable to assign them to the third quarter of the seventeenth century, an assumption which is supported by the design of the gates themselves, though the little lead figures may very well be of some fifty years later. It was not until the

222.—CUPID AT TEMPLE DINSLEY.

Revolution of 1689 and the accession of William III that lead statues came into the great vogue which they enjoyed until 1787, when John Cheere died and his leadyard at Hyde Park Corner was closed. He was the successor in business of Jan Van Nost, a Dutchman who followed William to England, and turned out figures in such great numbers that they can still be traced in a score of English gardens. It is not necessary to attribute every lead statue to him, as he had competitors in Scheemakers, Charpentier and others; but many of the most popular types can safely be attributed to him.

Another illustration shows one of a delightful pair of leaden Cupids at Temple Dinsley, which stand not on the piers of the gates themselves, but at the end of the curved stretches of railing which enclose the forecourt. These figures are of about 1720, and though, like most of the similar work of the period, they lack any marked distinction *qua* sculpture, they have the pleasant sentimental air which befits garden ornaments.

The pictures show how attractive the piers of entrance gates, otherwise uninteresting, may be made by the addition of little figures. Lead or stone vases are also suitable to give the same sense of finish; but a word of warning may be added. Such vases should not be of a type that seems to demand use as a flower-pot.

223.—A BLUECOAT BOY IN LEAD

224.—SIMPLE STONE VASES AT HARTHAM PARK

The writer recently saw a gateway adorned by replicas of the famous open vases on the terrace at Hampton Court, and the effect was distinctly unhappy. If a vase is to be used, it should either be of the type pictured in Fig. 224 or of the covered urn pattern   L. W.

225.—AT HALL PLACE, MAIDENHEAD.

STATUES ON BUILDINGS.

The Filling of Empty Niches—An Old Statue in a New Niche—Christ's Hospital, Hertford —
Samuel Taylor Coleridge on Pudding—Charles Lamb's Silence—In Praise of Modern Statues.

THERE are so many empty niches on houses of the eighteenth century, and on modern houses designed in the same spirit, that it is worth while to consider how such voids may be filled. Christ's Hospital, Hertford, supplies examples, the more interesting because one of them shows an old statue occupying a new niche. They have ripe associations, for both of those illustrated adorn that branch of the Hospital which is now wholly devoted to the girls of the Foundation, though a part of the buildings has a larger history. When the great school was founded, the

226.—AN OLD STATUE IN A NEW NICHE.

beneficiaries of the City of London's charity were not only "children under education," but "children out at nurse." By the seventeenth century it had become the practice to send the little children to Hoddesdon, Ware and Hertford, to houses which were in charge of matrons. In 1697 most of the Ware and Hoddesdon children were moved to Hertford, where the hospital buildings had been reconstructed and greatly enlarged a few years earlier; but the Ware premises continued in partial use for a considerable period. Over the Ware front gates was originally placed the figure of a Bluecoat Boy, now fixed in the niche on the front of the School Hall at Hertford. In the old days of the Foundation practically all the Bluecoat children were first sent to Hertford. Every year in March the Treasurer and two or more of the Governors would go there and pick out about fifty boys and twenty girls to be moved to London, and this continued in a modified form as late as 1891. After the removal of Christ's Hospital to its country home at Horsham, the Hertford buildings were wholly given over to the girls' branch. The buildings have been lately reconstructed, leaving practically nothing of the old work except the delightful gatepiers and that part of the original girls' school which faces the street. Here, standing in plain brick niches, are two most attractive figures of Bluecoat Girls, which date from about 1780. The very notable feature of these and of the boy on the School Hall is their material—oak. The figures on the gatepiers (illustrated in the last chapter) are of lead, which is far more usual; but despite the more perishable nature of oak, the girl and boy which appear in the accompanying picture are in admirable repair. Though all three are rather minutely carved, their surfaces have suffered but little with age. The characteristic garb of the boy, in Charles Lamb's words. "as it is antique and venerable, feeds his self-respect," while the little cap and dress of the girls give them a demure aspect altogether delightful. The sculptor, whoever he was, evidently saw no signs of "the unruly and disorderly carriage and behaviour of the Girls" which so vexed the Treasurer on his visit in 1715. From the little roll which the child holds in her hand, it is clear that he

227.—A MODERN STATUE AT BARNET.

wished to emphasise the work of the Writing Master rather than of the Matron, whose duty it was to see that they learnt to knit and use their needles. Samuel Taylor Coleridge spent a year at Hertford before he was moved to London, and wrote of it, " I was very happy on the whole, for I had plenty to eat and drink, and we had pudding and vegetables almost every day " : an Elysian state of things which did not always obtain in the historic home of the Blues in London. It is odd that Charles Lamb never went to the Hertford school, because he was only seven years old when he was entered. Odder still, that with all his passion for Hertfordshire in general, and for Blakesware in particular, he never referred to the schools at Ware or Hertford, though Blakesware was so near the former. One almost nourishes a grudge against that gentle spirit for ignoring the little statue at Ware that he must have seen so often. Neither in his " Recollections of Christ's Hospital " nor in " Christ's Hospital Five and Thirty Year Ago " does he as much as mention the existence of the Hertfordshire schools, and we are left to Coleridge, " the *inspired charity boy* " of the latter essay for some of the little knowledge we have of them.

In the example of a modern statue in a modern niche the architect of the house which they adorn has designed the niche in a simple vein, and very charming is the little sportsman, evidently bent on very

228.—AT CHRIST'S HOSPITAL, HERTFORD.

moderate bloodshed.   Just the right note seems to be struck by this treatment.   With the Georgian manner taking deeper root in our domestic architecture, such niches will become more usual features of house design, and it will be unfortunate if they are left untenanted.   In the great grave mansions of two centuries ago, Hercules and the Cymbal Player, Venus de Medici and the Apollo Belvedere found their homes on stately pedestals in the shadow of lofty niches ; but these heroes and goddesses " all standing naked in the open air ", are little suitable for the small country houses of to-day.   Rather would one adopt the graceful conventions of such little clothed figures as make gracious the walls of Barnet Court.   The child illustrated and his sister, a little girl regarding a frog which rests on her hand, are cast in lead, a suitable material, far more durable than the oak of which the Bluecoat children at Hertford are made. It needs no painting and, indeed, should be spared the indignity, but will take on with time a silvery patina that will stand out the more pleasantly as the rich red of the brickwork behind it darkens and mellows

L. W.

229.—THE CYMBAL PLAYER AT ROUSHAM.

HARD COURTS FOR LAWN TENNIS.

Tennis all the Year Round—The Influence of Hard Courts on an Improved Game—Detailed Instructions for the Making of Hard Courts.

IN an eloquent lecture on the advantages of being an Englishman, Mr. G. W. E. Russell included among them our climate, on the ground that, bad as it might be for games, it was good, in that it made us Northerners able to play the supreme game of give and take. It is precisely our climate that has invented the hard tennis court, and our love of games the necessity for having it. There can be no doubt that lawn tennis would be much more played than it is if one could only depend on the weather ; but with many wet summers it becomes a hazardous business to rely on the ordinary grass court. As most people are out to get a game, rather than to practise patience under difficulties, it becomes a question how it can be played without reference to the weather. This is answered by the hard court, upon which play is possible unless it is actually raining, or after a frost, when the surface is apt to kick up. It gives us lawn tennis (or, rather, hard court tennis) for twelve months in the year. One of its effects is the possibility of exercise during the winter, and its general adoption would bring a general improvement in the game. A good many men play badminton now for practice in the off-season ; and inasmuch as lawn tennis is only an adaptation of badminton, as first played in India, there may be something in the idea. There is, however, no comparison between the games—the one played in the fresh air, with all the consequent exhilaration, the other in a stuffy hall in a dust-laden atmosphere. Also, there is a very fundamental difference between the line of flight of a tennis ball and that of a badminton shuttlecock, so that an eye trained to take the shuttlecock may miss the ball. If, then, our lawn tennis players could play the game all the year round, there would be a marked increase in their numbers, consequent on the greater certainty with which fixtures may be made. Players would improve their

230.—A HARD TENNIS COURT.

game and more men of promise be discovered to graduate eventually at Wimbledon and represent us against Colonial cousins.

As to the joy of the game played on a hard court on a winter's day there can be no doubt. To don flannels and take a racket from the press seems a startling thing to do in November, and you slink off in overcoat to the astonishment of passers-by, who clearly doubt your sanity. Until you warm to the game the north-east wind treats the tennis shirt as a covering of little moment, but at " fifteen. all," this hardly troubles, and at the end of the set you will have to be sternly advised to get into your overcoat again because you are so hot. There is no pat-ball on a hard court, and the service comes off the billiard-table-like surface as true and hard as a bullet. Hard courts are not as expensive to make in the first case as grass courts, and are much easier to maintain. As to the making, care should be taken to choose as level a part of the garden as possible so as to save expense in digging. An area one hundred and twenty feet by sixty feet is needed. The first step is to remove the top soil one spit deep all over. This should be wheeled away for use in making up borders, or it can be sold, and the proceeds go to reduce the cost. It is essential that the top spit be taken off, as the whole idea of the hard court is that rain shall readily drain through it, and so leave a dry surface fit to be played upon ; if underneath the ballast one leaves this layer, which is full of vegetable matter, the final result will not be satisfactory.

The nature of the subsoil is the next determining factor. In any case it must be levelled, and a dead-level court is to be prepared. It spoils the game if, as a result of guessing " rough " or " smooth " correctly, a move is made to one side of the nest which has an advantage of level over the other. Also, in a hard court, it is absurd to expect that any fall in the actual surface will help to drain—rain goes through at once, so draining must be dealt with underneath. If the subsoil is a stiff clay, the upper surface of it must be graded to fall to channels. In these are placed ordinary agricultural draining-pipes, which need to be taken to a ditch or soak-away sump hole. Where the subsoil is sand or gravel the only necessary precaution is to take off the vegetable top spit, which would serve to keep the moisture from draining through into the subsoil. This stage successfully passed, there remains the provision of the materials for the formation of the court, and those indigenous to the neighbourhood will obviously be the cheapest. The essential quality is that they should not disintegrate by reason of climatic influences, and that they should have the further property of packing down hard and not easily becoming loose or friable.

Perhaps a description of the materials used in the court which is illustrated may serve as guidance in judging how far local materials may be suitable. The bottom layer was of gas clinker—this was put on six inches thick, and rolled down with a heavy horse-roller to about four inches, all large pieces being broken with a hammer. The second layer was of burnt clay ballast, three inches thick, rolled down to two inches with a lighter roller pulled by three men, and water was prodigally used to consolidate the mass. The court as finished is very successful, but there is always the danger that clay ballast may not be thoroughly burnt, and so show a tendency to revert to clay. Another material very suitable for the second coat is the refuse left after a clamp of bricks have been burnt and cleared away, and there is less fear of reversion here, as the heat generated in a brick clamp is fiercer and more constant than in burning ballast.

The final coat was two inches of sifted burnt gravel, put on and rolled with a lighter roller (again with much water) to a thickness of one inch. A local brickfield burns gravel by means of rubbish, and this, again, is safer than the burnt clay ballast. It was at first feared that little splinters of flint, caused by the burning, might cut the balls, but the result has proved otherwise, and this final coat is very satisfactory and hard-wearing. To mark the line of demarcation between ballast and grass, pieces of wood four inches by two inches were set up edgeways, the top being level with the court and nailed to uprights let into it. All the wood was tarred, and on this line the ten-foot galvanised wire netting was set up with iron standards, as balls must not be allowed near damp grass.

The only remaining details are the fixing in concrete of sockets to take the net posts, as the ordinary attachment would, of course, pull up out of the ballast ; and the addition of a little plaster of Paris to the whiting when the court is marked out, which makes the lines last longer. A general point to be remembered is that in the making and the after maintenance of the court rolling cannot be overdone.

Enough has been written to show that it is a comparatively simple matter to form a hard court, and that its success depends mainly on the suitability of the materials used. As to the labour, any agricultural labourer or gardener can easily do the work.   C. H. B. QUENNELL.

USES OF REINFORCED CONCRETE.

A New Form of Construction—Its Suitability for Country Estate Work—Stables and Mangers—
Garden Retaining Walls and Tanks—Culverts and Bridges.

IN the last fifty-five years there has been a gradual growth of a novel form of construction, which only began to show real development in this country in the past ten years. This revolution in construction, for it is no less, is not yet in full bloom. For those to whom concrete is nothing but a name, it may be explained that it is a mixture, in certain definite proportions, of a hard, inert aggregate and a cement. The aggregate will be broken brick or stone, or, generally, gravel of regulated size with a proportion of sand; the material which binds the whole together will be lime or Portland cement, according to the purpose for which the concrete is required, Portland cement being used always for reinforced concrete. These ingredients, thoroughly mixed together with a sufficiency of water, form a kind of pudding that sets into an exceedingly hard and practically imperishable mass. Concrete has often been used in conjunction with steel to protect it against fire and corrosion. The new method of construction, called reinforced concrete, is, however, very different from ordinary steelwork, though it employs steel in conjunction with concrete. Steel is a material strong both in tension and in compression; concrete, on the other hand, is comparatively weak in tension, but strong in compression—in other words, it is strong but brittle. For resisting compressive forces concrete is much more economical than steel, provided that its greater bulk does not preclude its use. In a reinforced concrete beam steel is put on the tension side, embedded in the concrete, which itself serves to take the compression; in the combination, therefore, both concrete and steel are serving the functions for which they are respectively adapted in an economical way. If steel is introduced into a concrete pillar, the tendency for the tensional forces to snap the brittle concrete is counteracted. In arch construction we may have either pure compression or a combination of bending and compression; in either case the reinforcing of the concrete by small sections of steel is very advantageous. Though the advantages thus secured are very considerable, the amount of steel is notably small in all reinforced concrete construction, amounting only to about one per cent. in bulk. In general considerable economy in first cost is effected, while, furthermore, the concrete has the property of protecting the steel from corrosion and renders the structure fire-resisting, so that economy is effected both in the upkeep of painting and in reduction of fire risk. Reinforced concrete will serve in almost all cases in place of steel, stonework, brickwork, or other structural material.

231.—CATTLE STALL DIVISIONS.

Reinforced concrete has been applied to so many and varied purposes, and has made such tremendous strides, that it is difficult to forecast its future limitations. Even where there is no saving in first cost, reinforced concrete is often preferable to other materials because of its durability, its fire resistance, hygienic quality and general efficiency. In the present chapter a few of the applications of reinforced concrete in and about the country house will be described, though the list cannot be exhaustive, for every day it is being put to fresh uses.

In the building of the house itself reinforced concrete is very suitable for constructing floors and roofs, which are thus made fire-resisting and durable. Buildings have often to be erected on very soft and treacherous subsoils; and thin rafts of reinforced concrete can be constructed to distribute the weight of the building evenly over a large area. Internal staircases have been built in reinforced concrete, as well as flights of external concrete steps for gardens and terraces. Reinforced concrete cow-houses, piggeries and chicken-houses have been found of advantage, as also fruit-houses, greenhouses and root cellars. The roofs of such buildings are constructed of slabs and beams of concrete with steel rods embedded therein, such roofs being either sloping, curved or flat. Reinforced concrete is useful for greenhouses. The glass is sustained on sloping beams butting into a ridge piece, all moulded in concrete reinforced with steel. In fruit-houses, in sheds, and often in wine-cellars, shelving may be constructed in reinforced concrete, for it is impervious to liquids, not subject to decay, clean, sanitary and fire-resisting. Dairies are required to be cool in summer, warm in winter and scrupulously clean ; therefore the material of which they are built should be one that is easily cleansed, otherwise excessive labour will be necessary in their management. Reinforced concrete is just the material for such purposes; the whole of the floors and walls can be of concrete, and the surfaces when finished will be hard and durable. They can be moulded so as to leave no room for the lodgment of dirt, and to enable the interior to be washed out frequently. Such appliances as washing troughs can

232.—STABLES.

be built of the same material. In connection with the garden, concrete is used for laying out ponds, waterfalls, steps, etc., and also for the building of rockeries. Safes and strong-rooms are often constructed of reinforced concrete, the reinforcement effectively preventing both fire and burglars from getting at their contents.

On the farm modern science emphasises the immense importance of studying hygiene. Animals, if they are to be kept fit and healthy, require as cleanly surroundings as human beings. A few instances will show the hygienic value of concrete on the farm. On an estate in Ireland a dung-pit during the winter months was nothing less than a swamp, in which cattle sank up to the body. The pit was covered over by erecting concrete pillars and a roof, and the floor concreted with a gradual fall to a concrete tank. The liquid that ran into this tank was pumped out and used in the gardens and upon the farm. In summer the shed served as a shelter for the cattle, and in rough weather the men were put in to turn the manure, while the shed was also used for shearing sheep, for lambing ewes, and for young lambs in the early spring. The reconstruction work cost two hundred and fifty pounds, and the direct return on the money invested was more than ten per cent. The stone-paved floor in a boiler and mixing house on another farm was always foul owing to fragments of roots, etc., falling between the stones and decaying there. The cattle food left on the floor for even a short time became tainted and thus imperilled the health of the animals, while it was difficult to shovel up the food into the feeding baskets and buckets ; the cost of repaving with concrete was well repaid. In such floors it is preferable in many cases to employ reinforcing rods or meshwork, so as to prevent cracking, due to expansion and contraction, or to local settlement at a soft point in the foundations. Another typical instance of the value of reinforced concrete was the

233.—RETAINING WALLS.

construction of a dipping-trough and pens with a long, sloping stairway, with concrete grips for the feet of the sheep on their way into the draining-pen. The latter had a concrete floor sloping towards the trough. Thus, as the sheep shook the fluid out of their fleeces, it found its way back into the tank with very little loss.

Reinforced concrete is particularly useful in the construction of stables and mangers. The stable picture (Fig. 232) shows a range of stalls for horses in a large stable block, itself constructed throughout in reinforced concrete. The beams and floor slabs of this material are seen at the top of the view. The divisions of the stalls are of concrete two and a-half inches thick, reinforced with steel rods which run into the cast-iron posts, which in turn are set in bases embedded in the concrete floor. The floor is finished in granite chippings and cement, and grooved to prevent slipping. These stables have been in use for a number of years without damage from kicking horses.

The range of cattle-mangers and stall-divisions illustrated was constructed in reinforced concrete at Burderop Park, Swindon (Fig. 231). It is worth noting that the building shown was destroyed by fire in November, 1909, yet the whole of the reinforced concrete work remained in position, and did not even need repair when a new structure was built. In the reconstructed building concrete was used throughout for the walls, mangers, partitions and water-troughs, both the original mangers and the cattle-sheds being reinforced with steel bars.

234.—CULVERTS.

There is an interesting application of reinforced concrete in the construction of fences and fence-posts. Wooden fence-posts have been almost universal in the past, but they are subject to decay and do not withstand the effects of water, frost or fire. Iron posts are frequently used, but they are subject to corrosion and need painting from time to time, thus entailing a continual expense for upkeep. Reinforced concrete has been found to meet all requirements and to be a very inexpensive substitute. The posts are easily moulded to any form and reinforced to ensure any desired strength.

Another application to estate purposes is the building of retaining walls to hold up earth where excavated, or to retain materials in a bin or some similar position. The old-fashioned way of building such walls in brick or stone was not economical because it required a great bulk. A retaining wall in course of construction is illustrated in Fig. 233. The wall is seen to be reinforced with sheets of expanded steel. In ornamental gardens where appearance is of importance such a concrete wall can be faced with brick or stone.

Retaining walls are often required in sunken tanks, which may at some time be empty, though when they are full the water counteracts the thrust of the earth. The view of a circular-covered reservoir at Horsley Park, constructed in concrete reinforced with sheets of expanded steel, shows an interesting work, for which Messrs. A. M. Mackenzie and Son were the architects (Fig. 235).

Of a similar nature is a wall to hold up water, such as a dam or the sides of a tank raised above the ground. By the adoption of reinforced concrete considerable economy may be effected. On rocky hillsides, too, it would be costly to excavate the ground for a tank, an unnecessary course when a tank can be built in reinforced concrete quite capable of withstanding the pressure from any head of water.

Storage cisterns and wells may be lined with reinforced concrete, while elevated water-tanks of reinforced concrete have been built to a great height and in all sizes, one of the largest in this country containing three hundred thousand gallons. In connection with estate roads works, reinforced concrete culverts have come into general

235.—RESERVOIRS.

favour. Bridges for small or large streams are economical and durable in reinforced concrete construction, either of beam or arched form.

Shore protection, groynes, conduits, water mains and sewer-pipes are carried out in reinforced concrete on an extensive scale. Fig. 234 shows a reinforced concrete pipe in course of construction. It clearly indicates how the expanded steel sheets are put in position over a timber centre, and how the concrete is applied, the centre being afterwards removed and put in position further along for the next section of the work. Such sewers are very economical. Water mains and culverts for carrying surface water or draining low-lying land are constructed in a similar manner.

H. KEMPTON DYSON, C.E., Secretary of the Concrete Institute.

INDEX

COUNTRY LIFE

THE Journal for all interested in Domestic Architecture and in Country Life & Pursuits

UNTIL the advent of COUNTRY LIFE, the premier English illustrated paper, few people had realised the treasures possessed by the Old Country in the way of country houses and gardens. In some cases even the very owners did not fully know the artistic, architectural and antiquarian value of their own possessions; and in spite of the exercise of the most fastidious and scrupulous care in selection, the number of old houses possessing instructive and interesting features seems unending. One of the aims of COUNTRY LIFE is to purify and improve taste, and the surest way of doing this is to show what is fine. The houses themselves are often equalled in interest by the wealth of furniture and pictures which they enshrine. The historic mansion is, however, for the few, while there is a great and increasing public which is deeply interested in the "Lesser Country Houses of To-day." Articles on these and on small houses of yesterday which have been repaired and enlarged to make them suit modern needs appear every week in COUNTRY LIFE.

By this means the public at large becomes acquainted with the best work of the architects of the day who have revived and are carrying to their logical development those building traditions of England, so diverse and full of vitality, which give to each county its distinctive architecture. A study of the articles in COUNTRY LIFE in the two series of "Country Homes and Gardens Old and New" and "Lesser Country Houses of To-day" will go to establish a truth too long forgotten—that Architecture is the Mistress Art.

The above notes on COUNTRY LIFE, appearing as they do at the end of an architectural book, naturally emphasize that side of its activities. It is hardly needful to remind readers that the paper, week by week, presents country life in all its aspects and illustrates agriculture, gardening, sport, and natural history with a fulness attempted by no other journal.

In view of the increasing number of visitors to England from the United States, who take delight in its ancient homes and country pursuits, it is not remarkable that the number of American subscribers to COUNTRY LIFE is increasing by leaps and bounds.

PUBLISHED WEEKLY

Subscription Prices—Per annum, post free, to any address in the United States and including Double Numbers

$11·50

Published at the Offices of COUNTRY LIFE, LTD., 20, Tavistock Street, Covent Garden, London, W.C., or from GEORGE NEWNES, LTD., 8-11, Southampton Street, Strand, London, W.C.

SMALL COUNTRY HOUSES OF TO-DAY

Edited by LAWRENCE WEAVER

Price $5.00 net.

THE two reduced facsimile pictures given here, and the specimen illustrations reproduced opposite, full size, chosen from three hundred which illustrate this handsome quarto volume, serve to indicate its scope. It fills a distinctive place, because not only is **the picked work of more than 40 of the best architects of the day** shown by plan

A THATCHED COTTAGE

and photograph, but is discussed in detail, frankly yet sympathetically. As the houses illustrated, nearly fifty in all, vary from whitewashed **week-end cottages costing less than $2,500 to dignified country homes costing $25,000,** all sorts of internal arrangement and architectural and garden treatment are brought under review. Not least important are the chapters which deal with the right way to repair and add to old country cottages and farmhouses. **To all of moderate means who contemplate building or altering a country house, this book,** which treats the subject clearly and in a large spirit, yet in an untechnical way, **will be of the utmost value.**

A FINE BRICK HOUSE

Published in England at the Offices of COUNTRY LIFE.   New York—CHARLES SCRIBNER'S SONS.

A SIMPLE PLASTERED HOUSE

A Surrey Porch   A Fine Staircase

IN ENGLISH HOMES

Edited by H. AVRAY TIPPING, M.A.

The internal character, furniture, and adornments of some of the most notable Houses of England depicted from Photographs taken by CHARLES LATHAM.

Volumes I., II., and III. now ready

Price $15.00 net each

These three notable volumes form together an unequalled pictorial survey of the domestic architecture of England of every style and period. They are, moreover, a treasury, not only of the life stories of the notable men and women who have lived in our historic homes, but of those county and village traditions which throw so much light on the larger issues that have made the history of the nation.

The following are the principal Houses illustrated in the work :—

VOLUME I.

Agecroft Hall, Lancashire
Apethorpe, Northamptonshire
Audley End, Essex
Belton House, Lincolnshire
Birtsmorton Court, Gloucestershire
Boston House, Middlesex
Bowood Park, Wiltshire
Bradfield, Devonshire
Bramall Hall, Cheshire
Bramshill Park, Hampshire
Broughton Castle, Oxfordshire
Burton Agnes, Yorkshire
Cassiobury Park, Hertfordshire
Castle Ashby, Northamptonshire
Castle Howard, Yorkshire
Chastleton House, Oxfordshire
Chawton House, Hampshire
Cobham Hall, Kent

Combe Abbey, Warwickshire
Crewe Hall, Cheshire
Drakelowe Hall, Derbyshire
Dunster Castle, Somersetshire
Eastnor Castle, Herefordshire
Gifford's Hall, Suffolk
Godington, Kent
Goodwood House, Sussex
Grimsthorpe, Lincolnshire
Groombridge Place, Kent
Haddon Hall, Derbyshire
Hampton Court, Middlesex
Hardwick Hall, Derbyshire
Hatfield House, Hertfordshire
Hewell Grange, Worcestershire
Holme Lacy, Herefordshire
Kedleston Hall, Derbyshire
Kingston Lacy, Dorsetshire

Knowsley Hall, Lancashire
Lanhydrock, Cornwall
Levens Hall, Westmorland
Littlecote, Wiltshire
Longleat, Wiltshire
Melbury House, Dorsetshire
Old Place, Sussex
Oxburgh Hall, Norfolk
Parham Park, Sussex
Ragley Hall, Warwickshire
Red Lodge, Bristol
Rufford Abbey, Nottinghamshire
Rushbrooke Hall, Suffolk
Saltram, Devonshire
Sandringham, Norfolk
Smithills Hall, Lancashire
Speke Hall, Lancashire
Stanway House, Gloucestershire

Stoke Park, Buckinghamshire
Stourhead, Wiltshire
Sutton Place, Surrey
Sydenham House, Devonshire
The Deanery Gardens, Berkshire
The Vyne, Hampshire
Tythrop House, Oxfordshire
Waddesdon Manor, Buckinghamshire
Wakehurst Place, Sussex
Wentworth Castle, Yorkshire
West Dean Park, Sussex
Westwood Park, Worcestershire
Wilton House, Wiltshire
Wolfeton House, Dorsetshire
Wroxton Abbey, Oxfordshire

VOLUME II.

Adlington Hall, Cheshire
Aston Hall, Warwickshire
Athelhampton, Dorsetshire
Baddesley Clinton, Warwickshire
Beningbrough Hall, Yorkshire
Blickling Hall, Norfolk
Bolsover Castle, Derbyshire
Burton Constable, Yorkshire
Canons Ashby, Northamptonshire
Chicheley Hall, Buckinghamshire
Clouds, Wiltshire
Gotehele, Cornwall
Dorton House, Oxfordshire

Drakelowe, Derbyshire
East Sutton Park, Kent
Glynde, Sussex
Hanford House, Dorsetshire
Hever Castle, Kent
Hill Hall, Essex
Hoghton Tower, Lancashire
Holland House, Kensington
Hornby Castle, Yorkshire
Hutton-in-the-Forest, Cumberland
Ightham Mote, Kent
Knebworth House, Hertfordshire
Langleys, Essex

Lyme, Cheshire
Marshcourt, Hampshire
Maxstoke Castle, Warwickshire
Methley Hall, Yorkshire
Newburgh Priory, Yorkshire
No. 12, Welshback, Bristol
Park Hall, Shropshire
Prinknash Park, Gloucestershire
Quenby Hall, Leicestershire
Ragdale Old Hall, Leicestershire
Ribston Hall, Yorkshire
Rothamsted, Hertfordshire
St. Donats Castle, Glamorganshire

Samlesbury Hall, Lancashire
Sizergh Castle, Westmorland
Stockton House, Wiltshire
Temple Newsam, Yorkshire
Treasurer's House, Yorkshire
Welbeck Abbey, Nottinghamshire
Westonbirt House, Gloucestershire
Woodsome Hall, Yorkshire
Woollas Hall, Worcestershire

VOLUME III.

Apethorpe Hall, Northamptonshire
Badminton, Wiltshire
Barnsley Park, Gloucestershire
Blenheim Palace, Oxfordshire
Boughton House, Northamptonshire
Broome Park, Kent
Castle House, Oxfordshire
Cefn Mably, Glamorganshire
Chatsworth, Derbyshire
Clumber, Nottinghamshire

Deene Park, Northamptonshire
Ditchley, Oxfordshire
Dorfold Hall, Cheshire
Duncombe Park, Yorkshire
Easton Neston, Northamptonshire
Forde Abbey, Dorsetshire
Gilling Castle, Yorkshire
Halswell Park, Somersetshire
Heveningham Hall, Suffolk
Holkham Hall, Norfolk
Holme Lacy, Herefordshire

Houghton Hall, Norfolk
Hursley Park, Hampshire
Kirklees Park, Yorkshire
Newby Hall, Yorkshire
Nostell Priory, Yorkshire
Oulton Park, Cheshire
Petworth, Sussex
Ramsbury Manor, Wiltshire
Rainham Hall, Norfolk
Rushton Hall, Northamptonshire
Stoke Edith Park, Herefordshire

Stoneleigh Abbey, Warwickshire
Stowe House, Buckinghamshire
Sudbury Hall, Derbyshire
Swakeleys, Middlesex
Thorpe Hall, Northamptonshire
Tredegar Park, Monmouthshire
Tyttenhanger, Hertfordshire
Wentworth Woodhouse, Yorkshire
Wimpole Hall, Cambridgeshire
Wolterton Hall, Norfolk

Published in England at the Offices of COUNTRY LIFE.   New York—CHARLES SCRIBNER'S SONS.

IN ENGLISH HOMES

A Specimen Illustration

·Published in England at the Offices of COUNTRY LIFE.   New York—CHARLES SCRIBNER'S SONS.

GARDENS OLD AND NEW

(The Country House and its Garden Environment)

Edited by H. AVRAY TIPPING, M.A., the illustrations being from Photographs specially taken by CHARLES LATHAM. Crown folio (15 in. by 10 in.). Handsomely bound in cloth, gilt edges.

Volumes I., II., and III. now ready

Price $12.00 net each

These three volumes illustrate the relationship between house and garden, and the beauties of every type of garden, both formal and natural, in a way never before attempted. They afford a complete survey of the whole history of garden design and garden architecture, considered from every point of view, historical, artistic and horticultural.

The following are the principal Houses illustrated in the work :—

VOLUME I.

Alton Towers, Staffordshire	Compton Beauchamp, Berkshire	Holme Lacy, Hereford	Prior Park, Bath
Ashbridge Park, Great Berkhamstead	Condover, Shropshire	Ightham Mote, Kent	Ragley Hall, Warwickshire
Athelhampton Hall, Dorchester	Drayton House, Northampton	Kelly House, Tavistock	Renishaw Hall, Chesterfield
Barlborough Hall, Chesterfield	Elvaston Castle, Derbyshire	King's Weston, Gloucestershire	Risley
Belton, Grantham	Fountains Hall and Abbey, Yorkshire	Kingston Lacy, Dorsetshire	Rous Lench Court, Worcestershire
Blickling, Norfolk	Franks, Kent	Levens Hall, Westmoreland	St. Catherine's Court, Bath
Brickwall, Sussex	Great Tangley Manor, Surrey	Lilleshall, Shropshire	Shipton Court, Oxford
Brome Hall, Norfolk	Guy's Cliff, Warwick	Longford Castle, Wiltshire	Stoneleigh Abbey, Warwickshire
Broughton Castle, Banbury	Hall Barn, Buckinghamshire	Loseley Park, Surrey	Studley Royal, Yorkshire
Bulwick Hall, Northampton	Hall, The, Bradford-on-Avon	Lypiatt Park, Gloucestershire	Sutton Place, Guildford
Casa de Pilatos, The, Seville	Ham House, Richmond	Melbourne Hall, Derbyshire	Sydenham House, Devonshire
Charlton House, Kent	Hardwick Hall, Derbyshire	Montacute, Somerset	Tissington Hall, Derbyshire
Chatsworth, Derbyshire	Heckfield Place, Hampshire	Newstead Abbey, Nottingham	Trentham, Staffordshire
Cleeve Prior Manor, Worcestershire	Henbury Court, Gloucestershire	Norton Conyers, Yorkshire	Ven House, Somerset
Clevedon Court, Somerset	Heslington Hall, York	Old Place, Lindfield	Wilton House, Salisbury
Clifton Hall, Nottingham	Hever Castle, Kent	Panshanger, Hertfordshire	Wollaton Hall, Nottinghamshire
		Penshurst, Kent	

VOLUME II.

Agecroft Hall, Manchester	Easton Hall, Grantham, Lincs	Kentwell Hall, Suffolk	Packwood House, Birmingham
Albury Park, Surrey	Eaton Hall, Cheshire	Leighton Hall, Welshpool	Pain's Hill, Surrey
Aldenham House, Herts	Eydon Hall, Northants	Linton Park, Maidstone, Kent	Parham Park, Sussex
Amesbury Abbey, Wiltshire	Frogmore and Windsor	Littlecote Hall, Berkshire	Penrhyn Castle, N. Wales
Balcarres, Fifeshire	Grimston Park, Yorkshire	Lochinch, Wigtownshire	Penshurst, Kent
Harmeluith, Lanarkshire	Groombridge Place, Kent	Longleat, Wiltshire	Pitchford Hall, Shropshire
Barrow Court, Somerset	Gwydyr Castle, Denbighshire	Mapperton House, Beaminster	Powis Castle, Montgomeryshire
Brockenhurst Park, Hants	Hackwood Park, Hants	Margam Park, Glamorganshire	St. Fagan's, Cardiff
Castle Ashby, Northants	Haddon Hall, Derbyshire	Marks Hall, Essex	Sedgwick Park, Sussex
Chastleton House, Gloucestershire	Hadsor, Worcestershire	Melford Hall, Suffolk	Shrubland's Park, Suffolk
Chirk Castle, Denbighshire	Hampton Court, Middlesex	Mere Hall, Droitwich	Smithill's Hall, Lancashire
Chiswick House, Middlesex	Harewood House, Yorkshire	Moyns Park, Essex	Stoke Erith Park, Hereford
Compton Wynyates, Warwickshire	Highnam Court, Gloucestershire	Munstead, Surrey	Stoke Rochford, Lincolnshire
Cranborne Manor, Dorset	Hoar Cross, Burton-on-Trent, Staffordshire	Newbattle Abbey, Midlothian	The Vyne, Hants
Drakelow Hall, Staffordshire		Okeover Hall, Derbyshire	Westwood Park, Droitwich
Drumlanrig, Dumfriesshire	Inwood House, Somerset	Orchardleigh Park, Somerset	Wickham Court, Kent
Drummond Castle, Perthshire	Kedleston Hall, Derbyshire	Orchards, Surrey	Wilton House, Wiltshire

VOLUME III.

Athelhampton Hall, Dorsetshire	Montacute House, Somerset	Keevil Manor, Trowbridge	Lyme Hall, Cheshire
South Wraxall Manor, Wiltshire	Hatfield House, Hertfordshire	Stibbington Hall, Huntingdonshire	Castle Howard, Yorkshire
Faulkbourne Hall, Essex	Holland House, Kensington	Hutton-in-the-Forest, Cumberland	Wotton House, Aylesbury
Layer Marney Towers, Essex	Bradfield, Devon	Treworgey, Cornwall	Bowood, Wiltshire
Giffords Hall, Suffolk	St. Catherine's Court, Somersetshire	Newton Ferrers, Cornwall	Arley Hall, Cheshire
St. Osyth's Priory, Essex	Canons Ashby, Northamptonshire	Wilton House, Salisbury	The Deanery Gardens, Sonning, Berkshire
Speke Hall, Lancashire	Llangedwyn Hall, Denbighshire	Bramham Park, Yorkshire	Easton Lodge, Essex
Great Tangley Manor, Surrey	Gayhurst, Buckinghamshire	Wrest Park, Bedfordshire	Goddards, Surrey
Castle Ashby, Northamptonshire		Bicton, Devonshire	

Published in England at the Offices of COUNTRY LIFE.   New York—CHARLES SCRIBNER'S SONS.

GARDENS OLD AND NEW

A Stone Urn at Margam Park, Glamorganshire
(Reduced specimen illustration.)

" These beautiful books owe their charm to the wonderful collection of photographs of gardens and ga den architecture which such a paper as COUNTRY LIFE has had a unique opportunity of making. The principle conveyed in the letterpress is that held by all great gardeners and architects—that house and garden are, or should be, intimately associated, and that the character of the possessors should be reflected in both. The accounts of lovely garden after lovely garden are most agreeable reading. There is no country in the world where man created sylvan beauty can be found comparable to this in England, and as albums of charming pictures for the garden lovers and a mine of elegant suggestion to the garden-maker, these volumes are the best thing of their kind we have ever seen."—*Daily Chronicle*.

Published in England at the Offices of COUNTRY LIFE.   New York—CHARLES SCRIBNER'S SONS.

A LEAD VASE

*A Book for all owners
and lovers of gardens.*

English Leadwork
Its Art and History

By LAWRENCE WEAVER, F.S.A.

Price $7.50

LEAD is essentially the English material for garden ornaments. It takes its place as faithfully and naturally as marble does in Italy. While this volume deals as well with the more purely architectural uses of lead for pipe-heads, fonts, etc., many of its chapters are devoted wholly to garden statues, vases, cisterns, sundials and the like. No one who is interested in the Renaissance of formal gardening can afford to overlook this important work. It goes far to identify the statues and vases of the sculptors of the XVIIth and XVIIIth Centuries, who did so much to beautify old English gardens. The illustrations, of which three are reproduced here in reduced facsimile, number four hundred and forty.

LEAD BUST OF PAN

LEAD JARDINIÈRE

Published in England at the Offices of COUNTRY LIFE.
New York—CHARLES SCRIBNER'S SONS.

AN ILLUSTRATED

History of English Plate

ECCLESIASTICAL & SECULAR

IN WHICH THE DEVELOPMENT OF FORM
AND DECORATION IN THE SILVER AND
GOLD WORK OF THE BRITISH ISLES
FROM THE EARLIEST KNOWN EXAMPLES
TO THE LATEST OF THE GEORGIAN
PERIOD IS DELINEATED AND DESCRIBED

BY

CHARLES JAMES JACKSON, F.S.A.

AUTHOR OF " ENGLISH GOLDSMITHS AND THEIR MARKS "

In Two Handsome
Volumes, each con-
taining about 600
pages, bound in half
morocco,
$60.00 Net

Published in England at
the Offices of COUNTRY
LIFE.

New York—
CHARLES SCRIBNER'S
SONS.

*A Specimen Illustration, one of nearly sixteen hundred,
of which seventy-six are Photogravure Plates*

CAUSERIES

ON

ENGLISH PEWTER

BY

ANTONIO DE NAVARRO

$3.75 net.

A Specimen Illustration.

Published in England at the Offices of COUNTRY, LIFE,   New York—CHARLES SCRIBNER'S

"Country Life" Library of Garden Books

GARDENING MADE EASY

By E. T. COOK. *An instructive and practical gardening book of 200 pages and 23 illustrations, all showing the way certain garden operations should be performed. Every phase of gardening is included. The beginner will find this a most helpful guide in the cultivation of flowers, vegetables and fruits. It is the A.B.C. of gardening.* 40 Cents.

" It contains a vast amount of information in easily understood language that will be most helpful to persons who love to look after their own garden."—*Scotsman.*

ROSE GROWING MADE EASY

By E. T. COOK. *A simple Rose Guide for amateurs, freely illustrated with diagrams showing ways of increasing, pruning and protecting roses.* 40 Cents.

THE FRUIT GARDEN

By GEORGE BUNYARD and OWEN THOMAS. 507 *pages. Size,* 10½ *in. by* 7½ *in.* $3.75 Net.

" Without any doubt the best book of the sort yet published. There is a separate chapter for every kind of fruit, and each chapter is a book in itself—there is, in fact, everything that anyone can need or wish for in order to succeed in fruit growing. The book simply teems with illustrations, diagrams, and outlines."—*Journal of the Royal Horticultural Society.*

THE CENTURY BOOK OF GARDENING

Edited by E. T. COOK. *A Comprehensive Work for every Lover of the Garden.* 624 *pages, with about* 600 *illustrations, many of them full-page* 4to (12 *in. by* 8½ *in.*). *Art* Canvas. $7.50 Net.

" No department of gardening is neglected, and the illustrations of famous and beautiful gardens and of the many winsome achievements of the gardener's art are so numerous and attractive as to make the veriest cockney yearn to turn gardener. If THE CENTURY BOOK OF GARDENING does not make all who see it covet their neighbours' gardens through sheer despair of ever making for themselves such gardens as are there illustrated, it should, at any rate, inspire everyone who desires to have a garden with an ambition to make it as beautiful as he can."—*Times.*

GARDENING FOR BEGINNERS

(*A Handbook to the Garden.*) *By* E. T. COOK. *With nearly* 100 *diagrams in the text, and* 90 *full-page illustrations from photographs of selected specimens of Plants, Flowers, Trees, Shrubs, Fruits, etc. New and Enlarged Edition.* $3.75 Net.

" One cannot speak in too high praise of the idea that led Mr. E. T. Cook to compile this GARDENING FOR BEGINNERS, and of the completeness and succinctness with which the idea has been carried out. Nothing is omitted. . . . It is a book that will be welcomed with enthusiasm in the world of gardeners."—*Morning Post.*

WALL AND WATER GARDENS

By GERTRUDE JEKYLL. *Containing instructions and hints on the cultivation of suitable plants on dry walls, rock walls. in streams, marsh pools, lakes, ponds, tanks, and water margins. With* 133 *full-page illustrations. Large* 8vo, 186 *pages.* $3.75 Net.

!' WALL AND WATER GARDENS. He who will consent to follow Miss Jekyll aright will find that under her guidance the old walls, the stone steps, the rockeries, the ponds, or streamlets of his garden will presently blossom with all kinds of flowers undreamed of, and become marvels of varied foliage."—*Times.*

COLOUR IN THE FLOWER GARDEN

By GERTRUDE JEKYLL. *With over* 100 *illustrations and planting plans.* $3.75 Net.

." Miss Jekyll is one of the most stimulating of those who write about what may be called the pictorial side of gardening. . . . She has spent a lifetime in learning how to grow and place flowers so as to make the most beautiful and satisfying effects, and she has imparted the fruits of her experience in these delightful pages."—*Daily Mail.*

ROSES FOR ENGLISH GARDENS

By GERTRUDE JEKYLL and E. MAWLEY, *with* 190 *full-page illustrations.* $3.75 Net.

" A delightful proof of the increased devotion shown to rose-growing. There is a happy combination of authorship, for no one can better suggest the artistic value of garden roses old and new than Miss Jekyll, while the Secretary of the Rose Society, Mr. Edward Mawley, is a Rosarian who would satisfy Omar Khayyam."—*Manchester Courier.*

LILIES FOR ENGLISH GARDENS

Written and compiled by GERTRUDE JEKYLL. $2.30 Net.

" LILIES FOR ENGLISH GARDENS is a volume in the COUNTRY LIFE Library, and it is almost sufficiently high commendation to say that the book is worthy of the journal. Miss Jekyll's aim has been to write and compile a book on Lilies which shall tell amateurs, in the plainest and simplest possible way, how most easily and successfully to grow the Lily."—*Westminster Gazette.*

FLOWER DECORATION IN THE HOUSE

By GERTRUDE JEKYLL. $2.00 Net.

"Country Life" Library of Garden Books

THE UNHEATED GREENHOUSE
By Mrs. K. L. Davidson. $2.50 Net.

" An infinity of pleasure can be obtained from the due use of an unheated house built under proper conditions, and it is the function of Mrs. Davidson's book to provide hints and directions how to build such a house, and how to cultivate the plants that can be cultivated with advantage without artificial heat."—*Pall Mall Gazette.*

THE ENGLISH VEGETABLE GARDEN
By various experts.   Cheap edition, $2.50 Net.

CHILDREN AND GARDENS
By Gertrude Jekyll. *A garden book for children, treating not only of their own little gardens and other outdoor occupations, but also of the many amusing and interesting things that occur in and about the larger home garden and near grounds. Thoroughly practical and full of pictures.* $2.00 Net.

ROCK AND WATER GARDENS
THEIR MAKING AND PLANTING
With Chapters on Wall and Heath Gardens. By the late F. H. Meyer. *Edited by* E. T. Cook.
$2.00 Net.

TREES AND SHRUBS FOR ENGLISH GARDENS
By E. T. Cook. $3.75 Net.

" It contains a mass of instruction and illustration not always to be found altogether when required, and as such it will be very useful as a popular handbook for amateurs and others anxious to grow trees and shrubs."—*Field.*

MY GARDEN
By Eden Phillpotts. 207 *pages.* 60 *full-page illustrations.* $3.75 Net.

" It is a thoroughly practical book, addressed especially to those who, like himself, have about an acre of flower garden, and are willing and competent to help a gardener to make it as rich, as harmonious, and as enduring as possible. His chapters on irises are particularly good."—*World.*

A GARDEN IN VENICE
By F. Eden. *An account of the author's beautiful garden on the Island of the Guidecca at Venice. With* 21 *collotype and* 50 *other illustrations. Parchment, limp.* $3.75 Net.

" Written with a brightness and an infectious enthusiasm that impart interest even to technicalities, it is beautifully and rarely pictured, and its material equipment is such as to delight the lover of beautiful books."—*Glasgow Herald.*

SEASIDE PLANTING OF TREES AND SHRUBS
By Alfred Gaut, F.R.H.S. *An interesting and instructive book dealing with a phase of arboriculture hitherto not touched upon. It is profusely illustrated, and diagrams are given explaining certain details.*
$2.00 Net.

" Mr. Gaut has accomplished a piece of very solid and extremely useful work, and one that may not be without considerable influence upon the future development of coast-side garden work and agriculture."—*Liverpool Courier.*

CARNATIONS AND PINKS
Edited by E. T. Cook. $1.25 Net.

" Those who add this volume to their library of garden books will obtain more information concerning the interesting family of garden and wild pinks than is to be found in the majority of books that have come under our notice."—*Westminster Gazette.*

SWEET VIOLETS AND PANSIES
AND VIOLETS FROM MOUNTAIN AND PLAIN
Written by several authorities, and Edited by E. T. Cook. *This interesting subject has never been treated in the same way as set forth in this illustrated book. The information is thoroughly practical. A dainty gift-book to gardening friends.* $1.25 Net.

" Altogether excellent, and must be useful both to the grower of prize flowers and to the amateur."—*Guardian.*

THE BOOK OF BRITISH FERNS
By Chas. T. Druery, F.L.S., V.M.H., *President of the British Pteridological Society.*
$1.25 Net.

" The book is well and lucidly written and arranged ; it is altogether beautifully got up. Mr. Druery has long been recognised as an authority on the subject."—*St. James's Gazette.*

THE DISEASES OF TREES
By Professor R. Hartig. *Royal 8vo.* $3.75 Net.

Lightning Source UK Ltd.
Milton Keynes UK
UKHW02f1841100818

327077UK00014B/829/P

9 781333 573225